# Praise for *The Rare Earths Era*

"Chomón undertakes a deep dive into the rare earth metal supply chains which form the material underpinnings of the modern world, and skillfully articulates how these are impacting Western geopolitical priorities. . . ."

MARK CAZELET, Editor in Chief, *European Security & Defence*

"Chomón's academic and international experience gives him the authority to reach valuable conclusions on such a complex and delicate subject. He is not half-hearted when it comes to pointing out the risks for the West of the Chinese monopoly on rare earths. His ability to disclose is accompanied by accurate data that compel us to reflect and for public authorities to act."

E. FIGUEREDO, journalist, *La Vanguardia,* specialized in security matters

"Juan Manuel Chomón immerses us in the exciting reality of rare earths, revealing the West's dependence on minerals controlled for now by China and explaining how they could redefine global hegemony, spark resource wars and influence the energy transition. He asks: are we ready to understand how these strategic elements are redrawing the global geopolitical landscape?"

CHRISTIAN D. VILLANEVA, CEO, *ArmiesMagazine.com*

"Interviews, visits, and trips were carried out around the world. The expeditionary spirit is accompanied by investigative scientific rigor. Thanks to an elegant exercise of analysis and disclosure, Chomón fuses and synthesizes information from many different sources and reveals with great amenity to the reality that lies behind these strategic and critical elements. He demonstrates his brilliant knowledge with respect to so many strategic as well as security issues in the rare earth context bridging the gap between theory and practice."

STEFAN BAYER, PhD, Head of Research German Institute for Defence and Strategic Studies and Co-Course Director of the Master of Military Leadership and International Security of the Helmut Schmidt University, Hamburg, Germany

# More Praise

"Chomón embarks us on a fascinating journey into the unknown world of rare earths. His multidisciplinary approach and penetrating view reveals to us the essential role these critical metals play in some of the biggest challenges the world faces in our days. Listening to his call to diversify supply chains and to comply with the global obligation of international collaboration is as crucial as it is urgent."

ARNAULD AKODJENOU, Senior Advisor for Africa of the Kofi Annan Foundation and Former Inspector General of the United Nations High Commissioner for Refugees

# THE RARE EARTHS ERA

## Strategic Metals Dependency & World Order

Juan Manuel Chomón

Clarity Press, Inc.

ISBN: 978-1-949762-89-1
eBook ISBN: 978-1-949762-90-7

In-house editor: Diana G. Collier
Book design: Becky Luening



DISCLAIMER: All opinions expressed in this book are my own and do not reflect the official policy or position of the Spanish Air Force, the Ministry of Defense, or the Government of Spain. *The information provided within this book is for general informational purposes only. While I try to keep the information up-to-date and correct, there are no representations or warranties, express or implied, about the completeness, accuracy, reliability, suitability or availability with respect to the information.*

Library of Congress Control Number: 2023948442

Clarity Press, Inc.
2625 Piedmont Rd. NE, Ste. 56
Atlanta, GA 30324, USA
https://www.claritypress.com

# Table of Contents

# Acknowledgments

Halfway through the dream journey . . . When I was a child, I dreamed I wrote a book that began with these five words: Now I know how it continues:

Halfway through the dream journey . . . I have been finding wonderful people to share it with; others were always there and others emerged as flesh of my flesh. Some of them have made this book possible (and many other things). Thanks to my mother for being my mother and for contributing her vision as a chemist, to Isabelle for being a real woman, for her unconditional support and for daring to read the first drafts, to my children for illuminating my days with their smiles and my nights with their existence, source of motivation for writing and for everything. To the friends who have helped me: A thousand thanks to Craig Hymel for carrying out the first English edition of this book, an exceptional work motivated only by friendship; to Sebastian Janeras for our unforgettable inspiring and enlightening conversations, which helped me to set the course of some chapters; to Brendan Diazma for his support in this project, especially in the research trips I made such as the one to Uganda and for transmitting his contagious enthusiasm to me; to the staff of the Spanish Geological and Mining Institute for giving me a little bit of their wisdom; to the members of the company Europe Strategic Minerals for their hospitality, sincerity and transparency; to the Rwenzori Metals team; and to the staff of NEO Performance Materials and especially to their CEO, Constantine, for opening the doors not only to their factory in Estonia but also to an unparalleled knowledge and experience in the world of rare earths.

And last but not least thanks to Jermy Phifer and Andreaas Ganser for their contribution to this work, sometimes well accompanied by barbecues and laughter, a fundamental part of this trip.

# Author's Note

Almost no aircraft in the world today could fly without rare earths, which is how I first came across them. I'm a military pilot by trade, and in 2013 I was working on my Master's in Peace and International Security. As part of the curriculum, I was analyzing the implications of these curious elements, and internalizing the fact that the aircraft I was flying could not function without them. At that time, in addition to being an aircraft commander in the Spanish Air Force, I was the chief of maintenance for a search and rescue (SAR) squadron. Three years prior, China had cut off its supply of rare earths to Japan as a result of a territorial conflict. Naturally, I began to wonder, what would have happened if instead of Japan, Europe was the victim of this rare earth embargo? How long would my fleet have remained operational? Almost 11 years have passed since then, during which I acquired a second Master's in International Security from Helmut-Schmidt-Universität and put a General/Admiral Staff Course at the German Ministry of Defense Leadership Academy under my belt. During these years I have focused a large part of my research and study on rare earths, and I am currently devoting myself to a PhD on the same topic.

This book is the culmination of my past few years of research, comprised of interviews with experts, site visits, field research experiences and the fruit of rigorous academic investigation. As for why—beyond the professional implications these metals pose to a pilot and my innate curiosity, I believe that, given that the defense and safety of citizens of the West depend on rare earths, their role in our security has been gravely underestimated. I hope that this book will serve to give them the relevance they deserve and assist Western governments with developing policies that account for their implications to defense, security and national strategy. The global security situation since I joined the General Air Academy in 1996 has evolved appreciably, and with it the threats that have grown out of its conventional framework. Globalization in particular leaves all of humanity exposed to risks related to food security, medical security, energy security, and so on. These risks enter incognito through the back door of many democracies.

Incredible as it may seem, today many aspects of our lives are in the hands of a few metals. Today, the problem of rare earths is already an urgent problem that, despite having a start date of 2025, has yet to find a solution. In a globalized world where specialization is synonymous with success, no one knows where to place these multidisciplinary threats. An understanding of the implications of rare earths requires input from the fields of geopolitics, chemistry, geology, industry, economics, technology, law and environmental protection… So, what is to be done?

*Juan Manuel Chomón*
September 2023

# Preface

## No rare earths, no paradise!

The current fight against climate change seeks to ensure our survival and that of our descendants. But the struggle against climate change requires numerous approaches to curb global warming. Renewable energies and electric cars are among the current projects whereby we hope to achieve the decarbonization of our economies. Both require chemical elements that are critical because of their scarcity and strategic relevance; these elements go by the name of rare earths. With their miraculous properties they can endow other materials with an unalterable super magnetism, an amazing hardness or robustness, a unique luminescence or fluorescence and a special conductivity.

But today's crucial questions are: to what extent is extraction of these metals itself detrimental to the climate change effort, who presently controls access to most of earth's rare earths, and what will it mean for countries who cannot ensure such access?

In the face of a predicted shortage, and without strong global action, the energy transition could be severely delayed, and the effects of climate change would continue to grow.

Bear in mind: without this set of 17 metallic elements, many of the most modern weapons systems will not be able to function, nor would many of the technological elements that shape our daily lives, from our cell phones to our televisions, computers and medical scanners, to name just a few examples. These metallic chemical elements allow us to continue to worship our new humanistic demigods such as communication and information and to maintain a highly technological and electrified lifestyle. More importantly, without their proper supply, international, national, and human security would be put at serious risk.

Such is their importance, that rare earths currently play a key role in the struggle between the U.S., seeking to maintain hegemony, and China, seeking to acquire a geopolitical weight equivalent to its population, territorial dimensions, and economic power. These metallic elements form the physical basis of many of the disruptive technologies that act as levers for global leadership.

The unbridled race for mineral resources with rare earths at the forefront is redrawing the global geopolitical map. But these metals also have their dark and little-known side, the environmental damage caused by their extraction. Western (and non-Western) mining companies are also sometimes complicit in illegal activity. In such instances, the damage inflicts a catastrophic impact on indigenous populations, ecosystems and local flora and fauna.

Neoliberal humanism run amok, in the form of almost unlimited free trade and exalted capitalist globalization, has put the sustainability of planet earth in jeopardy. As globalization explodes, supply chains grow larger and more complex. However, the survival of Western culture seems to depend on the procurement of these indispensable metals, which are almost entirely produced outside its borders and monopolized by China. It is an existential problem that requires solution. The struggle for access to rare earths has begun. Whether it can be pursued without wreaking inestimable damage on humanity, without recourse to damaging economic or military means, depends on the questionable wisdom of our world´s leaders.

# 1. RARE EARTHS, THE HOLY GRAIL OF THE 21ST CENTURY

Today, it isn't easy to imagine our modern life without the 17 esoteric elements known as rare earths. Aside from a growing chorus of defense and policy experts, rare earths are not exactly a topic of daily conversation. But the modern life we now enjoy would be impossible without these elements. Our mobile phones, personal electronics, satellites, and cars simply do not work without them. They are the quintessential material of modern technology. The importance of rare earths in technology likewise applies to high-tech arsenals. Our precision munitions, communications, and almost everything else requiring super magnets and semiconductors are intrinsically tied to rare earth metals.

These omnipresent rare earth metals comprise 17 elements on the periodic table; the 15 elements of the lanthanide group, as well as scandium and yttrium, are further classified as light or heavy rare earths according to their atomic weight. The light rare earths are lanthanum, cerium, praseodymium, neodymium, promethium, and samarium. Heavy rare earths, which are rarer and consequently more valuable, include europium, gadolinium, dysprosium, holmium, erbium, thulium, ytterbium, and lutetium, together with scandium and yttrium.

The term referring to this new technological holy grail, rare earths, is surrounded by a certain ambiguity. Understanding the different meanings associated with its use is essential to understanding how their supply chain works and their strategic relevance. Whether out of ignorance or a desire to simplify key points for the population at large, both politicians and journalists erroneously use the term rare earths to refer not only to rare earths, but also other "green metals" necessary for the green energy transition, such as lithium, cobalt, and nickel.

While these green metals are certainly important for our envisioned green future and are inexorably intertwined with rare earths, we focus here largely on true rare earths, seeking to focus on the details regarding their most interesting secrets, and the devils hidden therein.

The critical strategic importance of rare earths is slowing emerging into the public forum, yet for all of their importance their procurement is concentrated in just two countries, China and Australia. Even then, the Asian giant controls 80% of the rare earths market, and if we look specifically at heavy rare earths, these figures nearly reach 100%. In the context of supply chain security, it's a figure that is as alarming as it is astonishing to contemplate. Given the growing tensions between China, the U.S., and the rest of the western world, it's understandable why there is a growing chorus of defense and policy experts concerned about China's rare earth monopoly. But why should the lay person going about their everyday life care about rare earth metals?

At an individual level, they have slipped under our skin and injected themselves into our lives without our realization. You carry them around with you every day. In your wallet, your banknotes are marked with europium in order to prevent counterfeiting. For those not inclined to carry cash, you could pay with your cell phone, which is full of rare earths (usually lanthanum, terbium, neodymium, praseodymium, europium, and dysprosium) or pay with your smart watch, which essentially contains the same elements. If you are listening to music with the latest model of wireless headphones, the technological miracle of their miniaturization and lightness is based on the use of internal magnets manufactured with neodymium and praseodymium.

Let's imagine that by some magic all those rare earths you're carrying disappear. Faced with the inability to shop and no handheld entertainment, you decide to return home. If you live in an apartment with an elevator, it is very likely that the electric motor of the elevator works with neodymium and praseodymium super magnets. Bad news, dear reader: your elevator is useless without these magnets, but if you're able-bodied and not overburdened with a baby stroller or the day's groceries, a little exercise is in order. If you were inclined to calculate, as you climb the stairs, the amount of rare earths in your house when you entered it, the amount would probably not exceed one kilogram. Yet neither your TV, nor your refrigerator, nor the dryer, nor the vacuum cleaner, nor the light bulbs (fluorescent or LED), nor the internet signal through the fiber optic, would function.

Swallowing your disappointment, you decide to take your internal combustion vehicle (if it is electric or hybrid, you need not bother trying to use it) to go visit a friend in the countryside. Perhaps your friend has survived the technological hecatomb, isolated in the countryside. But without rare earths your internal combustion vehicle would not start either, and even if it did, it certainly won't function to a degree that it is safe to drive it. The small electric motors in your car contain rare earths, and your vehicle's catalytic converter won't work without the elements lanthanum or cerium.

"Enough!" you think, and in desperation decide to light up a cigarette, but your lighter stone is composed of a rare earth alloy called mischmetal containing cerium, lanthanum, neodymium, and praseodymium. If you finally do succumb to panic, it's not worth calling 112 in Europe or 911 in America, because like any computerized communications system, it too depends on rare earths. This story could end up in taking a long walk to a hospital, itself in chaos, and without a GPS to guide you. I think this is sufficiently illustrative of the impact removing these innocuous metals from our lives would have. In short, our modern world cannot function without rare earths. If our industries at-large suffered a shortage of these materials, and if government response were not as early and forceful (or not) as with COVID, this hypothetical situation would rapidly begin mirroring reality. We could see power outages, cold chain breakages, ATMs out of service, potable water shortages in cities, defective heating systems, disarticulated maritime and land traffic networks, collapsed sanitary systems, etc.

The future simply cannot do without these materials, which are physically present in the bases of virtually all emerging technologies, some of them potentially disruptive.[1] Their unrivaled properties, even in minute quantities, make them an irreplaceable holy grail for technology industries. Their varied properties include magnetic fields ten times stronger than traditional magnets, resistance to high

1 European Commission, "Science rocks – the rare earths that technology can't live without," EU Research & Innovation, *Horizon,* March 2015. https://ec.europa.eu/research-and-innovation/en/horizon-magazine/science-rocks-rare-earths-technology-cant-live-without

temperatures (coercivity), luminescence, fluorescence, and electrical conductivity, among others.[2] Without them our western techno-culture would collapse. The disappearance of super magnets alone would render it impossible to manufacture anything requiring high-performance electric motors, like automobiles, washers and dryers, vacuum cleaners, refrigerators, air conditioners, or our aforementioned elevator. Thanks to the elements neodymium, praseodymium and dysprosium, the so-called permanent magnets crucial to many economic sectors, engineers have drastically decreased the form factor and energy consumption of their products. They are used both for the motors of missile fins and for our air conditioning and electric vehicles, as well as for hard disks. Modern satellites could not function without them either.[3] Likewise, the electronics who hold us in thrall cannot function: TV screens, barcode scanners, computers, cell phones, digital cameras, portable stereos, and hard drives would all be affected, and this is just a fraction of the everyday items containing rare earths.

## THE NEW AGE OF METALS

The significance of this marriage between rare earths and technology was not apparent to the Swedish Army lieutenant who discovered them in 1787 in the town of Ytterby. Unlike today, there was no "gold rush" to seize these precious metals; their use was initially limited to incandescent lamps, and the chemically based techniques required to separate them from their natural oxides, at the time simply called "earths," was challenging and costly. This misleading designation of "rare earths" (as opposed to the perhaps more accurate "rare oxides"), refers to their low concentration within the mined oxide. From 1787 to 1947, the civilized world discovered 17 "rare metal oxides." Continued research breakthroughs in the fields of atomic physics, quantum physics and chemistry resulted in growing importance attached to these elements, while advances in spectroscopy made it possible to classify rare earths within the periodic table. The last of these elements wasn't discovered until 1947, when three American scientists came across

2 Nawshad Haque, Anthony Hughes, Seng Lim, and Chris Vernon, "Rare Earth Elements: Overview of Mining, Mineralogy, Uses, Sustainability and Environmental Impact. *Resources,* 2014. https://www.mdpi.com/2079-9276/3/4/614

3 Magnetpartner, "What are some of the uses of permanent magnets?" https://magnetpartner.com/blog/uses-permanent-magnets, accessed January 2022.

it while developing the first generation of atomic bombs. This timid element, produced when uranium decays, was baptized with the name promethium and is today used in pacemakers, watches, portable X-ray equipment and even nuclear batteries.

These "supermetals" have also become a key resource for the modern-day green energy transition, with demand for them skyrocketing.[4] They are used in fuel cells and increase the strength of the magnets equipping electric vehicle motors and wind turbines. An average hybrid or electric vehicle uses between 2 and 6 kilograms of rare earth magnets. They are commonly referred to as neodymium-iron-boron (NdFeB) magnets, but in addition to neodymium they also contain praseodymium, dysprosium, and ytterbium. These four metallic elements account for only 20% of rare earths extracted but 90% of rare earth economic value.

Rare earths, together with other metals such as lithium, have become the "green gold" needed for renewable energies and electric vehicles. They are gradually replacing petroleum, the legacy "black gold," as the material strategic to our livelihood. As this dark, oily substance became the world's star commodity, its production and use redrew our lives. Its energy powered machinery that avoided the use of animals as a means of transportation, and in agriculture it replaced the physical labor of people. Factories were opened that concentrated labor in the cities, and the slave labor previously utilized thankfully disappeared. Manufacturing led to the organization of labor, and from there to higher salaries in the workforce. Without petroleum energy there would have been no modern middle class. And it. gave many people both the time and means to engage in leisure activities.

Through rare earths, our modern society is attempting a similarly revolutionary transformation. But this revolution also comes with eerily similar ecological and sustainability issues, starting from the very first step in the procurement process—mining. Although Rare earth deposits are abundant throughout the world, access to many is not economically viable. There are many deposits not considered reserves because of their insufficient size or concentration—their grade. The exploitation of such deposits simply isn't profitable. Conversely there are also many deposits in the world that aren't exploitable, not for lack

4 Roskill, *Rare Earths. Outlook to 2030,* 20th Ed. (March 2020), 3.

of size or quality but because of the excessive costs of extracting and separating the minerals, or technological and logistical challenges, or the generation of heavy environmental pollution. All these factors make rare earth elements a scarce commodity in the metals markets.

The supply chain for these elements begins with the extraction of their associated oxides from the earth. Most of these ores are extracted in large open mines, using techniques such as drilling and rock blasting to fragment the rocks and ore into manageable sizes for processing. But this is only the first step, and mining ventures must now expend staggering amounts of power to crush and grind the ore, and tons of water to separate the oxides by leaching (pouring acids over the ores) and concentrating them via froth flotation. On average, with rough calculations, it takes always more than 1.000 tons of mined earth to produce enough material for a single wind turbine's magnets. This concentration of rare earth oxides is then transported to processing plants.[5] This requires further expenditure in the form of petroleum for trucks and trains, and there is also the inevitable loss of material in transit. This final concentrate leaving the mines contains between 30% and 70% of the total rare earth oxides.[6]

Depending on the rare earth element contained within, ores are classified as either heavy or light rare earth ore. Heavy rare earths are much less abundant than light rare earths.

An example of the difficulty in obtaining heavy rare earth elements can be found in the name of one such element, dysprosium. It is an indispensable material for permanent magnets, deriving its name from the Greek *dysprositos,* meaning inaccessible. Dysprosium and other heavy rare earths are not found in monazite ore, the main source of light rare earths as found, for instance, in the Mountain Weld mines of the Australian Lynas Company. This elusive metallic element is instead found in bastnasite ore mined in China, Inner Mongolia and in the U.S. Mountain Pass mine in California. The concentration of heavy rare earths in these ores is so low that the total mineral content

5 Vitalij K. Pecharsky and Karl A. Gschneidner, Jr., "Rare Earth Element." *Encyclopaedia Britannica,* Jan. 17, 2019, Accessed Dec. 1, 2021. https://www.britannica.com/sciencrare-earth-element

6 U.S. Geological Survey Agency, "National Minerals Information Centre, Rare Earths Statistics and Information," 2021. https://www.usgs.gov/centers/nmic/rare-earths-statistics-and-information.

before concentration does not exceed 2%. If we add the difficulty of separating these elements, due to their similar properties, we can understand why barely 100 tons of dysprosium are produced in the world per year.

Because typical concentrations of rare earth elements are so low, one solution is to extract them as a secondary target when extracting another metal such as aluminum through bauxite ore, which also contains traces of rare earths.[7] But, according to some rare earth experts at the Spanish Geological and Mining Institute, one of the other major problems in extracting rare earths is that there are only accurate refining flowsheets (technical diagrams of the processes for refining ore) for a few types of minerals, such as monazite and bastnasite. The rest of the flowsheets must be constructed from theoretical models and laboratory experimentation, with no guarantee of success. If a company does generate a successful flowsheet, it usually becomes an industrial secret to guard that company's revenue stream from competitors.

Ultimately, the underlying problem is that the world's open reserves of rare earths, whether light or heavy, are not sufficient to meet the expected global demand, and converting a deposit into a rare earth producing reserve (a working mine) has become the kind of venture for investors and mining companies that usually takes more than 10 years, even assuming the process is successful.

## ROAD TO SELF-SUFFICIENCY—OR TO THE PRECIPICE

The Chinese consultancy Shanghai Metals Market (SMM),[8] a leader in the analysis of metals-related information in China, confirms a deficit between global supply and demand for rare earths products. SMM's analysis shows that the deficit will not diminish in the near future. Worse, this deficit will very likely soon turn into a severe shortage of rare earths supply, which has already been predicted by

---

7 Institute for Bauxite and Strategic Metals Extraction, "REE as a by-product of bauxite mining," 2021,

8 SMM, "SMM: predicts that there is still a gap between supply and demand of rare earths in 2022 and that prices will be consolidated at a high level [minutes]," January 21, 2022. https://news.metal.com/newscontent/101733464/smm-predicts-that-there-is-still-a-gap-between-supply-and-demand-of-rare-earths-in-2022-and-that-prices-will-be-consolidated-at-a-high-level-minutes

the European Commission and by specialized consultancies such as Adamas Intelligence and Goldman Sachs. Other specialized agencies such as the Roskill Institute[9] or IRENA[10] also warn of the exponential increase in demand for rare earth metals in the coming years and of their scarcity before the end of the decade.[11] As IRENA points out: *"The key to scarcity is therefore not reserve levels, but the development of new mining capacity."* Adamas strengthens IRENA's words with hard figures and forecasts that global demand for NdFeB magnets will increase annually by 8.6% until 2035 but over the same period, global production of neodymium, praseodymium, dysprosium, and terbium will collectively increase at a slower annual rate of just 5.4%. Supply struggles to keep up with demand.

In the event of a curtailment of rare earth supplies, problems would not be immediately apparent to a consumer. Issues would instead manifest slowly, as companies' warehouse stocks dwindled without replenishment. In the framework of modern "just-in-time" logistics, companies typically only stock about two months' worth of parts and materials, so beyond this timeframe, the consequences grow more serious. Governments and companies would naturally react, but without new sources of rare earths, according to different sources I've consulted, within a year they may find themselves with little room to maneuver.

---

9 Roskill was acquired in June 2021 by Wood Mackenzie, the leading global research, consultancy, and data analytics business powering the natural resources industry. Through the acquisition, Wood Mackenzie has expanded the West's commodity capabilities, augmenting our existing metals and mining offering, especially in battery and electric vehicle materials, while aligning with our strategic investment in the energy transition.

10 The International Renewable Energy Agency (IRENA) serves as the principal platform for international co-operation, a center of excellence, a repository of policy, technology, resource and financial knowledge, and a driver of action on the ground to advance the transformation of the global energy system. An intergovernmental organization established in 2011, IRENA promotes the widespread adoption and sustainable use of all forms of renewable energy, including bioenergy, geothermal, hydropower, ocean, solar and wind energy, in the pursuit of sustainable development, energy access, energy security and low-carbon economic growth and prosperity. https://www.irena.org/

11 Dolf Gielen and Martina Lyons, *Critical Materials For The Energy Transition: Rare Earth Elements,* International Renewable Energy Agency (IRENA), Technical Paper 2/2022. https://www.irena.org/Technical-Papers/Critical-Materials-For-The-Energy-Transition-Rare-Earth-elements

In the meantime, without these metals, several industrial sectors that directly or indirectly guarantee our security would be damaged. Imagine how many of our sophisticated military weapons systems could not be produced and the extent to which the existing ones, without adequate spare parts, would lose their operational capacity. Hospitals would not be able to continue receiving new and modern equipment such as scanners to diagnose by magnetic resonance, nor maintain their scanners properly. We would stop receiving radars for airports and the existing ones would gradually stop working, risking the collapse of access to airspace.

The consequences of an inadequate functioning of our satellite constellations, such as the GPS system, could be catastrophic. Our energy distribution networks, transport and sometimes water or some foodstuffs systems, are supported by them. They also ensure the operation of computerized time and attendance systems or payment terminals, among others. Most of the satellites currently in orbit depend on rare earths for many of their components and for their communications both by microwave and laser systems.[12] The same would be true for computers whose average life span is six to ten years. In other words, in less than a year without manufacturing new units, their operating quantity would fall by more than 10%. Our terrestrial communication networks, on which so many things depend: police, fire departments, emergency units, etc., would likewise be impaired.

Compounding the situation, the lack of rare earths used as catalysts in refining crude oil would sharply increase fuel prices. And the energy transition without new wind turbines and solar panels would come to a halt. The climate will continue to change with its dramatic human and security consequences such as droughts, famines, natural catastrophes, and migratory waves.[13]

Alarmingly, this dystopian future bereft of critical metals is not the fruit of a science fiction movie but corresponds to the chronicle of a problem already announced. Without adequate power availability, with faulty computers and personal telephones, with satellite

---

12 James B. Hedrick, *U.S. Geological Survey Rare Earths in Selected U.S. Defence Applications.* http://www.cecdarchive.umd.edu/publications/Argonne%20 Lab/Defense%20applications%20of%20Rare%20Earth.pdf

13 David S. Abraham, *The Elements of Power: Gadgets, Guns, and the Struggle for a Sustainable Future in the Rare Metal Age* (Yale University Press, 2015).

communication breakdowns and non-functioning transportation networks, the world, as we know it today—and the countries of the West in particular if lacking rare earths access—would progressively collapse.[14] In the time it would take to react, we would begin a return to the 1970s, when rare earths still had marginal technological applications, such as giving color to the images on our televisions.

In the attempt to survive without rare earths, the first step would be to try to replace them. However, due to the lack of elements providing the same performance and the time required to change production lines on a large scale, a complicated, bumpy process of racing against the clock would be initiated, while simultaneously dealing with widespread disruptions to basic services on which every citizen currently relies. Some countries would be forced into measures such as cannibalization and triaging the use of rare earths to ensure national security, which would leave other domestic sectors completely unsupplied. In the midst of a possible or even likely "every man for himself" scenario evolving from the attempt to stock up on rare earths, cohesion among allied countries could be threatened. This was the case at the beginning of the COVID crisis and the race for self-sufficiency in masks, respirators, tests, and vaccines.

In the face of escalating tensions, pressure by corporations could lead governments to take more aggressive action by initiating conflicts or armed movements to obtain rare earths. The choice would be between mining in their own backyards in the face of opposition by public opinion and environmental groups, or targeting weaker and less governable states, leading to yet another chapter in the history of conflicts over resources, in which the interests of different nations and corporations intersect. This would give rise to proxy conflicts (proxy wars) for obtaining these critical materials.

As with the COVID crisis, China will once again find itself in the eye of the hurricane, being the central country in a global crisis. Due to the lack of rare earth supplies, Beijing could be also a fundamental part of the equation to solve it, were the West to approach the matter with diplomacy rather than with economic sanctions. China dominates the processing of lithium, rare earths, cobalt, and other metals used to make batteries. These metallic elements would not be

14 Guillaume Pitron, *The Rare Metals War: The Dark Side of Clean Energy and Digital Technologies* (Scribe US, 2020).

the first materials for which nations have competed, even going to war to obtain what they considered the physical foundations of their civilizations. Similar conflicts occurred, for example, in the name of black gold—oil. Although most readers are familiar with the bombing of Pearl Harbor by Japanese aircraft in 1941, the causes that led to the surprise attack on the Americans are much less well known. Japan's rapidly expanding global ambitions were threatened when the United States, for geopolitical reasons, imposed restrictions on the export of a key raw material that the Empire of the Rising Sun could not obtain domestically and autonomously: oil. Desperate, Japan was forced to secure a crucial supply chain through the proactive use of violence. The global consequences were devastating. And we should ask ourselves if the action of some western countries in Middle East was not also partially driven by oil interests. Today, the resource has changed, but conditions are alarmingly similar. Many countries have proved many times throughout history what they are willing to do to secure control over key resources.

## THE MOST STRATEGIC METALS: FROM BLACK GOLD TO GREEN GOLD

The last raw materials super-cycle we have witnessed this century has been led by China. Its urbanization and industrialization would not have been possible without its access to huge quantities of iron, steel, and coal, not only from its own mines but also from Australia, Brazil, Russia, and several emerging economies. The global technology and western renewable energy booms look set to outlast China's urbanization and industrialization. Now the Asian giant is also gobbling up the rare metals that make these booms possible, fueling its position as a world manufacturer of wind turbine components, solar panels, batteries, and countless other technological products. Remarkably, since 1985, China has consistently gained near-total control of the global rare earth supply chain.[15] While petroleum has heretofore been the key material which provided easily accessible energy to the post-war

15 Brendan P. Dziama, Juan Manuel Chomón Pérez, and Andreas Ganser "Rare Earths: Fighting for the Fuel of the Future," *The Diplomat,* January 2022. https://thediplomat.com/2022/01/rare-earths-fighting-for-the-fuel-of-the-future/

world, in the future the watts will flow not from barrels, but from batteries, and it is China that has these new barrel replacements.

The strategic nature of rare earths stems not only from their scarcity and difficulty of extraction but also from the difficulty of accessing them in what are becoming largely manipulated and controlled strategic markets in an array of sectors. At present China exercises monopoly, dominance, and control over the entire supply chain, from the mine to the final products. These metals have been kept out of the usual Western commodity trade circuits. As the U.S. seeks to manipulate to its advantage some of the markets it partially controls, such as the chips industry, China is well placed to respond, as it has done most recently, by placing export limits on germanium and gallium.[16] That said, had they been available, due to their scarcity, their price could well have led to constant fluctuations with sharp price rises and falls, leading to uncertainties in the costs of product production.

This strategic importance becomes particularly relevant when compared to a similar historical monopoly exercised by the Organization of the Petroleum Exporting Countries (OPEC). Today, OPEC controls 41% of oil production and as a result has gained enormous geopolitical clout over the decades. Leading member Saudi Arabia produces 10% of the world's oil and has 16% of the world's reserves. As a prime example of the power OPEC wielded, their oil embargo in 1973 crippled the U.S. economy and contributed to President Jimmy Carter's defeat in the 1980 U.S. presidential election. Even today, Saudi Arabia uses production cuts to impact the price of oil.

By comparison, China alone controls approximately 75% of rare earth production. If we refer to heavy rare earths that control reaches the extraordinary figure of 95%. One can argue that part of OPEC's comparative advantage is that its member states own[17] almost 80% of identified oil reserves, while only 37% of known rare earth deposits are in China. But China's real strength lies beyond the mines. China,

---

16 Mai Nguyen, "China's rare earths dominance in focus after it limits germanium and gallium exports," Reuters, July 5, 2023. https://www.reuters.com/markets/commodities/chinas-rare-earths-dominance-focus-after-mineral-export-curbs-2023-07-05/

17 OPEC, "OPEC share of crude oil reserves," Annual Statistical Bulletin 2022. https://www.opec.org/opec_web/en/data_graphs/330.htm

a single country, has absorbed 85% of the separation of rare earth oxides and 90% of the manufacture of these precious 17 metals; it holds the monopoly on manufacturing the final product.[18] As China was consolidating its monopoly, most of the world was abandoning these costly and environmentally challenging processes in pursuit of short-term financial gains, it made sense to outsource these problematic processes to a then-developing economy. Thus, popular pressure to combat pollution in the West helped to create the Chinese monopoly on rare earths, now strategically unparalleled in today's world of raw materials. Incongruously, the more addicted we became to a technology that depends on these metals, the more we banished them from our borders. China pursued, developed then marketed them. Today China is reaping the benefits. Imagine if Saudi Arabia, in addition to possessing the world's largest oil reserves, managed to acquire almost all the world's crude oil and then refined and sold it to the West without a regulated international market. This is exactly what China has accomplished with rare earths.

Beyond shortages resulting from exponential unmet demand driven by our crusade against climate change[19] there are other factors threatening to disrupt supply to the West. The first is China's weaponization of rare earths, its limited export in the form of quotas or denial of access to certain Western countries. In a tit-for-tat response to U.S. actions against the Chinese company Huawei, in 2020 China's top legislature passed a law on export control, allowing the government to ban exports of strategic materials and advanced technology to specific foreign companies on its equivalent of the U.S. Department of Commerce's Entity List.[20] This will enable China to use its monopoly of the world rare earths market as a geopolitical card. And even if many western communications are not under Chinese's influence

---

18 Xianbin Yao, "China Is Moving Rapidly Up the Rare Earth Value Chain," *Brink News,* August 7, 2022, https://www.brinknews.com/china-is-moving-rapidly-up-the-rare-earth-value-chain/

19 Ryan Castilloux (lead author), Adamas Intelligence, *Rare Earth Elements: Market Issues and Outlook,* Q2 2019. https://www.adamasintel.com/wp-content/uploads/2019/07/Adamas-Intelligence-Rare-Earths-Market-Issues-and-Outlook-Q2-2019.pdf

20 Iori Kawate, "China passes export control law with potential for rare-earths ban," *Nikkei Asia,* October 19, 2020. https://asia.nikkei.com/Politics/International-relations/US-China-tensions/China-passes-export-control-law-with-potential-for-rare-earths-ban

because of security reasons, Huawei sales continue to grow despite sanctions, as it expands to new arenas.[21]

A second threat to western access to rare earths is the increase in worldwide social awareness of the damage caused by mining. This environmental epiphany could lead to political action to block the opening of new mines or the closure of existing ones in western countries.[22]

Finally, an unintended disruption of Chinese supply chains could also lead to a shortage of precious metals. A new health emergency, an internal conflict in China, a civil war or any natural disaster affecting the Middle Kingdom, in whose basket all our rare earth eggs are found, could cut off Chinese production or export capacity. It doesn't take much stretch of the imagination to project the impact of a new biological threat in the form of a pandemic from China or elsewhere in the world. How long would China's borders remain closed this time? Simply closing its major ports would already have a huge impact on the shipment of critical materials. Although total national autarky or absolute self-sufficiency in our times is a pipe dream, China, via its "Made in China 2025" plan, has set a goal of 70% self-sufficiency in its high-tech industry.

China can afford such aspirations because it is the country with the greatest mastery and control over the materials that provide the physical basis for this self-sufficiency. China is a leading power in both the refining and processing and the mining of various metals and minerals, with staggering world control rates of over 20%. Among them: rare earths, antimony, tungsten, bismuth, graphite, magnesite, fluorspar, germanium, coal, arsenic, gallium, lead, tin, barite, aluminum, vanadium, molybdenum, cadmium, zinc, iron, and manganese. Although it does not fall into the metals category, China also mines more than 30% of the world's phosphate annually, which is essential to fertilizer production. China's recent ban on phosphate exports serves as proof that self-sufficiency is a criterion with significant political

---

21 "Huawei's Sales Grow Again as New Arenas Mitigate Sanctions Hit," *Bloomberg News,* August 11, 2023. https://www.bloomberg.com/news/articles/2023-08-11/huawei-s-sales-grow-again-as-new-arenas-mitigate-sanctions-hit

22 Michael Penke, "The toxic damage from mining rare elements," *DW,* April 13, 2021. https://www.dw.com/en/toxic-and-radioactive-the-damage-from-mining-rare-elements/a-57148185

weight in China's strategy. The war in Ukraine, which also affected the shipment of Russian fertilizers in response to Western sanctions, places the world in a situation which, if not unblocked, will lead to great famines. According to OECD data, China and Russia are the world's largest fertilizer exporters and together with Canada, the USA and Morocco account for almost 50% of global fertilizer exports.[23]

As early as 1950, Isaac Asimov referred to phosphate as the neck of life. Similarly, rare earths are the neck of technology. And while more and more countries are opting for protectionist measures to protect their phosphates leading to an 800% price increase in recent years, the COVID crisis and the war in Ukraine show us the vulnerability of certain supply chains. We can no longer rule out a total, abrupt and sustained cut in the supply of rare earths, which would have devastating consequences. The current microchip shortage crisis that resulted in long waiting times to receive a newly purchased car serves as the proverbial canary in the coalmine, alerting us to the problems that could occur if our supply of rare earths (which, by the way, are also necessary for the manufacture of microchips) were cut off. It is therefore essential that nations give these elements the importance they require, ensuring their production and supply chains. This is the only way to prevent history from repeating itself in the form of new resource wars like those that took place in the past over oil.

## A NEW CRUSADE IN A GLOBALIZED WORLD?

Between the eleventh and thirteenth centuries, rivers of blood flowed in search of the Holy Grail and other relics, and to ensure access to the Holy Land. At that time, it seemed vitally important to sustain the religious foundations of Catholic civilization. Similarly, struggles over rare earths are on the horizon. As our almost religious infatuation with technology grows, our consumption of rare earth grows exponentially, with no end to the demand in sight. How far would our leaders be willing to go to ensure their populations' access to technology and communication? What battles are justified in order to obtain rare earths to fight climate change, to supply our armies, and in the name of the geopolitical power?

23 Observatory of Economic Complexity (OEC), *Fertilizers,* accessed June 30, 2022. https://oec.world/en/profile/hs/fertilizers

In hindsight, we can easily observe the futility of the medieval Crusades, However, we are in danger of repeating history. To become embroiled in conflicts to obtain these scarce metals, when a peaceful solution is still in our hands, would be to return to those crusades. Today the West, led by the American capitalist hegemon, fights to defend its liberal humanist culture and its new secular gods, technology, and communication. Rare earths form the technological lynchpin. Its rival, China, has used its system of socialist autarchy veiled with capitalist touches to hijack the supply of these critical materials. The race to curb climate change, the struggle for technological superiority, and the literal arms race of our militaries are largely based on these elements. In the scramble, governments and nations count among their ranks a handful of companies that move in these complicated rare earth arenas, the contemporary equivalent of the Order of Malta or the Order of the Temple. Their directors and chief executives are the equivalent of those Templars who tried to guarantee access to a Holy Land that today are the mines containing these precious minerals. Rare earths have become today, just as relics almost a thousand years ago, essential. They constitute our holy grail, a priceless resource to be rescued.

But if we are to repeat history, there are far better passages to choose from. Beginning in the 11th century, as a result of Middle Eastern incursions, Europeans began to enjoy some heretofore rare oriental products, among them, spices. The route to bring these products to Europe, known as the Silk Road, grew in size and relevance over the decade. In the 16th century, the importance of these products in Europe was at its peak, due to their use in preserving food, especially meat, as well as for medicinal use, such as antiseptics or digestives. Hence the importance (and modern-day prevalence) of these spices, such as cinnamon, cloves, pepper, nutmeg, and ginger. As is the case with rare earths, even small quantities yielded great benefits, but then demand outstripped supply. Thus, the Spice Wars broke out between the Portuguese, the English, and the Dutch. In order to consolidate access to these resources, the Dutch government formed the Dutch East India Company (Verenigde Oost-Indische Compagnie or VOC) in 1602 and bestowed upon it the power to govern the eastern territories, manage its own shipyards, build forts, maintain armies and make treaties. This civilian company held sway and dominated the spice trade until the end of the 18th century, establishing a monopoly so aggressive that it went so far as to destroy spice plantations not under its ownership. The important lesson of history is how these wars ended and how the Dutch monopoly was broken—not by violence, but by competition. Spice production began to increase in other territories, and their cultivation adapted to other climates. In 1770, Pierre Poivre, a French horticulturist and administrator, smuggled several shoots out of the Spice Islands to plant on the Ile de France (now Mauritius) and Ile Bourbon (now Réunion). Likewise, in 1812, an Arab named Harmali bin Saleh transplanted cloves in Zanzibar and established plantations that eventually covered most of the world's demand. Other European countries took note, and during the 19th and 20th centuries managed to acclimatize spices to other continents, where they began to be massively cultivated, lowering their price, and creating sufficient supply to meet demands.[24]

## RARE EARTHS PRODUCTION IN EUROPE: THE SILLAMAE FACTORY, ESTONIA

The political and religious leaders who launched the crusades—kings, popes, and bishops—would have been on the verge of a panic if, after securing their treasured relics, witnessed their disappearance overnight. All the effort, pain and sacrifice of their armed vassals and devoted parishioners would have been in vain. Without them it would be very difficult to justify the divine origin of the monarchy.

If, after waking up, I noticed that my computer, cell phone, television, tablet, etc. had disappeared, my feelings would probably be similar. My treasured belongings would have disappeared. New times, new gods, but similar channels of worship, materialized in objects. What would a future in which rare earths suddenly disappeared be like? It is obvious that food and water are critical for our existence; governments and citizens are clear that they need a continuous and uninterrupted flow of these. But few realize that without an adequate supply of certain metals their modern world would collapse. These metals constitute today, along with other critical materials, a

---

24 James Hancock, "European Discovery & Conquest of the Spice Islands," *World History Encyclopedia,* November 8, 2021, https://www.worldhistory.org/trans/es/2-1872/descubrimiento-y-conquista-europea-de-las-islas-de/

cornerstone, a *sine qua non*. Without them, many of our industries would have to cease production, a glimmer of which we saw during the COVID pandemic. Many of these affected industries are directly or indirectly related to human and/or national security.

The reality is that our modern-day relics, in the form of rare earths, have already disappeared; we simply haven't woken up to the fact. Within Europe, the Solvay plant in France and especially the Sillamae factory in Estonia are the only places where significant quantities of rare earths are separated. Having spent so much time studying rare earths, I felt compelled to experience the practical side of production first-hand. I needed to touch and smell the ore, and to personally experience the transformation from rock to refined product. Naturally, as a European, I could not refrain from visiting the facilities of the Silmet processing plant, seeing it firsthand, with my own eyes. So, I traveled to Estonia to visit this complex, owned by the Canadian company Neo Performance Material and located in the village of Sillamae.

My first impressions upon visiting this factory were reminiscent of the Cold War era. Its Soviet architecture and aesthetics gave me the impression that the factory could be a perfect backdrop to an old James Bond film. Its facilities could well be the property of a sinister post-Soviet oligarch, striving to manufacture the ultimate world-destroying bomb, while always on the lookout for a nosy British agent. An air of secrecy surrounds the buildings, draped in exterior pipes as archaic as they are resistant to the acids and bases they carry. These acids and bases feed the chains of mechanized tanks which, when linked together, progressively purify the product and separate the oxides from each of its individual elements—cerium, lanthanum, neodymium and praseodymium. This is known as a solvent extraction line from a series of stratification cells.

My analogy, as it happens, wasn't too far off. In these once-secret facilities from the 1980s, the Kremlin processed and enriched the uranium needed to manufacture nuclear bombs—these are the same plants and the same machinery with which today rare earths are separated.

My visit started with an introduction to one of the plant's operations managers. As he explained to me, the procedures used haven't changed much since the Soviet era and are in line with the inherited Russian machinery. The rare earth oxide concentrate coming from the mine starts to be processed in the third plant by using acids or basic solutions in precise and continuously controlled proportions. These same acids and bases are involved in other related hydrometallurgical processes such as roasting, leaching, solution purification, electrowinning, and smelting. The hydrometallurgical processing methods are described in a flowsheet that is specifically adapted to the chemical composition of a specific concentrate. The product leaving the Silmet separation plant is the carbonates of each of the rare earth elements contained in the initial concentrate from the mine, but already separated. Then, as he explained to me, the metal is fabricated, usually by electrolysis. The metals obtained can in turn be used to form alloys with other metals or elements.

The Soviets have long since departed, but Neo still employs Russian-speaking Estonians from the Estonian border city of Narva, from where it imports part of its rare earth concentrates. The factory itself is only 27 km away from the Russian border. Probably, if the facilities were expanded, it would be much easier to recruit skilled labor if the plant were to be located in Russia rather than in Estonia, or anywhere else in Europe at large. Europe has for too long been a stranger to the world of rare earths.

The importance of Silmet's strategic location in the Estonian town of Sillamae is commensurate with its past, present, and future. Connected by a railway and a small seaport, the factory is supplied with energy from the nearby shale oil power plant, an unconventional oil whose deposits were the origin of the settlement in 1927. Much of the region has electricity via a general network that was connected to the Russian energy network that provides electricity, largely of nuclear origin, at a very competitive cost. The manager is very much a hands-on director. A native of the region, he is aware of the importance of his roots and contacts in the region in managing the factory and solving any problems that may arise. His friendly and approachable character doesn't detract from a fantastic perspective on the world of rare earths, and an extensive background in mining. He relates that under Soviet ownership, the factory's proximity to the sea allowed them to dump the waste directly into it.

As an aside, this was not an exclusively Soviet practice. In the French tourist paradise of La Rochelle, Solvay, home of the only rare earth refinery in western Europe, the local plant also dumped its waste, rich in the radioactive element thorium, into the Atlantic in the early 1980s. With Solvay having been a frequent destination on my itineraries as an exchange flight instructor with the French Air Force, I became uncomfortably aware of the unwitting risk I took of enjoying a potentially radioactive seafood dinner then in Solvay—or indeed, now in Sillamae.

Despite a considerable degree of obsolescence, Silmet's existing facilities and machinery continue to fulfill their function. Their age doesn't detract from an appreciation of their uniqueness and strategic value; Silmet has for many years been the largest rare earths separation plant on western soil. The fall of the Berlin Wall and the disintegration of the USSR left Estonia with one of Europe's secret hydrometallurgical treasures. Even Lynas, the Western Australian leader in the rare earths market, has its refinery in Malaysia, despite having an otherwise complete vertical and integrated production chain. But unlike Lynas, Neo Performance Materials (NPM), the owner of Silmet, does not own its own mines. It must purchase its rare earth concentrates for processing at the Sillamae plant from other places.

## WESTERN COUNTRIES MUST REACT

A metals revolution is already underway and the competition for rare earths has already begun. The motives are very similar to those that led to the Spice Wars. To avoid a losing outcome, Western countries should learn the lessons of history and hasten to extract, separate and refine the precious rare earths on their own territory. Only by mastering this art absorbed and perfected by China will we be sure to escape possible violence and hardship caused by its scarcity. Even so, before the situation improves it is likely to get worse. We will quite possibly suffer a period of shortages before we can achieve large-scale production of rare earths, akin to the developmental process that occurred with the spices of Old Europe.

Our governments are beginning to adapt, but the inertia inherent in their traditional structures does not allow them to do so at the appropriate speed. Further, within a democratic system characterized by election cycles, leaders focus on short-term decision making, and often fail to fully realize, let alone address some issues that do not fit their immediate four-to-six-year timeframe. The national security organizations of many countries are trying to react in terms of energy security before globalization as we know it fragments completely. But many other actions are needed before the anticipated and likely inevitable multipolar order emerges, bringing a redistribution of power that will affect the world's financial institutions, rebalancing trade and volumes of reserve currencies and redesigning the world supply chains.

Some proactive independence is needed at the national level. Countries need to regain sovereignty over their phantom supply chains, refocusing and directing them to within allied nations. These supply lines are becoming more and more stretched and intertwined with each other. Citizens are ignorant of the provenance of resources critical for their lives, even sometimes preferring to remain ignorant. The temporary disappearance of products from some of these links, caused by the COVID pandemic and by the effects of the war in Ukraine, are symptoms of its fragility. Yet few in the public are aware of the actual causes—not just supply chain disruptions, but inability to access foundational resources.

Although the monetary value of the rare earths market is extremely low compared to other strategic markets like petroleum,[25] ensuring capitalist corporate disinterest, the strategic importance of rare earths has served to challenge major powers such as the United States as lack of access to oil challenged Japan in the past. It therefore becomes a priority to have a secure supply chain for these critical minerals for all states that want to maintain strategic autonomy. If trade war or military actions would escalate the Western countries will undoubtedly face a Chinese response via rare earth supply cuts and export quotas.

The creation of a secure supply chain, irrespective of issues with China, is even more imperative, as the rare earths market currently has no specific legislation or international agreements regulating its concrete function. We are years away from having a set of regulations and standards that regulate the rare earths market, such as those controlling, for example, the oil market with its set of international environmental laws regulating carbon dioxide emissions. The governments of Western countries (and the rest of the world in general) must

25 Approximately 190,000 tons of REO are produced annually in the rare earths market, with a current estimated value of $4.94 billion, based on $107,729 per metric ton. World rare earth prices from 2014 to 2025 (in dollars per metric ton). https://www.statista.com/

also consider in their security doctrines[26] a "worst-case scenario," i.e., an unexpected event with severe consequences, known in the bonding world as a black swan event.[27] As is, the current situation of Chinese monopoly and lack of regulation leaves Western countries exposed and vulnerable.

Among experts there is already a feeling of urgency or even alarm, but the rare earths problem, which has only grown over the past three decades, is too complicated a problem to be able to solve it in just a few years. While these experts are warning us that there is a cliff 10 kilometers away, we have decided to go forward at a breakneck pace, on the off chance that they were wrong. In the best-case scenario, technology, dependent as it is on these elements, may become part of the solution and save the day. But currently in this world there is no driver with sufficient overall responsiveness behind the wheel, and the precipice grows closer.

Perhaps the time of incremental change is over, and the time has come instead for a great reaction. If so, we must begin by understanding how we arrived at the problem in the first place. To know how to regain control over this supply chain we must first understand, how

---

26 Eugene Gholz, *Rare Earth Elements and National Security,* Council on Foreign Relations, October 2014. https://www.cfr.org/sites/default/files/pdf/2014/10/Energy%20Report_Gholz.pdf

27 Imagine the effects that the solar storm of July 23, 2012, would have had, if the face of the sun on which it occurred had instead been oriented towards the face of the earth. These types of geomagnetic storms, like the one that shook the earth in 1859, are episodes of increased solar wind emission accompanied by solar coronal mass ejections. Their effects upon reaching the earth are similar to those of the electromagnetic pulse from a nuclear bomb but occur in a more staggered manner over two days. If the 2012 solar storm had reached the earth, the magnetic radiation would have "melted" all the circuits and transformers on the face of the illuminated earth. Imagine a world plunged in gloom where not even electric pumps can pump water, nor power plants purify it, with no refrigerators or ovens, with a stopped distribution of gas and fuel—technology would regress two hundred years in so many days. How would countries react to such an event? A transformer has an estimated manufacturing time of two years, under normal conditions, from the time the order becomes firm. If most of the world's transformers and batteries are produced in China, it is very likely that China would close its borders and supply itself first in order to protect its citizens and prevent as many deaths as possible. That is the function of a government, engraved in its intrinsic nature, in the DNA of states. How will the rest of the world fare in the meantime? In February 2014, physicist Pete Riley of Predictive Science Inc. published an article in the journal *Space Weather* in which he analyzed solar storm records going back more than 50 years. He calculated the odds of a Carrington-class storm of 1859 hitting the Earth in the next ten years to be 12%.

did the Western world get into the situation of depending on China for the supply of the most critical and strategic of all materials? How did we let crucial resource access that was once in our hands slip away?

# 2. HOW CHINA CORNERED THE GLOBAL RARE METALS SUPPLY

It is not by happenstance that the only country in the world with a complete, localized, independent and autonomous supply chain is China.[28] This stems partly from the neoliberal capitalist perspective of the Western world, based on the "efficient market," which leaves the generation of its overall rare earth supply chain, to which ideally a proportionate value chain should correspond, in the hands of companies and private capital motivated primarily by the pursuit of profit. In contrast, China applies a wholistic, strategic and geopolitical perspective to its economic pursuits, entailing different rules of the game. Through state-level policies, it ignores the West's cost-based market approach to the rare earths value chain. Given the advanced state of globalization and economies of scale, this practice served as a funnel and succeeded in absorbing the entire rare earth supply chain with its associated value.

## A CULTURE WITH A TASTE FOR STRATEGY

While one-party control of the political process contributes to Chinese ability to employ a long-term strategy, there is a deeper, longstanding cultural influence on their strategic thinking. One major manifestation of this mindset lies in the so-called 36 Stratagems. These lessons of strategy, dating back to pre-Christian Chinese dynastic wars, have become part of the collective subconscious and extend to their way of doing business and their international relations. They're a staple of the Chinese educational system and are routinely referenced in the course of business. One of the major strands of these

28 Jack Lifton, "Jack Lifton on Rare Earth Supply Chains and Value Chains," *Investor News,* March 23, 2021. https://investorintel.com/markets/technology-metals/technology-metals-intel/jack-lifton-on-rare-earth-supply-chains-and-value-chains/

36 stratagems is deception. The utility of deception has deep roots in China, having been expressed by the general, Sun Tzu, in his foundational book on the topic, "The Art of War," more than 500 years before Christ, who instructed: "There can never be enough deception in war." This warrior philosopher is still considered today as one of the great masters of strategy and his teachings are a widespread staple of Chinese culture. Among the maxims he left us are "The art of war is to subdue the enemy without fighting," "You can win when no one can understand at any time what your intentions are," and "all war is based on deception."

This mindset contrasts itself with the Western perception of warfare, where deception is seen as a negative trait. Chivalric codes of honor, Augustinian just war theory, and decades of treaties and conventions governing acceptable conduct all characterize centuries of European warfare—at least in theory, with actual practice sometimes making these claims themselves seem a form of dissemblance. That said, these contrasting viewpoints play out, literally, when comparing the classic strategy games of both cultures, Chess and Go. In chess the goal is confrontation and assault, openly eliminating the opponent's pieces to secure a checkmate. The pieces are on the board from the start and, however complex the strategy, nonetheless follow rigid rules for movement. Strategy is focused on individual pieces working in concert, and while there are thousands upon thousands of permutations, only a small fraction of those create viable strategies. Competitive play requires thinking about discrete permutations, and only world-class players can routinely think more than a handful of moves ahead.

In Go, the objective is to surround the adversary, isolate him and obtain more territory than him. Unlike Chess, Go players place pieces on the board as the game progresses, with limitations on placement developing based on the opponent's own moves, rather than as prescribed rules of movement. If you are a chess player like me, your first game of Go will surely be a lesson in humility. Instead of Chess's discrete tactical nature, Go experts think in conceptual, strategic terms. Chess certainly employs general strategic lines such as "dominate the center," "develop pieces," "protect the king," which coexist with the actions of killing and being killed. But Go is dominated by a chain of strategic actions that at the end of the game show a greater or lesser dominance of the territory without the removal of any one piece or cluster of pieces leading to victory. The best chess players only resisted the onslaught of IBM's Deep Blue until 1997 but Go resisted until 2016 before being beaten by AlphaGo. Even then, an amateur player just this year developed a strategy to readily defeat that program.[29]

This fundamental difference between these two games underscores the differences in strategic outlook when it comes to understanding interwoven issues such as trade, security and geopolitics. Understanding this strategic mindset is fundamental to understanding Beijing's approach to supply chains such as rare earths. In China, the government manages the economy by setting a strategic direction and intervening directly in its enterprises. The economy is managed by first addressing national security objectives, securing the supply chain, and then maximizing the benefits of the value chain.[30] This "management" translates into a blunt manipulation of some markets, such as rare earths, which goes unnoticed due to its small size and the lack of transparency of its industry. China's ideal position in this market is none other than the one it has now. It sets a relatively low price that discourages the exploration of new resources outside China and a "prime" price for companies operating in China. Thus, it maintains *a metal production whose supply deficit only manifests outside its borders* and which, although not alarming, is sufficient to force companies that need them to choose between establishing portions of their business in China or losing competitiveness due to the procurement costs of the metals. China intelligently promotes its own development by prioritizing the use of its internal resources.

It took China 15 years to take over the entire rare earth supply chain that the U.S. abandoned in 1985. Rare earths were quietly ceded, with the Western world in the throes of globalization now a passive spectator to the Middle Kingdom's conquest of this key sector. China initially took over the most basic steps of mining, extracting generic concentrates of these metallic elements and separating each of them

---

29 Richard Waters, "Man beats machine at *Go* in human victory over AI," *Financial Times,* Ars Technica, February 2023. https://arstechnica.com/information-technology/2023/02/man-beats-machine-at-go-in-human-victory-over-ai/

30 Jamil Hijazi and James Kennedy, "Caught between rare earths and Chinese dominance," Mining.com, April 23, 2021. https://www.mining.com/caught-between-rare-earths-and-chinese-dominance

into oxides. Soon afterwards it absorbed the remaining part of the chain, concentrating the world's production of rare earth metals and alloys in its factories, including the finished refined products. Until 1980 the uses for these metals were limited to the industrial sector: glass production, catalysts and metallurgy; they lacked strategic relevance. It was China that later revolutionized their use, giving them a technological application, opening new horizons in technological fields such as communications and consumer electronics, and taking over the links in the production chain up to and including the final products.

Part of understanding the Chinese strategy is recognizing that the economic value obtained in each discrete link of the rare earth production, from the mines to the final product, is not proportional to the investments made. Large Chinese mining companies usually carry out only the mining and extraction processes, while smaller companies are involved in separation, refining and processing. Both operate at low profit margins. Mining companies try to gobble up any rare earth ore mined anywhere in the world, adapting to the most dangerous political scenarios such as in Afghanistan or Myanmar, or to the bureaucracy of countries such as the USA or Australia. But it is the refineries and separation centers that constitute a real global bottleneck. These factories are a strategic trap consciously devised by China and the yoke from which the West cannot currently escape. The Chinese government recovers its investment in the first links of the downstream value chain, thanks to the sale of the final products, where one finds the larger profit margins. Due to its state-planned and controlled industry, the Communist Party of China (CPC) can afford to have mining companies operating at marginal profit, or massively subsidize separation and refining, as it captures the supply chain of many end products made from rare earth metals. Some mining or refining companies must be sacrificed, entailing that they even operate in some periods with losses, but the state wins in the long run.

This monopoly also benefits China by implicitly obliging foreign companies to operate in China. Only in this way will they be able to enjoy a constant and secure flow of rare earths, the best prices for their products, and competitive advantages derived from the country's lax environmental and labor laws. The procedures for separating rare earth concentrates into their individual elements are an ugly business.

They are laborious and polluting, producing difficult to digest waste materials such as radioactive thorium. These separation processes were formerly the workhorse of some Western mining or metallurgical companies, who have since either gone bankrupt or opted to abandon this step of the value chain. Chinese companies absorbed this step, benefiting not only from cheaper labor costs and laxer environmental regulations, but also from strategic government support in the form of subsidies. China was and still is trying to eliminate competition by discouraging the creation of new rare earth separation centers. It is virtually impossible to fight Chinese rare earth prices without state support for separation and refining.

The French company Solvay serves as an example of failure due to lack of government support in the West, in this case in the processing of rare earths and their toxic by-products. Today, this company is the only European company, together with the Sillamae plant in Estonia, with sufficient capacity to process and refine rare earths, separating them from the radioactive element thorium and obtaining their metallic elements. During the 1980s, its La Rochelle factory, located in a beautiful and touristic French area, expelled waste byproducts containing thorium into the Atlantic Ocean. Before environmental groups took to the streets, many tourists "enjoyed" local seafood suspected of radiological contamination. Demonstrations against the company, then part of the former French public company Rhone-Poulenc, led to a policy of outsourcing the refining stages to China. The expertise required to refine rare earths evaporated in France but was quickly absorbed in the Cantonese Mandarin region.[31] The Solvay company, heir to Rhone-Poulenc, currently maintains a token rare earth separation capacity which it does not enlarge for fear of the kind of environmental backlash it endured in the 1980s.

Forty years have passed since this American and French political and business failure, stemming from lack of strategic vision, ceded requisite knowledge, technology, and jobs to China. Meanwhile, the Asian giant has exploited Western lethargy and mastered refining, becoming the largest importer of rare earth concentrates from mines in third countries. It thus extends its dominance over the first link in the chain beyond the 40% of the world's rare earths reserves located

---

31 Guillaume Pitron, *The Rare Metals War,* 102–106.

on its territory. In addition to maintaining the strength of this link in its supply chain, it also avoids a domestic environmental impact by outsourcing it. If necessary, in order to suppress competition, it can and does purchase rare earth concentrates at prices even higher than market prices.

## A DISGUISED MONOPOLY

China's real tool of control over the rare earths market is based on an overwhelming, consciously created, worldwide monopoly over the process of separating its elements and manufacturing the metals from their oxides. China extracts the oxides of the various rare earths from every ore concentrate that arrives at its refineries. Although they come from different parts of the globe and each one contains a particular and specific mixture of elements, China's accumulated know-how allows it to adapt and separate them from different kinds of minerals. Sometimes they are even just targeted as byproducts, the first extraction objective being other metallic elements such as iron.

At this stage, China already captures 85% of the world production of these oxides; if we refer specifically to heavy rare earth oxides, it controls a frightening 100% of production. But subsidies to these Chinese companies, tax exemptions, and environmental regulations[32] play out further in the manufacturing process of each of the metals, further increasing its monopoly of world production and raising it above 90%.

In the manufacturing phase, the concentrate of a given rare earth oxide (e.g., neodymium oxide) is refined into its metal. This stage marginally increases the value of the metal; one kilogram only increases in value by about $10, or 23%. This does not compensate for the production costs and is not profitable without subsidies and favorable tax conditions. But all the money that the Chinese state "loses" or rather "invests" through these companies is recouped in the next and final stage of the production of products based on rare earth metals. In particular, magnets[33] of neodymium alloyed with iron and boron (NdFeB) are the most valuable manufactured component. At

32 Jack Lifton, "Jack Lifton on Rare Earth Supply Chains and Value Chains."

33 Swiss bank UBS forecasts that demand for NdPr will soar by 300% by 2030, driven by the consumption of electric vehicles (an electric vehicle typically carries between 1 and 2 kg of NdPr in its engine) and wind turbines, which use about 200 kg of NdPr.

present, 95% of the profits made in the rare earths market come from end products such as these magnets.[34]

However, until 2023 no one could accuse China of throttling its rare earth exports; on the contrary, China had been increasing them. China has flooded the rare earths market with its metals, alloys and metal powders at subsidized prices that drive out competitors and prevent the entry of new companies.[35] It has achieved mastery in a commercial technique known as "dumping" but it has also achieved a mastery unparalleled on the planet in hydrometallurgy and chemical engineering. Despite these measures, export supply cannot meet the rapidly increasing global demand for rare earths. Thus, there is still a certain global shortage outside China's borders, but not within.

The latest events suggest that shortages could increase or even turn into supply disruptions. In February 2023, China imposed sanctions on two defiant American manufacturers over arms sales to Taiwan, Lockheed Martin Corporation and Raytheon Missiles & Defence, a subsidiary of Raytheon Technologies Corp. These sanctions came immediately after Beijing pledged to take countermeasures in response to Washington's downing of a suspected Chinese surveillance balloon that entered U.S. airspace at the end of January. Now these two entities will be added to China's sanctions list, meaning they are banned from importing, exporting, and investing in China.

In April 2023, China was considering prohibiting exports of certain rare-earth magnet technology in a move that would counter the U.S.'s advantage in the high-tech arena. Beijing officials were planning amendments to its technology export restriction list. The revisions would either ban or restrict exports of technology to process and refine rare-earth elements or manufacturing the magnetic alloys.

The tendency is clearly identified and seems consolidated, as at this writing the Asian giant has retaliated in response to the CHIPS Act by imposing export controls on eight gallium and six germanium products starting August 1, 2023.

---

34 Hijazi J.and Kennedy J., Caught between rare earths and Chinese dominance. April 2021. https://www.mining.com/caught-between-rare-earths-and-chinese-dominance

35 Assessing and Strengthening the U.S. Manufacturing and Defense Industrial Base and Supply Chain Resilience Report to President Donald J. Trump by the interagency task force pursuant to executive order 13806 Sept. 2018

It is no coincidence that the market par excellence for the sale of minor or rare metals, and the only one where rare earths can be bought and sold—the Asian Metal Market—is controlled and managed by the Chinese authorities. As it is the only point of sale, the world price of these elements is set by China. And meanwhile, the West is forced to continue to feed this voracious giant that controls the impregnable fortress of rare earths, irrespective of whatever sanctions or Taiwan-related threats it may direct towards China. All Western rare earth mining or processing companies can still be publicly bought; China simply exercises its right to purchase these companies. By contrast, none of the Chinese ones are for sale to foreign capital.

## THE SEVEN SISTERS AND THE "BIG THREE" AUTOMAKERS: CHINA COPIES THE U.S. OIL MONOPOLY PRECEDENT

It should come as no surprise that this CPC-sponsored modus operandi is a faithful reproduction of an old Western strategy. While Chinese industry is accused of having shamelessly copied some of our patents,[36] its government is reproducing the strategy historically followed by the Anglo-Saxon oil companies known as "the seven sisters." These seven companies (Exxon, BP, Chevron, Shell, Mobil, Texaco and Gulf) similarly held a monopoly of the crude oil market, reaching a share of 85% at its peak, having bought all available oil wells outside their territories and then transported the extracted crude to domestic refineries. The heirs of this monopoly, which operated from the mid-1940s until 1970, are none other than today's BP, Shell, Chevron and ExxonMobil.

By copying this method, China has outsourced much of the pollution generated in its rare earth supply chain[37] and taken control of the processing. For the past decade, the first step in the chain, mainly extraction and beneficiation (separation of ore and gangue[38]), has

36 Office of the United States Trade Representative, *2022 Special 301 Report* (April 2022), 44–53. https://ustr.gov/sites/default/files/IssueAreas/IP/2022%20Special%20301%20Report.pdf

37 Willis Thomas, Alex Tonks, and Juan Esteban Fuentes, "Why rare earths are vital for a low carbon economy," CRU, November 28, 2019. https://www.crugroup.com/knowledge-and-insights/insights/2019/why-rare-earths-are-vital-for-a-low-carbon-economy/

38 Gangue is generally an unwanted material or impurity that is present in an ore.

been carried out whenever possible outside its territory, in countries such as Brazil, Vietnam, Myanmar or the United States, which do not have rare earth processing plants. By the time they send the mineral concentrates of these elements to China, they have already left behind much of the associated environmental contaminants.[39]

The similarities between the origin of the growth in demand for rare earths and oil are also unavoidable. The oil rush began in 1859, but it was not until 1910 that demand for oil exploded worldwide, driven by the growing adoption of internal combustion engine automobiles. Similarly, it is today's electric vehicles that are high among the factors driving the demand for rare earths, which is increasing to a point where it cannot be fully satisfied. Curiously, this is similarly happening five decades after they began to have technological use, such as their incorporation in color televisions in the 1970s.

The comparison becomes even more interesting when one observes how, at the time of the world automobile boom in 1910, the USA not only led vehicle production, but also had a monopoly on fuel. On the one hand, oil was under the baton of John D. Rockefeller, with a world production share of between 60 and 70 percent, and on the other it also dominated automobile manufacturing, thanks to the "Big Three" triumvirate of Ford, General Motors, and Chrysler. Here, a single country pooled resources and production. One hundred years later, history is repeating itself and China has control of the critical resources with which to produce the most efficient motors and batteries to power electric cars. Rare earths, along with lithium and cobalt, are replacing petroleum as the lifeblood of transportation. As the sale of e-vehicles advances within China, its automakers specializing in electric vehicles are taking market share from Western brands. More than 25% of vehicles sold in China in July 2022 were electric vehicles, including hybrids.[40] If the electric vehicle market continues this trend, it is likely that with a population of nearly 1.4 billion, two or even three

---

This can be found in ore deposits where the mineral is present. During the process of extraction, these impurities are mixed up with ore in the form of stone, sand, rock, etc.

39 Tom Daly, "China becomes world's largest importer of rare earths: analysts," March 13, 2019. https://www.reuters.com/article/us-china-rareearths-idUSKBN1QU1RO

40 "China's Love of Local EVs Is Bad News for Foreign Carmakers," *Bloomberg News,* August 31, 2022, https://www.bloomberg.com/news/articles/2022-08-31/electric-car-sales-in-china-ruled-by-byd-great-wall-tesla

of the "Big Three" will be replaced with Chinese manufacturers within the next two decades. Domestic candidates such as BYD, Geely and Chery are already on the horizon. A growing middle class, cheap labor and state subsidies strategically targeted at "made in China" vehicle manufacturers represent a great springboard for globally competitive mass production.

## CHINA'S PROGRAM 863

The Beijing government has not only succeeded in securing the rare earths supply chain from capitalist competitors by using the same ruse as the Seven Sisters, but also wants to put that to similar use by dominating the automobile industry. China openly envied[41] what Volkswagen did for Germany, what Toyota did for Japan and what General Motors did for the United States. It recognizes that all the members of the G8 reached their positions due in part to owning a significant share of global automotive manufacturing. China's Ministry of Science and Technology knew that it had little hope of competing against these companies in the conventional car market. Therefore, in 2006 it decided to revamp its State High-Tech Development Plan, known as the 863 Program, and focus on "new energy vehicles," to include hydrogen-powered vehicles. This program involves not only automakers, but also suppliers, universities, and independent Chinese laboratories. Even Chinese banks are working closely with the central government on the program. With the help of their financing, Chinese suppliers of critical materials for the electric vehicle industry acquired ownership interests in mines and processing facilities in Africa, Australia, Europe, North America, and South America.[42] As a result, China has developed a vast network of influence over the most challenging links in the automaking supply chain. The distinct advantage over already lagging U.S. and European competitors is the shielding of its own critical resources via state control.

---

41 Keith B. Belton, John Graham, and Suri Xia, *"Made in China 2025" and the Limitations of U.S. Trade Policy,* July 30, 2020 (posted Sept. 11, 2020), 12. https://papers.ssrn.com/sol3/papers.cfm?abstract_id=3664347

42 John D. Graham, Keith B. Belton, and Suri Xia, "How China Beat the US in Electric Vehicle Manufacturing," *Issues* XXXVII, no. 2 (Winter 2021). https://issues.org/china-us-electric-vehicles-batteries/

To maintain this materials supremacy, the Communist Party of China avoids as much as possible "wasting" its precious national rare earths, especially the critical heavy rare earths. Therefore, if we add the imports[43] from outside its borders to its domestic resources, the Chinese monopoly of these minerals amounts to about 140,000 tons, approximately 75% of the world production. This figure shows that China overwhelmingly dominates the first link in the rare earth chain: the minerals in which rare earths are to be found. Having captured the next stages, its domestic downstream industry is also its main consumer of rare earth metal products. These, once manufactured, are needed for countless end products. The Asian country's industry absorbs more than 70% of these metals resulting from global manufacturing, followed by Australia (11%) and the United States (8%).[44]

China's efforts to nurture its domestic electric vehicle producers and suppliers are similar to the efforts it has made, and continues to make, to supply other flagship industries. Thanks to government support they are placed in a dominant position in the global trade of a wide range of products and services. These include, among others, solar panels, industrial robots, 5G repeaters, telecommunications technology, and artificial intelligence. The Belt and Road Initiative (BRI), and the New Silk Road formerly known as OBOR (One Belt, One Road), launched in 2013, is the perfect springboard to boost trade and transport of rare earths and associated products. The pipelines of the future are the railroads that transport minerals to the ports that China is inaugurating halfway around the world. This network of communications and infrastructures favors both imports and exports, underpinning its global monopoly.[45] This initiative will enable China to become the center of gravity for 100 countries from which it will absorb its critical and strategic materials.

---

43 Adamas Intelligence, *Rare Earth Magnet Market Outlook to 2030,* August 2020. https://www.adamasintel.com/report/rare-earth-magnet-market-outlook-to-2030

44 Natalia E. Gómez Gabás, "Geostrategic implications of Chinese hegemony in the rare earths market," Global Strategy Report, 43/2020, Sept. 2020. https://global-strategy.org/consecuencias-geoestrategicas-de-la-hegemonia-china-en-el-mercado-de-las-tierras-raras/

45 George Barakos and Helmut Mischo, "The Potentials of Scientific and Industrial Collaborations in the Field of REE through China's Belt and Road Initiative," *International Journal of Georesources and Environment* 4(3), July 2018.

The Beijing government is learning from our past Western colonial history. China's neo-colonization has so far produced no bloodshed. It pursues its interests but establishes flexible and adaptable relations with third countries. Its trade agreements are more attractive to many developing country governments than IMF and World Bank loans and aid programs conditioned on structural or domestic policy changes. A good example are the railways built by Beijing's state-owned companies in the Great Lakes region (Uganda, Rwanda, Burundi, and the Democratic Republic of Congo) that transport minerals to the port of Mombasa in Kenya. Despite Kenya's vulnerability to having its port taken over in compensation for its non-payment of its accumulated debt, while this is presumably an option for China it nonetheless appears to be one China has not as yet pursued. Nevertheless, it gives China officials a leverage position towards Nairobi government, to negotiate, for instance, extraction or transport rights of its minerals.

China is not content with securing its monopoly in the short term; it is planning for the long term to dominate intellectual property. Proof of this is that since 1996 China has become the world leader in the registration of patents related to rare earths. This ensures technological dominance associated with the generation of patents. China's investment in the field of research and development related to these metals has followed a geometric progression in recent years, while in the rest of the world it has decreased. If Western governments have not invested their public funds in research and development in this domain of rare earths, it is because this veiled threat has either not been on the radar of many countries until recently or has not been given sufficient importance in national policy.[46]

## HOW THE WEST'S GLOBALIZATION DROPPED THE BATON

Not all the Western regions or powers started from the same position when it comes to addressing their strategic collapse as it concerns access to rare earths. Some were unaware, others naïve, others

46 Jakob Kulik, *Unter dem Radar. Die Strategische Bedeutung Seltener Erden für die wirtschaftliche und militärische Sicherheit des Westens,* Arbeitspapiere, Bundesakademie fur Sicherheitspolitik, 13/2019. https://www.baks.bund.de/de/arbeitspapiere/2019/unter-dem-radar-die-strategische-bedeutung-seltener-erden-fuer-die

pursued only short-term interests, but all of them let the Holy Grail slip through their fingers and into the hands of China.

The first to wake up to this self-inflicted wound to the world's critical supply was Japan, which sought the support of a mining-friendly country such as Australia. The Sino-Japanese conflict over the Senkaku Islands, in which rare earths were militarized by China in the form of a supply cut-off, led to their mutual alliance. As a result of this alliance, since 2010 they have been trying to escape the yoke of the Chinese monopoly and have achieved a certain degree of independence in their production and supply chain.

It was not a historical blunder that left the West's access in the hands of China, but a lack of strategy dedicated to rare earths and other materials. Chinese leaders have been better able to read and interpret history and prehistory, noting how in the past the discoveries of new metals have led to major cultural shifts and transfers of power, giving rise to the metal ages. These 17 metals escaped the strategic radar of the West. Despite being their discoverers, they were not given the relevance they required. After the fall of the Berlin Wall, our Western industries gradually became oblivious to the production of critical metals. In a rush to accelerate post-Cold War prosperity, Western countries gladly embraced the brave new world of globalization, feeling certain that their American big brother protected them. With an unrivaled navy, the leader of the NATO alliance had secured the world lines of supply through the seven seas.

Democratic liberal countries welcomed, among other commercial procedures, the techniques derived from the Japanese "just-in-time" business culture. This supply chain orientation eschews stockpiling necessary parts and materials, and instead develops supply chains that can deliver these goods right as they're needed, thus avoiding costs associated with storing excess material. It seemed a win-win proposition for companies looking to reduce overhead costs. On one hand, China was not even a shadow of a threat at that time, and the West was outsourcing the supply chains of many critical metals to the Middle Kingdom. On the other hand, it avoided the negative environmental impacts of extracting and processing them, while enjoying the benefits of low labor costs in China. At that time our environmental concerns finished mainly at our borders, and we disregarded the dark and hidden side of this arrangement: the devastation of large areas of China[47] dedicated to rare earths mining. Although nowadays the Chinese government has progressively modified its environmental regulations,[48] a great deal of damage has already occurred, and it would be disingenuous of the West to deny that it had benefited indirectly from it.

The West opted for "low cost at any cost" and our theoretically efficient market, based on liberal capitalism, abandoned the rare earth supply chain.[49] China not only strategically captured the first links in the supply chain (mining and refining) through its directed market, but progressively developed the next links up to the finished products. It also created new uses for these elements, cornering this market, building its monopoly and making the rest of the world "metal-dependent" on its products. As the doses of rare earth metals required were increasing, our self-sufficiency was becoming almost non-existent. Today, whether we like it or not, many critical elements no longer behave under the laws of the capitalist free market because they are under the power of another system, that of the Chinese. And the uncertainty generated by fighting against a directed market goes against the basic profit requirements of our Western mining companies. The principles of *"Realpolitik"* should show the West how vulnerable it is to the blow of a baton in the hands of the Beijing government, which has the rare earths Holy Grail confined within its walls.

## CHINA'S UNNOTICED STRATEGY

The Chinese fortress that encloses the world of rare earths did not come about via fortuitous accident but as part of a strategy beginning in 1986 with its "National Technology Research and Development Plan." Since 1984 China has doubled its Gross Domestic Product (GDP) by a staggering 26 times. It has been driven not only by its strategic plans but also by demographic and productivity changes,

---

47 Michel Penke, "The toxic damage from mining rare elements," *DW,* April 13, 2021. https://www.dw.com/en/toxic-and-radioactive-the-damage-from-mining-rare-elements/a-57148185

48 Ministry of Ecology and Environment, he People's Republic of China, "Emission Standards of Pollutants from Rare Earths Industry," October 1, 2011. https://english.mee.gov.cn/Resources/standards/water_environment/Discharge_standard/201111/t20111101_219415.shtml

49 Sophia Kalantzakos, China and the Geopolitics of Rare Earths (Oxford University Press, 2017). https://academic.oup.com/book/25755

which for much of its history have made it one of if not *the* most powerful nation in the world. As the famed strategist Napoleon Bonaparte mentioned, "China sleeps there, God have mercy on us if she wakes up. Let her sleep!"

Western nations tend to think policy in time spans equating to election cycles, but the Chinese Communist Party has the luxury of developing truly long-term strategies. The fruits of this vision are many of the rare earth utilities that were little more than a laboratory dream in the 1980s. These new uses have become a reality thanks to strategic state subsidies which, from the late 1990s to date, have contributed to China's establishing itself as holding undisputed domination in rare earths. However, these metals are only the tip of the iceberg, since two-thirds of the processing of the strategic materials needed for the energy transition is carried out in China. Downstream, the situation does not improve as control of production reaches, among others, more than 80% of lithium batteries and more than 80% of the production of solar panels that are often only assembled in Western countries. Same happens with some more specific elements which fall outside of the governments' radars: 60% of smart inverters regulating the energy obtained by rooftop panels connecting them to the internet, for instance.[50]

Insofar as this strategic vision and control over metals extends from renewables to electric vehicles, China is thus taking the opportunity to "greenwash" their industries, presenting them as ecologically friendly. Its purported goal is to champion global decarbonization. Indeed, it just so happens that China can carve a niche in the automotive market, where it was heretofore unable to compete with Volkswagen, Toyota, or Ford at the end of the value chain. By developing electric vehicles, China is also reducing its dependence on oil imports from abroad. Thus, for the first time in two decades oil imports have decreased from 73.6% in 2020 to 72% of total consumption in 2021[51] As we can see, the control of these metals is not a peripheral thing. Rather, it allows

---

50 Andrew Brown, "Coalition says inverters in rooftop solar systems are national security risk," Jul 22, 2023, https://reneweconomy.com.au/coalition-says-inverters-in-rooftop-solar-systems-are-national-security-risk/amp/

51 Zheng Xin, "China's oil dependence on imports sees drop," *China Daily,* Feb. 24, 2022. https://www.chinadaily.com.cn/a/202202/24/WS6216e135a310cdd39bc889be.html

China to progressively restructure or reshape the global automotive and renewable energy markets. These tectonic plate shifts in world trade do not occur at random but are the result of a calculated and developed strategy that is part of Chinese culture.

## SOFT POWER VERUS HARD POWER

Some Western-allied countries neighboring China, intimidated by its growing power, are arming themselves with nuclear submarines (e.g., Australia). Their hope seems to have been channeled towards security alliances such as NATO or AUKUS (Australia, U.K., U.S.). The West emphasizes hard power and the development of state-of-the-art weaponry, deploying frigates and aircraft carriers in the Indo-Pacific region. Even Japan has begun negotiations to join the AUKUS military alliance. But these organizations have not mastered the language of energy security, nor do they know how to jointly secure the supply chain of rare earths or other strategic materials. In short, they have not mastered the language of soft power.

Diplomatic, economic and information domain measures may be discussed in their Security Councils or equivalent bodies, but countries act individually and sometimes prioritize their national interests. NATO has some soft power tools such as its strategic communication center, but their scope is very limited for these purposes. Bluntly put, it will not be Western security organizations that will penetrate China's rare earth fortress.

Meanwhile, China, for its part, continues with its principle of non-interference in military affairs beyond its borders. Its geopolitical offensive is in actuality a real exercise of soft power and extends by placing pieces on the board little by little, silently, conquering territories without the need to use any weapons. Its strategy is more subtle and elaborate. The best of China's aircraft carriers, which ensure deterrence beyond its borders, do not need to emulate its U.S. and U.K. competitors by "showing the flag" worldwide.

Compared to the more than 20,000 tons of "diplomacy" exercised by U.S. aircraft carriers deployed in the oceans of the globe, the Chinese state-owned giant China Rare Earth Group exercises another, more practical deterrence. The company was created in December 2021 by regrouping three rare earth mining companies (Aluminum

Corporation of China, China Minmetals and Ganzhou Rare Earth Group). This new conglomerate exercises direct control over 70% of rare earths in the People's Republic of China and allows China to effectively control the amount of ore mined, adjust the production volume of refined metals, set export quotas more accurately, and centrally enforce export tariffs.

All this gives China enormous power to set global rare earth prices. It not only gives the Beijing government greater control over world prices, but also helps it to combat its existing black market for rare earths. The PRC thus increases the efficiency and responsiveness or use of this soft weapon. It will be its leader, Xi Jinping, who will decide the degree of lethality and its use in proportion to the threat to China's national security or interests. In other words, the rare earths supply chain has been taken hostage and may be executed depending on the behavior of governments opposed to Beijing.

However, the China Rare Earth Group should not be considered in isolation. In fact, there are no less than 97 Chinese state-owned companies that move under the governmental baton of the State-owned Assets Supervision and Administration Commission of the State Council (SASAC), directly under the State Council. Other Chinese instruments include the chemical giant Sinochem, the satellite communications company China Satellite Communications Co. Ltd, the electronics company China Electric Equipment Group and the logistics company China Logistic Group. The scale of these companies is compounded by their low cost of labor and the support of their government, which is reflected in the appropriate regulations. State subsidies are the icing on the cake, giving them great power to distort the free market and great advantages over their Western competitors.

The ability to "militarize" the use of these entities isn't limited to the military sphere, as restrictions or cuts in the supply of many products including rare earths are also useful during the intermediate stages of pre-conflict. These measures could also be part of a gray zone conflict characterized by cyber-attacks, information campaigns, embargoes, etc. Used with caution, they prevent the conflict from escalating into a conventional war. They are an invaluable weapon to possess in times like the present superpower competition and trade war. Those who consider the high-performance semiconductor chain the most relevant in this globalized world, focusing exclusively on its most vital production center—the Taiwanese Taiwan Semiconductor Manufacturing Company (TSMC)—may fail to consider the significant role of the China Rare Earth Group which almost exclusively provides the heavy rare earths required for TSMC to operate.

Thus, like a seasoned Go expert playing against novice western players, China has masterfully maneuvered itself into a position to exert soft power to nullify western hard power before a conflict even begins. We now find ourselves desperately trying to salvage a viable strategy to prevent encirclement.

# 3. THE WEST WAKES UP

## DE-GLOBALIZATION: NEW WALLS OF PROTECTION AND STATE AID

Whether it is due to "ideological goodwill," Western ignorance or the natural consequence of neoliberalism, the fact remains that in combination with China's monopolistic strategy, defined in the mid-1980s, China's production of rare earth metals has progressively increased, to the detriment of the rest of the world. For more than two decades, China kept production prices so low that no other country was willing to compete with its companies. Such competition would also have meant accepting a high environmental price that the West was unwilling to pay. China seized this opportunity to take the initiative and bought foreign companies stumbling under economic difficulties.[52]

Today, there are fewer than 30 Western mining companies with rare earths mining projects,[53] and fewer still produce rare earths in significant quantity. These few holdouts will have to prove their economic viability whilst fighting against Asian competition. This is a tall order, as they must both resist the impetus to sell their concentrates to China, as well as fend off a Chinese state that either absorbs many of their products or purchases stakes in their businesses. But the trend may have begun to change. For as the thrust towards globalization fails, protectionism may re-enter the scene with a vengeance. The West may have no choice but to resort to Realist politics and push its more constructivist ideologies off the stage.

52 David Pérez, "China monopoliza todas las 'tierras raras' esenciales para la tecnología," *El Confidencial,* January 28, 2014. https://www.elconfidencial.com/tecnologia/2014-01-28/china-monopoliza-todas-las-tierras-raras-esenciales-para-la-tecnologia_81222/

53 Melissa Pistilli, "How to Invest in Rare Earths" (Updated 2023), *Investing News Network,* October 12, 2023. https://investingnews.com/how-to-invest-rare-earths/

Although it comes late, the reaction to undo the Chinese refining bottleneck has already begun. Aware that the most sensitive link in the chain is refining, certain countries have decided to encourage its expansion. As a result, supported by the EU, the Mkango company aims to set up a rare earth refining plant in Poland for the whole of Europe by working with the Polish company Grupa Azoty Pulawy, a leading producer of fertilizers and chemicals. The required ore will come from its planned project in Malawi, giving access to Neodymium and Praseodymium, but also to the precious heavy ones, dysprosium and terbium.[54]

On the other side of the Atlantic, the Canadian government has opted for the creation of a state-funded rare earths refining plant. In this case, state intervention comes in the form of investment by the regional government of Saskatchewan, which has financed it to the tune of 31 million Canadian dollars. This will enable its mining companies to process minerals with a high rare earth content, as well as by-products from the extraction of other metals. These processing plants are essential not only to feed local supply chains but also to export to allied countries. Canada is also forcing Chinese shareholders with stakes in lithium mining companies in its territory to sell them. Other countries could follow suit.

Brazil is also betting big. If its products do not end up in the Asian giant, it could play a fundamental role in wresting control from China, as it has one of the world's largest reserves of rare earths and huge quantities of mining bargains containing these metals. Its government is carrying out a study (the Regina project)[55] together with the German company Fraunhofer, one of the world leaders in technological innovation. The objective is to develop a vertical and integrated supply chain from the mine to the magnets. In March 2022, the company Auxico[56]

54 Mkango Resources Ltd., "Mkango to Create European Rare Earths Hub in Poland with Grupa Azoty Pulawy, Poland's Leading Fertiliser and Chemicals Company," *Globe Newswire,* June 7, 2021. https://www.globenewswire.com/news-release/2021/06/07/2242420/0/en/Mkango-to-Create-European-Rare-Earths-Hub-in-Poland-With-Grupa-Azoty-Pulawy-Poland-s-Leading-Fertiliser-and-Chemicals-Company.html

55 "REGINA Rare Earth Global Industry and New Applications," *CLIENT II,* Federal Ministry of Education and Research (BMBF) (accessed July 2022). https://www.bmbf-client.de/index.php/en/projects/regina

56 Auxico Resources Canada Inc., "Auxico Reports Thorium Extraction Results on Rare Earth Concentrates from Tin Tailings, Massangana Project, Brazil," *Cision,*

announced its intention to build a thorium and uranium extraction plant, also on Brazilian soil, to take advantage of the gangue from the Massangana tin mines, which are rich in rare earths. Finally, the most promising Brazilian project of the mining company is Sierra Verde which, with state support, includes heavy rare earths in its extraction and processing, considered the most critical for expansion.

But this Western reaction comes after decades of disinvestment in mining in their territories and in some branches of the metallurgical industry, the result of an outsourcing evident in the drastic decrease of open mines and processing centers in Europe or the United States. This disinvestment has been inversely proportional to the growing dependence on many critical materials from mining that began to have a strategic weight just two decades ago. The lack of investment in research and development patents, along with the lack of associated patents, is symptomatic of national strategies failing to adequately address rare earths. The West has watched impassively as the existing talent in this field has been drained from its European and American universities. Mining is increasingly being pushed into a corner and rare earth-related specialties are virtually non-existent. However, the battlefield for these metals extends to laboratories, and very few Western companies in this sector have research centers. Neo Performance Materials, with two research centers, one in Singapore and one in Estonia, is certainly an exception and a guiding light in the midst of the storm.

Large Western companies are today trying to secure the supply of rare earths, either by controlling their mines or simply by acquiring their ores or concentrates. The pressure has been growing, due to supply shortages or outages and their consequences. Competition is becoming increasingly fierce. These geological rarities are not only scarce and difficult to locate but require an average of 10 to 15 years from discovery and exploration to being fully operational.[57]

It is not surprising that the new mines will not be enough to meet future mineral demand. The companies that decided to bet on

---

March 16, 2022. https://www.newswire.ca/news-releases/auxico-reports-thorium-extraction-results-on-rare-earth-concentrates-from-tin-tailings-massangana-project-brazil-882472483.html

57 Fred Sveinsson, "How to build a mine," *Resource World,* March 24, 2017. http://resourceworld.com/how-to-build-a-mine/

them a little over a decade ago had to seek financing for fifteen years ahead, dodging the effects of the 2008 world economic crisis. They also invested without being able to provide a rigorous "macro" forecast of the amount of green metals needed for our disjointed energy transition. And they did all this without state aid, while competing against the Asian giant. Many of those that tried succumbed in the attempt. One of them was the American rare earths flagship Molycorp that shipwrecked in 2014. But it was not the only company to suffer damage from competition with the Asian giant. This time downstream in the supply chain, Magnequench, the U.S. manufacturer at the time of the best super rare earth magnets. was acquired earlier, in 1995 by Chinese capital. There's no one better than the current chief executive of Neo Performance Materials, who experienced these first two battles firsthand, to describe those turbulent times. As Constantine Karayannopoulos points out in several of his speeches, he still bears the scars on his back from that struggle, in which China managed to dismantle the American rare earths stronghold Molycorp. What follows is the result of much research and cross checking through interviews.

## MAGNEQUENCH CASE STUDY: INDUSTRIAL ROBBERY, POLITICAL BUCK-PASSING, OR SIMPLY GLOBALIZATION?

In 1986, General Motors held the patents for the most powerful of permanent neodymium magnets, manufactured by what was the most underrated jewel in the American rare earth crown, the Magnequench company. This Indiana-based company supplied products with the highest quality standards to numerous customers, including the U.S. Military. However, the 1995 purchase of Magnequench was approved by the U.S. Committee on Foreign Investment during the Bill Clinton administration. Just over six years later the company moved to China, from where it still operates today. The acquisition was made through the Sextant Group Inc, founded by Archibald Cox, Jr. and financed by a Canadian holding company, MQI, which served as a front for two Chinese state-owned companies, Beijing San Huan New Materials High-Tech Inc. and China National Non-Ferrous Metals Import & Export Corporation, each one headed by one of President Deng

Xiaoping's sons-in-law. Just months before the Magnequench acquisition, San Huan New Materials was cited by the U.S. International Trade Commission for patent infringement and corporate espionage. The company was fined $1.5 million.[58]

It was not by chance that Magnequench, along with all its patents, came to serve the purposes of China's 863 Program, the afore-mentioned state plan for high-tech development. After 2001, when the American production line closed, the U.S. Army no longer had a domestic supplier of the magnets that equipped 85% of its precision-guided ammunition; Magnequench had moved to China. But the problem went unnoticed and was much deeper and much more relevant to security than a single production line. Virtually all computer systems depend on these small, powerful magnets for data storage. Without them, no weapons system could be assembled.

In the absence of a strong reaction from the U.S. government, Magnequench was subsequently acquired by Onfem Holdings. The veil had already fallen. This holding company was owned by Chinese state-owned companies related to the mining and metallurgical sector, and in addition to being based in Hong Kong was again headed by one of the then Chinese president's sons-in-law. When in 1992, the 88-year-old leader of the Asian giant Deng Xiaoping remarked, "The Middle East has oil, China has rare earths," nobody paid any attention to him outside his country's borders. However, his vision would become a reality that has transcended with immense force to the present day.

In 2005, Magnequench, now under Chinese ownership, merged with the Canadian rare earths company AMR, in which Constantine Karayannopoulos was a founding member, creating the company Neo Materials Technologies Inc. with the latter at the helm as chief executive officer. After Neo was bought and absorbed by Molycorp, the fall in prices engineered by China brought down this new American bastion of rare earths. The wreck was picked up in 2015 by the American private equity group Oak Tree, a giant specializing in high-risk convertible debt. These factories were then regrouped around the new company Neo Performance Materials, whose board of directors

58 Richard Mills, "Magnequench has left the building," *FNArena,* February 9, 2012. https://www.fnarena.com/index.php/2012/02/09/magnequench-has-left-the-building/

was initially led by Constantine. Just a few years later he became the head of the management team.

In 2008 Magnequench became a political sticking point in the election campaigns. Senator Hillary Rodham Clinton, in her battle for the Democratic presidential nomination against Senator Barack Obama, recriminated against him for what had happened with the company when located in Valparaiso, Indiana. Perhaps she forgot that it was actually her husband's administration that had authorized the purchase of Magnequench. But leaving the political context aside, the Magnequench case is a perfect illustration of the problems inherent in globalization. It is one example amongst many of the security implications of American deindustrialization via offshoring and its replacement by a FIRE (finance, insurance, real estate) economy, with the attendant loss of its supply chains.

In July 2008, the Washington-based Economic Policy Institute (EPI) presented a shocking study on the loss of manufacturing jobs to China.[59] The study concluded that the United States had sent 2.3 million jobs to China since 2001. As globalization has progressed, the U.S. has been losing manufacturing jobs and 78.7% of the population now works in the service sector. There has been a massive human capital flight from several rungs of the supply chains at a time when the U.S. had no rivals of its stature in the world since the fall of the Berlin Wall. At the time the ownership of Magnequench migrated, China was no match for America. Years later, with the rise of the Asian giant and the awakening of social awareness of the fragility of U.S. supply chains, Magnequench became a politicized scapegoat. But with a minimal amount of digging, it's easy to find similar cases. It would be enough to follow the trail of all the materials that are critical today for national defense and of the factories that used them for Department of Defense production—materials which weren't considered critical in 1980 because they were extracted and processed on American soil.

What makes this case so striking is the fact that ever since the underestimated Chinese government's gambit of pretending to set up shop in American territory in order to subsequently acquire one

59 Robert E. Scott, "The China Trade Toll: Widespread Wage Suppression, 2 Million Jobs Lost in the U.S.," EPI Briefing Paper, no. 219 (Washington D.C.: Economic Policy Institute, July 30, 2008). http://www.epi.org/briefingpapers/219/bp219.pdf.

of the opponent's chess pieces, China's rare earth fortress has grown and become impregnable, while the West has rested on its economic laurels.

To return to the story of Constantine Karayannopoulos, Neo CEO survivor of all acquisitions, mergers and shipwrecks, participant of these battles, he and his company were granted in 2015 the most valuable jewels in the world of rare earths, inheriting not only factories that have a strategic nature but also the problems of having to deal with the echoes of the past Magnequench leak and the speculation surrounding it.

The reality is that Neo, despite having factories in China, has developed a complete and vertically integrated international chain, "from the mine to the magnets" outside of China. In the end, Constantine's business strategy reflects the reality of the rare earth world in which the West cannot move forward either with or without China. Like it or dislike it, it seems that at the moment Neo is as much part of the problem as part of the solution. In addition to the Silmet factory in Estonia, there is the Thai rare earth metal and magnetic powder factory developed by AMR more than 25 years ago and a state-of-the-art patent research and development center in Singapore.[60] Neo Performance Materials has continued to secure Western access to China's precious magnets and is a bridge to the advanced Chinese rare earth world within its walls.

After visiting the Silmet factory in Estonia, I had the pleasure of meeting Constantine personally and interviewing several of his managers. On the outskirts of the plant, in a mansion-restaurant in the middle of a Baltic forest and gathered around a huge wooden table in the purest medieval style, were the chief executives of each of its factories and centers spread throughout China, Canada, USA, Estonia, Singapore and Thailand, gathered for dinner.

Surely there is no more authoritative voice in the world of rare earths in the West than Constantine. He knows the trade from every angle, having spent the last 30 years both inside and outside China. This chemical engineer of Canadian nationality but Greek origin has the air of a respected military leader about him. His managers treat

---

60 John Tkacik, "Magnequench: CFIUS and China's Thirst for U.S. Defense Technology," The Heritage Foundation, May 2, 2008, https://www.heritage.org/asia/report/magnequench-cfius-and-chinas-thirst-us-defense-technology

him with a respect that stems more from admiration than from his position in the business hierarchy. In turn, Constantine reciprocates with a trusting manner delineated by an invisible line that everyone recognizes and knows not to cross. In conversations with his management team, it's clear that they are aware of both the important role they will play in the coming years and the complexity of the world in which they operate.

Constantine's experience, coupled with a privileged vision, has allowed him to develop a fundamental business survival strategy in this intricate rare earths business. His strategy allows him to benefit from the huge rare earths market within China, but also to be a candidate to take advantage of the huge growth margin provided by the Western market. While many Western companies in the major sectors such as automobiles and IT are currently investing their know-how by setting up on Chinese soil, Neo can draw on the rare earth expertise it has developed intensively over the last thirty years to retain independence. In fact, Neo's Western customers are already benefiting from this know-how. So far, Neo has not needed its own mine because it has its own suppliers of rare earth concentrate. This reduces its vulnerability to price fluctuations, as its business is to add value through processing and manufacturing.

Despite Neo's symbiosis with China's complicated semi-public rare earths network, it remains a Western company based in Canada and owned by Westerners. Proof of its relevance are the requests for support it has received from different Western governments studying supply alternatives. But having visited the aging facilities of the Sillame plant and its obsolete rare earth processing machinery it seems clear to me that Neo, despite having one foot in China, is limited in its actions. Surely if it could obtain and extract from China the best machinery necessary for separation and refining, it would have already done so. This type of state-of-the-art machinery is available in the Asian country at very competitive prices that make it an object of desire for other Western companies, many of them neophytes in the sector. Building new industrial machinery specifically designed to carry out hydrometallurgical separation processes outside China can be very costly and involve lead times of more than 3 years, without guaranteed results of the same quality.

Finally, as unique as his company is, Constantine knows that it is not enough *to produce* in the rare earth world. Whether inside or outside China, he must have customers to whom he can sell either his metals or his finished products, such as super magnets. This is where the Neo strategy gives access to both exclusive Western and Chinese customers. Neo supplies Samsung and other Asian companies, but many of its super magnets can also be found in Western-made electric vehicles. Should the Beijing government decide to go on a rare earth price-cutting offensive, Neo would probably be one of the only Western companies with a chance of survival. The Chinese branch of his company would allow him to weather the storm until the waters calm down. But Constantine and Neo are not alone in this rare earth crusade.

## TESLA

Tesla, one of the world's leading companies in the electromobility market, is also a major player when it comes to the procurement of rare earths. Without rare earths, the path to electrification of transport, essential to reduce the global carbon footprint and combat climate change, would be really rugged. The challenge is no small one. In the words of the company's CEO, Elon Musk, the complete electrification of the global automotive sector alone would require doubling the current electrical output.[61] The implications of such a challenge are truly staggering, because a large part of this electricity, stored in the batteries of electric cars, will come from renewable sources. At the same time, these will also require enormous quantities of certain "green metals" requiring their extraction to be greater in the next three decades than in the last three centuries of history. One of the first repercussions is that we will leave some metals, such as copper, in danger of extinction, following the fate of animal species that are currently protected. It is not without reason that pressure is growing in the USA to declare copper a strategic metal.

If we refer to rare earths, one need only look at a traditional car to see the magnitude of the importance of these magnets. Supermagnets

61 Reuters Staff, "Tesla CEO says electric cars will double global electricity demand," Reuters, December 1, 2020. https://www.reuters.com/article/us-tesla-electric-germany-idUSKBN28B5Q8

are found not only in the motor and battery system of electric vehicles, but in many of the systems internal to conventional combustion vehicles: the climate control system, transmission, steering and brakes, various sensors, security systems, cameras, window and door controls, entertainment systems (speakers, radio, etc.), and in the fuel and exhaust system of hybrids.

Elon Musk himself, aware of the looming problem, breaks standards, or rather recovers the older standards of Ford or General Motors and enters the deepest rungs of the supply chains. Tesla is gradually cutting out the middleman and directly procuring 95% of lithium, 50% of cobalt and 30% of nickel needed for its cathodes, which represent almost 50% of the value of its car batteries. This leads it to sign contracts directly with some of the world's largest mining companies[62] such as Brazil's Vale S.A. Tesla does not resort to the rare metals markets of Chicago and Shanghai. By skipping the middlemen, it avoids as much as possible the problems of a trade subject to geopolitical fluctuations and manipulations. In the case of lithium, Elon Musk is not content to rely on these contracts and is starting the development of a processing plant in Texas. Strategically located near the South American lithium triangle, it will allow him to escape the 80% control rate of the world's lithium refining in China. But securing nickel in this case leads him to partner with a company with a dubious environmental reputation. The mining giant Vale S.A. has recently been involved in scandals such as the rupture of the Brumadinho dam in Brazil in 2019, which caused a human and environmental catastrophe resulting in 270 deaths.[63]

Similarly, the cobalt comes from a deal between Tesla and Swiss mining giant and trader Glencore Plc., which sources the ores from the Congo. Congo cobalt has long been considered a conflict mineral, associated with child slavery, corruption, and its use to fund non-state military groups. Perhaps for this reason, Elon Musk, after a first round of negotiations to acquire between 10% and 20% of the company, withdrew his offer, claiming only that the company's carbon footprint was excessively high. In addition to being a visionary, this

62 Tesla, *Impact Report 2021* (accessed May 17, 2022). https://www.tesla.com/ns_videos/2021-tesla-impact-report.pdf

63 "Vale dam disaster: $7bn compensation for disaster victims," *BBC News*, February 4, 2021. https://www.bbc.com/news/business-55924743

chief executive is well-informed, well-advised and well-aware of future strategic mineral shortages. Although he intends to reduce his dependence on cobalt in the coming years, before the competition for these metals begins, he has not only secured his mineral supply, but is even considering the idea of operating mines "made by Tesla." In this way, his company would avoid the deterioration of its social image by signing contracts with mining companies that move on the borderline of good and evil.

However, Elon Musk cannot employ this strategy with the rare earths that equip his vehicles. There is no company outside of China that manufactures all the necessary elements for his cars. Dysprosium, virtually unavailable outside of China, is essential for ensuring the coercivity of electric motor magnets, especially that of the main motor such as the one incorporated in his Model 3 since 2018. Tesla's factories in China have access to these elements and their motors, equipped with rare earth super magnets, provide better performance. Despite this, Tesla prepares some series of vehicles in factories outside China, with completely different induction electric motors designed to survive the shortage of rare earths. These induction electric motors equip Tesla's Model S and X. They use a copper or aluminum cowling, just like the Audi e-tron model. But they are exceptions in an automotive industry increasingly converging towards permanent magnet designs for their superior efficiency and energy density.

Thus, in 2020, 77% of the electric car market used permanent magnet motors. This proportion has remained fairly constant over the last 5 years. This is one of the main reasons for the forecast growth in demand for neodymium, which will increase elevenfold between 2022 and 2032.[64] A less efficient motor also requires a larger and heavier battery, further reducing performance. In contrast, the weight of the super magnet-equipped motor is lower, and the power provided higher, increasing range and power. In addition, motors containing rare earths made in China are no more expensive than those made in the U.S. or Germany without them. These competitive Chinese prices are a consequence of their government's strategic subsidies and the discount of sales taxes within their territory to these and other "green

64 James Edmondson, "Rare Earths in EVs: Problems, Solutions and What Is Actually Happening," October 28, 2021, https://www.idtechex.com/en/research-article/rare-earths-in-evs-problems-solutions-and-what-is-actually-happening/25071

metals," with final prices lower than those paid anywhere else in the world.

Even if manufacturers were to refrain from using rare earths in their vehicles, there is little point in manufacturing them if they are not going to sell as well as vehicles equipped with rare earths and manufactured in China because they have lower performance and/or higher prices. After the signing of the largest free trade agreement in history by 15 Asian countries, the 2022 Regional Comprehensive Economic Partnership (RCEP), which eliminates most tariffs in the Indo-Pacific area, it seems natural that Chinese vehicle manufacturers will supply this entire market. Only European and U.S. manufacturers with subsidiaries in China in the form of joint ventures such as Tesla's will be able to enjoy these advantages. Even so, another new option announced by Tesla is to produce motors equipped with magnets that dispense with rare earths altogether. Although they do not have the same performance as their counterparts equipped with neodymium super magnets, Tesla will surely improve the inferior performance of their other induction electric motors.

Other Western companies trying to escape Beijing's control also set out in search of rare earths outside China. These are usually mining companies, which assume the risks of operating in countries where security may be questionable. In some countries, the poor level of governance is conducive to dirty business and corruption—or vice versa. An example is the English company Rainbow Mining, which is trying to operate a mine in Burundi with the self-purported greatest wealth (by concentration) of rare earths on the planet—not without risks, as we shall see.

## (ALMOST) ALL RARE EARTH ROADS LEAD TO CHINA

Although more and more Western companies are enlisting in this effort to try to break China's stranglehold on rare earths, as a result of China's strategic plan outside its walls, there are only two companies today that produce a significant amount of rare earths from their mines. They are the Australian Lynas Corporation and the American Mountain Pass Materials.[65] However, the U.S.-based MP Materials continues to

65 Mary Hui, "US rare earths miner MP Materials takes on China dominance,"

ship all of its rare earth concentrates to China for processing and a portion of the company (10%) is owned by Chinese capital, through the state-owned Shenge Resources Holding Company, which also retains exclusive sales rights. Furthermore, its announced processing capacity has heretofore been periodically delayed, so it is not known whether it will succeed where its predecessor company, Molycorp, failed.

Given the dimensions of this national and international security problem, the U.S. government's $35 million aid package to MP Materials seems insignificant compared to the company's own plans to invest $700 million to develop the missing part of the supply chain and achieve independent magnet manufacturing. Some media outlets announced in early 2023 that MP Materials had created a supply chain independent from China by shipping its concentrates to Japan through the intermediary, Sumitomo Corp., after processing them in a Vietnamese plant.[66] However, what they intentionally or ignorantly omit is that this plant, Vietnam Rare Earths Company Limited, is 80% owned by the aforementioned Chinese state-owned company Shenghe Resources.[67] In the world of rare earths things are not always what they seem. Behind the curtain of some theatrical announcements by companies promising "geopolitical salvation" or their "ecological posturing" is the search for public or private financing. Companies are neither patriotic nor ecological; they go where the money takes them. This reflects their intrinsic capitalist nature, unless they are state-owned enterprises, as are those of the Chinese.

In the case of the Australian company Lynas, although it is dedicated to the manufacture of rare earth metals, its capacity is limited compared to the sum of Chinese state-owned rare earths companies. Lynas mines provide monazite ores which contain only light rare earths. Therefore, it can only autonomously manufacture light rare earth metals. And, in terms of finished products, among all items, it focuses on the manufacture of Neodymium magnets. The profitability

---

*Quartz,* November 16, 2020. https://qz.com/1931653/us-rare-earths-miner-mp-materials-takes-on-china-dominance

66 Cecilia Jamasmie, "Only rare earths miner in US to bypass China in supply deal with Sumitomo," *Mining.com,* February 22, 2023. https://www.mining.com/us-only-rare-earths-miner-to-bypass-china-in-supply-deal-with-sumitomo/

67 Peak Rare Earths Limited, "Shenghe Resources to acquire a 19.9% interest in Peak Rare Earth" (ASX Announcement), February 14, 2022. https://wcsecure.weblink.com.au/pdf/PEK/02486046.pdf

and importance of these items is reflected, for example, in strategic alliances with companies such as the German Siemens AG, as it is the most required and profitable product. Heavy rare earth metals, which are not as economically profitable[68] but are critical to national security components, are not produced in-house.

Therefore, we can presently state that almost all countries except Australia sell for a small profit the rare earth mineral concentrates from their mines, either directly or through intermediaries, to China. China, in turn, after separating and refining them, sells them back the refined rare earths powders, metals or products with a large economic profit margin. If the Lynas processing center in Malaysia is threatened with closure due to unproven accusations of environmental damage, this dependency on Chinese refineries could be almost complete—at least before the different initiatives of Western processing plants turn into a reality and scale up.

The aforementioned company, Neo Performance Materials, has established what could be the right approach to the problem. In an agreement with the American company Energy Fuels, it receives tailings and gangue from other mineral extraction endeavors. These by-products are rich in rare earth elements. Energy Fuels first removes the radioactive element thorium, which is the 200-kilogram gorilla in rare earth mining projects. Neo then processes the rare earth concentrate, separating the elements at its main strategic asset, the Silmet plant in Estonia, then ships the processed concentrates to its mill in Thailand, where it manufactures the metals. It thus ensures a complete supply chain in line with the standards of respect for the environment, support for the governance of countries and their society, reflecting its consideration of Environmental, Social and Governance (ESG) criteria. Even so, its international chain "outside China" is not completely independent, as it must resort to the Asian giant, just like Lynas, for its supply of heavy rare earths.

---

68 Andy Home, "U.S. finds its Chinese rare earth dependency hard to break," Reuters, July 28, 2020. https://www.reuters.com/article/us-usa-rareearths-ahome-column-idUSKCN24T20J

## THE ASIAN GIANT IS SPREADING ITS NETS

Western policymakers should be cautious about investing in this business network. Mountain Pass Materials illustrates why making decisions without considering the company's relationship with each rung of the supply chain can lead to funding and thus increasing China's monopoly on rare earths. In 2018, according to consulting firm Argus Media, the U.S., through MP Materials, was the largest supplier of rare earths to China, only closely followed by Myanmar. Moreover, the quantities of concentrates of these were progressively increasing between 2018 and 2020.[69] A more extreme example, in this case referring to lithium, is the company Lithium Americas, which despite its name has as its majority shareholder the Chinese company Ganfeng Lithium, the largest lithium producer in the world.

As Mountain Pass Materials demonstrates, developing a comprehensive domestic supply chain "from mine to magnets" like the Chinese is no easy task. It requires more than a decade, large investments, and in most cases environmental policies and tax measures that are flexible or adapted to their production. So, although the U.S. possessed the seventh largest reserves in the world in 2016, it did not produce a single kilogram of rare earths. Although Mountain Pass Materials' efforts in 2017 saved the U.S. mine and restarted mining after acquiring it from its failed predecessor, 6 years on it has yet to produce significant quantities of separated rare earth oxides, let alone metals.[70]

Without government support, both regulatory and financial, the risk for a rare earth company is twofold. On the one hand, companies may go bankrupt as the Chinese government sets artificially low prices for longer than Western companies in the sector can maintain their liquidity, especially given their usual small size. Simultaneously, the Chinese government is trying, with little fuss, to acquire as many mining companies as possible that produce rare earths or their ores. The acquisition strategy differs from country to country. Unlike

---

69 "China raises US rare earth imports in 2020," *Argus Media,* January 22, 2021. https://www.argusmedia.com/en/news/2179624-china-raises-us-rare-earth-imports-in-2020

70 Samantha Subin, "The new U.S. plan to rival China and end cornering of market in rare earth metals," CNBC, April 19, 2021. https://www.cnbc.com/2021/04/17/the-new-us-plan-to-rival-chinas-dominance-in-rare-earth-metals.html

Western governments, China has the ability to adapt to regulations (or lack thereof). In Western countries, a company must comply with administrative procedures and at some point in the process it needs political approval. In the case of Karvenfeld in Greenland, the Chinese government attempted to purchase and obtain a permit to operate one of the richest rare earth deposits in Europe. The political decision to approve the Chinese offer did not leave the citizens indifferent and led to early elections. The ruling party that had initially supported the Chinese takeover in early 2021 lost, leading to the cancellation of the deal. The Chinese state-owned company behind the attempted phagocytizing was none other than the one that already owns 10% of MP Materials in the USA, the Shenge Resources Holding Company.

Throughout the process, Greenland was acutely aware of the environmental damage caused by irresponsible rare earth mining and the Chinese government's voracious attempt to maintain control over the rare earth market. Unfortunately, the same local government that stopped the Chinese advance from the opposition and subsequently won the elections is not encouraging the opening of this mine by Western companies for the time being, either. These companies, on their own and without government support, cannot take the entrepreneurial risk.

Lithium follows the same scheme, and the best example is Chile. In this South American country, the critical materials are nationalized, but 20% of the largest state-owned company SQM (Sociedad Química y Minera), which exploits Chile's lithium salt lakes, is owned by the Chinese Tianqui Lithium Corp., and SQM sends all its concentrates to China. There they are processed by refining centers in which Chileans can participate in the form of joint ventures or leave them in the hands of Chinese companies. The same has happened with Argentina's richest deposit. The 3Q project is located in South America's "Lithium Triangle." It is the fifth largest lithium brine project in the world and among the top three in terms of grade. In January 2022, the Chinese company Zijin Mining[71] announced that it had acquired the project. But Zijin also moves well in the shifting sands of low-governance countries and had created a joint venture with Congolaise d'Exploitation Minière (COMINIERE) that same month. This African "joint

71 Zijin Mining, "Zijin Mining Completes Acquisition of Neo Lithium," February 5, 2022. https://www.zijinmining.com/news/news-detail-119227.htm

venture" *has* launched the group's first lithium exploration project in the DRC, located on the periphery of the Manono lithium mine, the world's largest hard rock lithium mine.

China is taking over lithium globally and doesn't mind taking an initial loss on investment. By creating vertically integrated domestic supply chains internationally it recoups those investments later. It is quite possible that this company will sell its lithium to the Chinese battery giant CTL, which is opening a new factory in Germany and will sell to Volkswagen, among other customers. Almost simultaneously, the same thing happened with the company Lithium Millennial,[72] which owned 100% of the Pastos Grandes lithium project in Salta, Argentina. This project was acquired by Lithium Americas, which again is a Chinese company despite its misleading name.

Although Australia is still the territory where most lithium concentrates are produced, if we take into account the Chinese properties outside its borders, the calculations show a different reality. It would also be interesting to review the "theoretically private" shareholding of Australian companies. Because the other option left for China is to enter through the back door of a non-transparent shareholding, going unnoticed through the purchase of shares in mining companies.

The tool, as in the case of Magnequench, can be a "holding company" or an investment fund from other countries, acting as a screen, without disclosing the true origin of the buyer. Data from the U.S. Geological Survey Agency show that in recent years China has reduced its global share of rare earth mining production in terms of metric tons from 90% to 60%, but these calculations do not incorporate all the minerals belonging to its mines in other countries. Even if the Chinese government fails one way or another to gain ownership of the mining companies, there is always the final option of simply buying their products. Even Lynas, the Western rare earths powerhouse, bases much of its economic viability on selling metals to China.

---

72 Global Newswire, "Lithium Americas Completes Acquisition of Millennial Lithium," *Financial Post,* January 25, 2022. https://financialpost.com/globe-newswire/lithium-americas-completes-acquisition-of-millennial-lithium

## HOW THE WEST CAN ESCAPE THE CHINESE STRANGLEHOLD

The creation of a vertically integrated national company "from the mine to the magnets," with governmental, regulatory and financial protection, is the best choice from the point of view of national security. However, this option currently requires 15 years of patience, and it needs to be accompanied by palliative measures to solve the problem of dependence on China in the short and medium term. A more agile and less costly alternative for a government is the creation of international cooperative production agreements. That would mean following the example of Neo Performance Materials, with an internationally orchestrated production chain in which each factory in each country specializes in one step of the supply chain. A similar model is proposed as a solution by the EU, which identifies different projects in different member states for possible financial support. In an ideal capitalist world, by incentivizing and coordinating entrepreneurial initiatives, a complete supply chain could be created within Europe. Despite this proposal, which is part of the European Raw Material Alliance, there is as yet no European country willing to convert any of the few existing quality deposits into mines. In addition to the fight against a manipulated market, there is also a fight against environmental protection groups.

The exception to the rule was Ukraine. Before the Russian invasion, the EU had just signed, in July 2021, a strategic partnership with the Ukrainian government for the exploitation of its mining resources under the umbrella of its Critical Materials Action Plan. Ukraine's impressive potential in critical materials would enable it to secure access to the material bases to drive its European Green Deal and carry out its energy transition, based on renewable energies and electric vehicles. It was of ancillary benefit to Russia that its 2022 annexation of the Donbas region encompassed the center of metallurgy in Ukraine. This area was the birthplace of the first Soviet smelting furnaces. These facilities were pioneers in using coal, by importing the technique from England during the years of the industrial revolution.

It is not easy to determine to what extent imperialist forces are driving the engine of Russian autarky or the pursuit of resources related to its security as opposed to its complaint regarding the expansion of NATO, and its effort to protect Russian-speaking citizens in the regions it subsequently annexed. The U.S. companies Shell Oil Co. and Chevron Corp. were also interested in exploiting oil and gas fields in the Black Sea and were in negotiations with the Ukrainian government shortly before the invasion.[73]

Given the current situation, and without being able to count on Ukrainian mines and deposits, Europe's only refinery with significant capacity, Neo Performance Materials' Silmet refinery in Estonia, is forced to look outside Europe for suppliers of rare earth concentrates. Seeking to diversify its supply, it focuses on minerals from the American company Energy Fuels and in October 2022 also created a new strategic alliance. The signing of a pre-agreement with the mining company Australian Rare Earths Limited to accelerate the development of the Koppamurra rare earths in Western Australia will give it access to its key neodymium, praseodymium, dysprosium and terbium, deposits, amongst other elements.

Following in Neo's footsteps, other companies are making inroads in Europe with similar alliances. One of them is Norway's REEtec[74] which plans to build a new refinery that will be fed with minerals from Canada's Vital Metals, to provide the EU with 5% of the rare earth metals it requires. Behind the promises of many junior mining companies, however, is the attempt to keep the flame of shareholding alive. Only the extent of their financing will allow them to cover expenses and stay alive until they reach a tipping point where they either get funding and permits to start full-scale exploitation of their mines or are forced to wind down their company.

The Swedish mining company Leading Edge Materials exemplifies this complicated situation. Due to its geographical proximity, it could be the perfect supplier for REETec's new refinery, but its mining project has been put on hold by the government for environmental reasons. Among the young American companies, one of the great hopes is the mining company USA Rare Earths and Texas Mineral

---

73 Murray Brewster, "Natural gas, rare earth minerals: What's at stake for Ukraine in the territory Russia is trying to conquer," *CBC News,* May 27, 2022. https://www.cbc.ca/amp/1.6467039

74 REEtec, "REEtec raises NOK 1200 million for first industrial plant," November 8, 2022, https://www.reetec.no/artikler/reetec-raises-nok-1200-million-for-first-industrial-plant

Resources Corporation. If this company manages to exploit its unique Round Top Mountain deposit in Texas, it could obtain 16 of the 17 rare earth elements. However, due to the deposit's richness in Uranium the company will have to fight with all the regulations surrounding the mining and handling of this radioactive element in the USA.[75]

Beyond the promising young companies, including Australia's Iluka, with plans to have its own refinery, the reality is that if the major Western mining companies such as Rio Tinto, BHP, Fortescue, etc., decided to take advantage of the rare earths in their tailings or waste, the West has a good chance of rescuing these essential metals. Vale S.A. announced in 2019 its intention to use by-products from its copper mines to process rare earths. The British mining company Rainbow Mining also signed an agreement in 2022 with the Moroccan state-owned company OCP Group to extract rare earths from the gangue of its phosphate mines used as fertilizer.[76] Even so, these projects require time that the West lacks to solve the problem. The three closest buoys to hold on to before we witness the shipwreck are Lynas with its own mine and its new refinery project on Australian soil, Neo Performance Materials with the planned expansion of the Silmet facility and the American MP Material which could come in a few years to process heavy rare earths.

## THE WEAPONIZATION OF RARE EARTHS

In view of China's predominant control of rare earths, it is well situated to use this control to its advantage, countering perceived negative acts by the West against it. Its options include the threat to embargo rare earths sales to the West or, in its more subtle version, to establish restrictive export quotas or a ban on supplies to certain companies. Insofar as the struggle of Western mining and refining companies to obtain rare earths has not produced clear results, relations between China and the USA are becoming tense. In the competition for world leadership, "trade war" with tit-for-tat exchange of sanctions and tariffs marks a rivalry that spills over into the realm of foreign,

---

75 Richard Roy Blake, *The Rare Earth Crisis* (independently published, 2022).

76 Álvaro Escalonilla, "Morocco signs cooperation agreement with Rainbow, a leader in the rare earths market," *Atalayar,* June 6, 2022. https://www.atalayar.com/en/articulo/economy-and-business/morocco-signs-cooperation-agreement-rainbow-leader-rare-earths-market/20220823112957157889.html

security and defense policy.[77] Just as in the past the U.S. and oil-producing countries have used oil as a diplomatic and political weapon, so too rare earths have already been used as a weapon against strategic U.S. defense companies such as Lockheed (LMT) Martin Corporation and Raytheon (RTN) Missiles & Defense, a subsidiary of Raytheon (RTN) Technologies Corp.

Although there had already been threats against these companies in the past for selling arms to Taiwan, these sanctions came just after the Beijing government announced that it would respond to the downing of a Chinese "observation" balloon that had entered U.S. airspace without permission in January 2023. These two companies were added to China's "list of entities" that are unable to import, export or invest in the Asian giant. The key word this time is "import" as they will no longer be able to buy Chinese rare earths and other critical metals essential for the manufacture of weapons systems. This has always forced the U.S. to keep rare earths and their products off its tariff list.[78]

The implications for the Ukrainian war are so obvious that speculation leaves the door open to the idea that China intended with this measure to support Russia by decimating American arsenals and by extension those of the allied bloc of countries. If we approach the most "conspiranoid" theories, we could think that the balloons were a bait that the U.S. took, giving China the pretext to freeze part of the Western arsenals. Even so, the EU maintains an incoherent division in its relations with China and the U.S. between its economic interests that bring it closer to the Beijing government, and its moral values and its Western-style foreign and defense policy. The EU-China relationship is alarmingly similar to that of the EU with Russia before the outbreak of the war in Ukraine.

## THE WAR IN UKRAINE: VULNERABILITY AND DEPENDENCE IN EUROPE

The invasion of Ukraine not only sent the price of nickel into the stratosphere, but also jeopardized the EU's energy security due to its

77 The Chinese government recognizes leadership aspirations in the official publication, *Made in China 2025.*

78 Tom Daly, "U.S. Leaves Rare Earths and Critical Minerals Off China's Tariff List," *EuroNews,* May 14, 2019, updated December 9, 2019. https://www.euronews.com/2019/05/14/us-leaves-rare-earths-critical-minerals-off-china-tariff-list

dependence on Russian fossil fuels. The impact on strategic minerals held by Russia, especially nickel, was such that it forced the closure of the largest Western metals trading center, the London Metal Exchange, as its nickel warehouses ran out of stock. The Tingshan Holding Group, the world's leading nickel producer, attempted to cover its own back with a more or less standard trading technique –shorting the price of nickel. Faced with the huge price increase due to the scarcity of the metal, it was not able to respond to a margin call to maintain its positions. Several Western automakers, who needed Russian nickel for their batteries, had a difficult few months. The same happened to steel producers, for which nickel provides its anti-corrosion properties and resistance to high temperatures. Barely a month after the Russian invasion of Ukraine the price of a ton of nickel had risen fourfold to $10,000 a ton. Some nickel-rich coins were worth considerably more for the metal they contained than for their fiduciary value, among them the American nickel, worth at face value five cents on the dollar but containing 33% of the metal nickel.

Although the London Metal Exchange returned to normal operation in the weeks that followed, it seemed time for Tingshan to draw conclusions and lessons learned, or ...perhaps just cheat? When China can't get in through the front door, it usually finds a back door or an open window, as has indeed been the practice of commodity traders worldwide. The London Metal Exchange, the last trading center with physical transactions in the West, was bought in 2012 by the Hong Kong Stock Exchange, which was subsequently integrated in 2016 with the rest of the Chinese stock trading centers. Thus ended the London Metal Exchange's 135 years of independent operation. Now, the London Metal Exchange is part of a stock market regulated directly or indirectly by the Chinese government. It is no coincidence that the London Metal Exchange's largest logistics hub for metal storage is no longer Rotterdam, but rather Port Klang in Malaysia.

Both before and after the entry of Russian troops into Ukraine on February 24, 2022, the U.S. appeared to have its foreign, security and trade policies more strictly drawn than the European Union, dividing the landscape dichotomously between allies and non-allies, and pressuring allies to do the same. Prior to that, Europe had looked to Asia and signed in December 2020 the EU's largest trade agreement to date with China, the Regional Comprehensive Economic Partnership

(RCEP). Incoherently and almost simultaneously, sanctions were exchanged between the two large blocs arising from Western human rights claims concerning China's policy towards the Uyghur minority in the Xinjiang region.[79]

Although the trade agreement has not entered into force for the time being, it shows Europe's intention and economic interest in EU-China relations. Its ratification could lead to a policy consolidation for Germany, the largest economic and political power in the EU, which in July 2018 sponsored the signing of agreements by some of its most strategic companies (Siemens, SAP, Volkswagen, BMW, BASF) with some of China's business strongholds (State Power Investment Co., Alibaba Cloud Computing, Brilliance Group, and Anhui Jianghuai Automobile Group).[80] These deals are intertwined with other Chinese government plans such as the new China′s new Silk Road,[81] which aims to buy strategic infrastructure in Europe and influence its trade policy. The German government was paying the price for having China as its largest trading partner when in September 2021 some German companies, including Siemens, faced accusations of favoring forced labor of Uighur prisoners.[82]

The situation is again dramatically reminiscent of the situation before the Russian invasion of Ukraine in February 2022. The United States reminded its allied partners that the energy pacts with Russia implied their willingness to undertake a strategic alliance with an autocratic country with no respect for human rights and opposed to NATO. However, at that time, Germany was firm in its decision to finish the construction of the Nordstream 2 pipeline. Building the pipeline, the U.S. complained, was not simply creating or reinforcing an alliance with Russia, but also increasing Ukraine's vulnerability

---

79 European Union Parliament, "MEPs refuse any agreement with China while sanctions are in place," May 20, 2021. https://www.europarl.europa.eu/news/pl/press-room/20210517IPR04123/meps-refuse-any-agreement-with-china-whilst-sanctions-are-in-place

80 "German companies clinch Chinese deals at Merkel-Li meeting," Reuters, July 9, 2018. https://www.reuters.com/article/us-germany-china-contracts/german-companies-clinch-chinese-deals-at-merkel-li-meeting-idUKKBN1JZ1K9

81 Matthias von Hein, "China: Germany's difficult balancing act," *DW,* August 9, 2021. https://www.dw.com/en/china-germanys-difficult-balancing-act/a-59043815

82 "Rights group files complaint against German retailers over Chinese textiles," Reuters, September 6, 2021, https://www.reuters.com/business/retail-consumer/rights-group-files-complaint-against-german-retailers-over-chinese-textiles-2021-09-06

with respect to its Russian enemy. Today the EU is 98% dependent on Chinese rare earths and still has no open mines. So far, sanctions between China and the EU have been limited to the diplomatic sphere without affecting the wider economy. However, as tensions escalate the EU is aligning itself with U.S. foreign policy, and trade war with China is also reaching Europe as well. The export ban on germanium and gallium impacts also the EU as they are defined as strategic and critical for many industrial sectors.[83]

## CONFLICT OVER TAIWAN: THE U.S. RARE EARTHS ACHILLES HEEL

Just as Russia invaded Ukraine, China has also announced its intentions to further integrate Taiwan with the mainland. To date, while Taiwan is recognized as a region of China both in U.S. law and by the United Nations, it has been willing to proceed with this at a congenial pace. U.S. threats and actions in the region make that problematic. What happened with Russian nickel would be child's play compared to a possible cut in the supply of Chinese rare earths. An exchange of sanctions with China affecting rare earths would be near-fatal not only for Western economies but also for its security. Ostensibly, China should have no interest in imposing either quotas or export bans on rare earths. This would harm it economically and could trigger a further escalation in the mutual imposition of economic or tariff sanctions. Germany had used similar reasoning to support its Nordstream 2 decision—but its contradiction to U.S. interests made such an appeal to no avail.

However, the economic benefit factor may not be so relevant for China if we look at the extent to which China's economic dependence on the U.S. has been steadily declining in recent years. Proof of the reduction of the economic weight of the U.S. and Europe on China was the signing, at the end of 2020, of the world's largest free trade agreement, promoted by China. This agreement includes Japan, South Korea, Australia, New Zealand and all the countries of the Association of Southeast Asian Nations (ASEAN) and will now account for more

83 Marc Schmid, "Rare Earths in the Trade Dispute Between the US and China: A Deja Vu," *Intereconomics* 54, no. 6 (2019): 378–84. https://www.intereconomics.eu/contents/year/2019/number/6/article/rare-earths-in-the-trade-dispute-between-the-us-and-china-a-deja-vu.html

than 40% of world trade. In January 2021, the Regional Comprehensive Economic Partnership Agreement (RCEP) came into force, allowing 15 Pacific Rim countries to trade with each other at lower tariffs. Moreover, in a few years, more than 90% of trade in goods between approved RCEP member countries will be subject to zero tariffs. According to the World Bank, the agreement covers 2.3 billion people representing $25.8 trillion in output as well as $12.7 trillion in trade.[84]

In other words, China's trade dependence on the U.S. and Europe is decreasing. The economic motive alone will probably not be a strong enough impediment in the future to dissuade China from implementing rare earth export quotas if the West interferes with its foreign policy ambitions. Here, Lockheed Martin and Raytheon serve as bellwethers. China is surely not going to make public its withdrawal of rare earths from these companies just as the U.S. is not interested in the world knowing that they were buying them from China. The Beijing government does not want to accelerate the loss of its monopoly and the U.S. arms companies do not want to risk losing customers, stock prices or sanctions.

While the U.S.-led bloc of liberal democracies could impose sanctions that might slow China's technological development, China could respond by crippling virtually all Western industries by not shipping needed critical metals. It is a game in which everyone loses, as there is a strong economic co-dependency. Nonetheless, many conflicts can and still do happen, despite their apparent irrationality. In this case securing domestic supply chains and producing key technologies indigenously is the best way out to reduce vulnerability to the impact of these sanctions.

## EXPORT CONTROLS

China's ability to impose tariffs on the U.S. is now almost exhausted, as China imports far less from the U.S. than it exports to it. Therefore, China could consider other response options. Reducing exports of rare earths, vital in the technology industry, could be one.[85] It is no coincidence that the Chinese government has recently

---

84 "World's Largest Free Trade Agreement Takes Effect," *Environment News Service,* January 5, 2022, https://ens-newswire.com/worlds-largest-free-trade-agreement-takes-effect/

85 Barbara Lippert and Volker Perthes (eds.), "Strategic Rivalry between United

established the legal basis for taking these steps.[86] China currently has a tacit "veto right" over many Western factories.

Following the enactment of its new Export Control Law in January 2021, a "control list" was established that includes both military weaponry and dual-use items. These are detailed in its "Import and Export Permit Management Index for Dual-Use Items and Technologies," which also covers nuclear, biological, chemical and missile-related dual-use items.[87] As rare earth elements are present in many final components used in these sectors, China can now restrict, for example, the export of the highly valuable rare earth composite magnets. The world is on notice.

Reflecting the prevailing tension in the rare earths market, the prices of its metals had already soared in November 2020 in anticipation of their inclusion[88] in the items controlled by the Export Control Act. Understandably, in the context of the China-U.S. trade war, this law could well be seen as a response to the "Entity list" controlling U.S. exports. If vigorously enforced, countries and companies subject to China's export quotas would be forced to prioritize the use of prod ucts made from rare earths.

However, there is another reason that may deter China from imposing severe rare earth export quotas, and that is the loss of its precious monopoly. The forceful use of this weapon could provoke

States and China: Causes, Trajectories, and Implications for Europe," SWP Research Paper 4 (Berlin: Stiftung Wissenschaft und Politik German Institute for International and Security Affairs, April 2020). https://www.swp-berlin.org/publications/products/research_papers/2020RP04_China_USA.pdf

86 "China's Ministry of Commerce on September 19, issued 2020, a State Council approved Order on Provisions on the Unreliable Entity List that calls for the establishment of a new system" to identify and respond to entities that endanger China's sovereignty, security, or development; violate "normal" market transaction principles; and cause serious damage to the legitimate rights and interests of Chinese companies, organizations, or individuals. U.S. Congressional Research Service, Insight: "China Issues New Export Control Law and Related Policies," October 26, 2020. https://sgp.fas.org/crs/row/IN11524.pdf

87 U.S. Department of Commerce, Bureau of Industry and Security, "China Export Control Information" (accessed December 2021). https://www.bis.doc.gov/index.php/enforcement/oee/220-eco-country-pages/1040-china-export-control-informationconsultado

88 CK Tan, "China's export control law to become 'key dynamic' in US relations," *Nikkei Asia,* December 1, 2020. https://asia.nikkei.com/Economy/China-s-export-control-law-to-become-key-dynamic-in-US-relations

a sufficiently strong Western reaction as to pressure it to enhance the business expansion of its own global rare earths market. In fact, the movement to escape the yoke of China's rare earth monopoly has already begun and China is loath to accelerate it. The effects of the war in Ukraine and COVID on supply chains have acted as catalysts at the global level, diminishing confidence in supply chain links.[89]

To date, it seems that the possibility of China establishing a strong embargo or heavy export quotas on rare earth products is more of a potential weapon with a deterrent effect. If used, this weapon is more likely to be used with surgical precision. The target need not be a country, but could be a specific rare earth, as is the case with germanium, or a U.S. defense company, a Japanese electronics company, a European industrial company, or any company that would offend the Beijing government or go against its interests.[90]

As China moves steadily towards global hegemony, other major international players may see their strategic autonomy eroded by the lack of a complete rare earth supply chain. China has an economic, diplomatic and even military weapon that together constitute a Trojan horse. With it, it could even halt the production of the enemy's defense capabilities in a short time. The Chinese government, aware of rare earths' importance and Western weaknesses, can use them as a strategic card against the West. Moreover, this card could also be internationally defended as having a defensive character by acting as a protective shield to avoid the imposition of economic sanctions by Western countries, who are in turn fearful of embargoes, quotas or cuts in the supply of Chinese rare earths. This uncomfortable situation for the West is aggravated by the growing influence of the Beijing government in the UN and other international organizations, in which China has been progressively increasing its level of representation.[91]

---

89 Marc Schmid, "Rare Earths in the Trade Dispute Between the US and China."

90 James Stavridis, "U.S. Needs a Strong Defence Against China's Rare-Earth Weapon" (opinion), Bloomberg, March 4, 2021. https://www.bloomberg.com/opinion/articles/2021-03-04/u-s-needs-a-strong-defense-against-china-s-rare-earth-weapon

91 Yaroslav Trofimov, Drew Hinshaw, and Kate O'Keeffe, "How China Is Taking Over International Organizations, One Vote at a Time," *The Wall Street Journal,* September 29, 2020. https://www.wsj.com/articles/how-china-is-taking-over-international-organizations-one-vote-at-a-time-11601397208

Let me present just one hypothetical scenario of the many possibles ones to expose its strategic relevance: Western war arsenals are empty. The transfer of weapons to Ukraine has left them metaphorically shivering, as Western arms companies have not been able to replenish stocks at the required rate. The problem already stems from a shortage of rare earths and critical metals from China. The companies do not openly admit this predicament, because they know they are responsible for the savage outsourcing that has left their nations in the hands of the Asian giant. This shortage, as predicted by specialized analysis centers, is progressively worsening. Western countries are coming up against the wall of technological problems associated with shortages. On the other hand, however, these countries have invested significant focus on independence in microchip manufacturing. Thus, the Taiwanese giant that dominated their manufacture is no longer so relevant. China is exploiting the situation to take actions in the so-called "gray zone" aimed at bringing down the Taiwanese government. Therefore, Nancy Pelosi's provocative trip to Taiwan in 2022 was followed up "with Beijing imposing sanctions, initiating cyberattacks, launching large-sortie incursions into Taiwan's air defense identification zone (ADIZ) and across the Median Line of the Taiwan Strait, firing ballistic missiles over the island, and conducting 'encircling' drills around the island."[92] As the situation escalates Beijing cuts off rare earths supplies to the island. The aim is to replace the Taiwanese government with one that is more favorable to the PRC. Japanese, Lithuanian, German and EU officials have since paid visits to Taiwan followed by other officials, thereby exacerbating their precarious situation caused by rare earth scarcity. This strategic card in China's hands has failed to prevent such actions. In addition, some reports suggest that Israel, France, and Germany, who had also sold or transferred some weapons or components to Taiwan in the past, such as missiles, submarines, radars, and engines, could decide to do it again. China strikes back, using its new export law backed by its giant China Rare Earth Group. Within hours these countries are under

---

92 Adrian Ang U-Jin and Olli Pekka Suorsa, "Since the Pelosi Visit, China Has Created a New Normal in the Taiwan Strait," *The Diplomat*, August 10, 2023. https://thediplomat.com/2023/08/since-the-pelosi-visit-china-has-created-a-new-normal-in-the-taiwan-strait/

embargo of these metals. Any company in the world that tries to sell armaments to Taiwan risks the same fate.

Despite the relatively dreamlike nature of this scenario, it is not difficult to imagine similar scenarios in which the mere threat of China imposing restrictions on access to its rare earths could be used as leverage to strengthen its negotiating position at the international level. China could become more aggressive on such vital issues as the recognition of part or all of its claimed Exclusive Economic Zone in Pacific waters. Other aspirations included in its foreign affairs policy agenda could include the management of the "Global Commons" such as the Arctic, the moon, the ocean floor, or space. In turn, nations aligning themselves with the Asian giant could be favored by their inclusion as a preferred nation in its export laws, enjoying an adequate flow of rare earths.

## THE FIRST CONCERN FOR CHINA IS ... CHINA!

China is concerned first and foremost with supplying raw materials for the foundations of its economy and culture, and then for those of the rest of the world. The country's development in recent decades has led to the emergence and growth of a middle class with access to previously prohibitive technology. China may have difficulty securing its own supply in the medium term[93] and in order to shore up its world trade quotas and ensure its own domestic consumption, it is beginning to build a fortress around its rare earths. Meanwhile, outside the Great Wall no country has secured the materials for its electronic gadgets or its green technology devices. One could argue that this situation has come about because of a lack of planning. However, since 1949 China has been drawing up five-year plans that set out the country's economic and social goals. The strategic vision allows China, in its 14th Five-Year Plan (2021–2025), to set targets even for 2035. China, with its almost absolute control of the rare earths supply chain, could have increased its production significantly, but it has not done so at the same pace as world demand, creating a continuous deficit. What it has done is to become a major importer of its minerals and concentrates[94]

93 Mary Hui, "A US rare earths miner is staging a comeback to take on China," *Quartz,* November 16, 2020. https://qz.com/1931653/us-rare-earths-miner-mp-materials-takes-on-china-dominance

94 Stuart Burns, "Rare earths are the next geopolitical chess game," *MetalMiner,*

and to impose masked export quotas that could conceivably increase progressively, "legitimized" to supply its own domestic market for national security reasons, or simply as needed to satisfy the growing Chinese middle class for electronic gadgets or its green technology devices.

## OTHER STONES ON THE ROAD

The shortage situation may come sooner than some analysts predict due to the secondary effects of a Chinese real estate crisis whose scope and duration is difficult to foresee. The world's largest rare earth mines located in China, in the Bayan Obo region, owe much of their economic profitability to obtaining iron as a primary element. These iron mines helped provide the new Communist Party of China with the backbone of its industry and military during its first two decades. The rare earths also obtained there, as a by-product, were used primarily to harden alloys. Today, the slowdown in the construction sector has led to a decline in the demand for steel and thus for iron from the Batou mines in Bayan Obo. Although the Beijing government is supposed to have huge quantities of rare earths stored as a strategic reserve, if the situation worsens, it could also affect the amount of this invaluable by-product being produced. In other words, the restrictions on rare earths could be the consequence of a natural evolution of the Chinese domestic market, due to lower demand for iron or higher demand for rare earths. What is undoubtedly true is that these restrictions would have a greater impact outside than inside China. The export quotas or tariffs that would be applied will always follow China's national interests, as well as its production targets.

Another trigger point that adds further strain to China's rare earths muscle is the carbon dioxide emissions associated with the manufacture of its products. The EU Green Deal envisages the imposition of import tariffs on products from outside the European bloc based on their $CO_2$ footprint ("carbon border tax"). Although this measure has been conveniently postponed by the EU, its implementation could trigger a new trade war. In the worst-case scenario this new trade war could trigger restrictions by China or even a rare earth embargo on

February 16, 2021. https://agmetalminer.com/2021/02/16/rare-earths-are-the-next-geopolitical-chess-game/

Europe, or similarly on any other country attempting to impose tariffs. Turning the Western point of view on its head, China would rightfully argue the injustice of being "punished" with tariffs on its exports. It is true that the Western world has been enjoying its technological delights for decades without bearing the environmental cost of mining and metallurgy that have devastated entire mining regions such as Bayan Obo and throughout the Global South.

According to Gavin Thomson, vice president of Energy for the Asia Pacific region of the Wood Mackenzie consulting group, it is possible for the world to reduce its dependence on Chinese rare earth minerals to 50%, but he sets the date at no earlier than 2050 and warns that with China dominating the rare earth processing market, most of what is mined elsewhere will still be shipped to China for processing and manufacturing for decades.

With energy security now at the top of the Western political agenda following Russia's invasion of Ukraine, attention may soon begin to focus not only on reducing dependence on Russian hydrocarbons but also on reducing dependence on Chinese clean energy technology. This was indicated by a statement from the President of the European Commission, Ursula Von der Leyen in September 2022, when she announced the development of the Critical Raw Materials Act.[95]

> Lithium and rare earths will soon be more important than oil and gas. Our demand for rare earths alone will increase fivefold by 2030. [...] We must avoid becoming dependent again, as happened with oil and gas. [...] We will identify strategic projects along the supply chain, from extraction to refining, from processing to recycling. And we will build up strategic reserves where supply is at risk.

Although the EU's Critical Raw Materials Act came into force in March 2023, its ambitious objectives are to combat an extensive Chinese monopoly on many rare metals. This dependence dwarfs that of dependence on Russian hydrocarbons since Europe is supplied, for

95 European Commission, "Critical Raw Materials Act: securing the new gas & oil at the heart of our economy | Blog of Commissioner Thierry Breton," September 14, 2022. https://ec.europa.eu/commission/presscorner/detail/en/STATEMENT_22_5523

example, with 97% of its magnesium from China, which also has an absolute monopoly in the processing of heavy rare earths and graphite.

To achieve some autonomy, the EU aims to extract 10%, process 40% and recycle 15% of the critical metals it consumes annually by 2030. By then, no more than 65% of the consumption of any strategic metal can come from a single third country. Implicitly, the country to flee from will almost always be China. European law is cautious; it avoids imposing tariffs that could have the undesirable effect of denying access to materials and products that are the key to the main technology chosen for decarbonization. Instead, it has useful tools such as fast-track authorization of "strategic" projects within a maximum of two years for mines and one year for processing plants. These must be considered in the public interest for environmental impact assessment purposes. Other useful tools include the evaluation of existing reserves at both public and private levels, stress testing of supply chains to assess how many days they would last without a material, and multinational joint purchasing of critical materials. Only time will tell whether the degree of EU interventionism is sufficient. Inevitably, given its semi-federal nature, it leaves many decisions and actions in the hands of member states, some of whom have basic mining legislation almost as antiquated as that of the USA, whose General Mining Act dates back to 1872.

# 4. SECOND FRONT: THE STRUGGLE AGAINST CLIMATE CHANGE

A lack of government planning to carry out the energy transition without the requisite materials could well jeopardize not only the fight against climate change itself, but also put the West in a technological abyss. Western leaders have opted to accelerate this heretofore unhurried process that resulted from the lack of environmental awareness of their populations. But, at the same time many citizens suffered from the COVID crisis, they also went through a period of reflection and internalization of the effects of globalization and climate change. This viral pandemic highlighted the risk of not considering threats to human security globally. After going through stages of denial, lack of relevance, acceptance and finally a feeling of risk and alarm in this regard, inevitably governments drew parallels and related conclusions. Governments are reacting by stepping on the accelerator in the struggle against climate change, but they have not sufficiently studied the road ahead. The coronavirus has reinforced our identity as global citizens, and with it our ethical-ecological awareness and willingness to protect the environment. Governments seem to have channeled this crusade into an immense but dysfunctional push for renewable energies, which, beyond any considerations of good and evil, depends on China.

Let's face it. China's low labor costs and lax environmental laws drove down prices for photovoltaic and wind power, making them more competitive than fossil fuels. China is now both part of the problem and part of an ill-considered, bittersweet solution. The sweet side of this solution includes the promise of energy independence for third countries, drawing on the inexhaustible energy of the sun and wind, thus avoiding conflicts over energy resources such as oil. But the sour part leaves the West in the hands of the countries that have the necessary minerals or the capacity to process them, and increases the fateful exploitation of limited planetary resources, the rare metals. There's also the environmental cost of disposing of used products containing rare earths or other hazardous elements. Cheap Russian energy and Chinese strategic subsidies have concentrated the world of metals processing in these two countries. This implies that as globalization deflates, the roots of our supply chains must be rediscovered. We have ten years ahead of us to build a multitude of processing centers.

The final scientific calculations of the necessary quantities of each "green metal" (metals needed to produce renewable energies) are gradually coming to light. Although the alarming results show the insufficiency of mineral resources to carry out the green transition at the marked pace, the crusade continues and already seems unstoppable. The numbers have finally broken through from one narrative to another. Their grotesque figures show us the infeasibility of the West's struggle against climate change as we have currently conceived it. The envisaged energy mixes, i.e., the proportions of energy production of each state according to their different origins (nuclear, hydrocarbons, renewables, etc.), are often based in Western countries on large percentages of energy production from renewable sources. Specialized private centers such as Eurometaux, Metallic Dutch, international associations such as the International Energy Association[96] or state entities such as the U.S. Geological Survey or its Finnish counterpart, the GTK,[97] among others, provide data that challenge the scientific seriousness of the energy transition as envisaged.

The climate crusade began in 1992 when the United Nations Framework Convention on Climate Change set the basis for reducing $CO_2$ emissions. Three years later, the Kyoto Treaty included legally binding clauses that came into force in 2005. Renewable energies and electric cars were becoming progressively cheaper as they were mass-produced in China. Although organizations such as the U.S. Department of Energy annually forecast oil demand, neither the U.S. nor most Western nations were calculating the amount of metals needed to sustain the new national energy mix, much less the global

96 "Mineral requirements for clean energy transitions," IEA, March 2022. https://www.iea.org/reports/the-role-of-critical-minerals-in-clean-energy-transitions/mineral-requirements-for-clean-energy-transitions

97 Geologian tutkimuskeskus GTK. https://www.gtk.fi

one. We lived in a false utopia, conceiving of a planet with infinite and easily accessible metals. The Western world was writing a blank check that Gaia had to pay.

In 2012, European countries such as Germany, Spain and France already had a well-defined energy transition project, but no plan as to how to secure the necessary materials to make it possible. Today, despite the fact that the worrying accounts of global needs are already surfacing, no one seems to dare to pull the emergency brake. The wheel of the economy cannot stop, and the energy transition train is running at such a speed that a derailment would almost assuredly invoke an economic recession, or still worse, depression. Small wonder, when one references recent data showing how renewables have already overtaken fossil energy jobs in the West. Instead of changing course, the train is accelerating. If at best the Western energy transition bears fruit, it will only succeed in building a few isolated green bubbles. These will perhaps serve as an example, perhaps as a source of envy for other nations that either cannot finance similar bubbles or for which there are no minerals and metals left to implement their own green projects. In any case, these isolated spaces will not be sufficient globally, nor with bio-diffusion will they remain isolated. This will not achieve the global goal of effectively curbing global warming.

## SCIENCE AT STAKE

In the Middle Ages, when faith made its appearance in the room, scientific thought was cornered and if it raised its voice, it was liable to be purified at the stake. Our crusade against climate change has striking similarities. The average Western citizen has faith in the good cause of saving the earth from climate change, saving themselves and the generations to come. Our politicians, channeling the faith of their people, their votes, and their taxes, preach the holy crusade to the four winds. Finally, the companies, our climate warriors, come calling, in search of riches, subsidies, funding sources, lucrative profits and a pro-ecological reputation that for some may well resemble eternal life. To be brief: the crusade for rare earths is encompassed and propitiated by an even greater crusade, the crusade against climate change. But where is science—at the stake, as in the old days? How has the struggle against climate change been planned?

Isabel Pino is a geologist with an international profile and background like few others. I do not know if, had she been born in the Middle Ages, expressing her scientific knowledge would have condemned her to the pyre. What is clear to me is that her voice and that of her colleagues has not been sufficiently heard in planning this energy transition. No one has consulted them. Her eleven years working at the European Geological Survey back up her words when Isabel tells me that "the energy transition approach has not taken into account the cycles of exploitation of materials, the real possibilities of increasing production or even the finite nature of certain minerals." And she adds, "as planned, this transition also leaves us in the hands of China." Her training in Spain, Mexico and Brussels and the number of international projects she has been involved in have given her a privileged view of how the geology strings are pulled behind the scenes at the international level.

The world is stepping on the gas in its race to get rid of $CO_2$ and fossil fuels, but according to this scientist,

> It is no use for the Joint Research Center of the European Commission to define a list of critical materials for the economy and for different sectors such as energy if it is not then taken into account in making political decisions. EU politicians do not make good use of scientific tools. The deadline for the exploitation of a new mine always exceeds the periods of the electoral mandates. Why fight against the current to obtain a "social license" to open them, to convince the public opinion if it will not produce effects in the next two campaigns?

On the other hand, when asked about the interaction or coordination with the security field and its experts from the Common Security and Defense Policy of the European projects related to raw materials, her answer leaves no room for doubt: "I have never seen anyone from the security policy branch in these projects." In other words, despite the existing European rare earth projects (ERMA, European Raw Material Alliance, ERECON European Rare Earth Competition Network, EURARE, European Rare Earth and GloREIA Global Rare Earth Industry Association) security is not a factor taken into account.

There are no state or supranational entities which seem to be considering the creation of a list of materials or elements critical to human security (including energy security), or to national security, even though these are at stake. During at least the last 30 to 35 years, economics has always prevailed over security as the main criteria in the critical and strategic materials field. On the other side of the Atlantic, the plan does not change much. Despite the high risk of shortages or supply cuts, politicians such as President Biden, after being elected in 2021, strongly promoted the green agenda, although he did not release the throttle on the oil and gas industry. In fact, oil production in the United States will average 12.4 million barrels per day (b/d) in 2023 surpassing the previous record of 12.3 million b/d set in 2019.[98] Today the urgency of addressing the goals of the 2015 Paris Climate Summit, the EU's European Green Deal[99] of 2019 or the U.S. Green New Deal,[100] is more present than ever.

## GREEN PACTS WITHOUT GREEN METALS: WRITING BAD CHECKS

Perhaps it is a question of "having faith" as it was almost 1,000 years ago, but it goes against reason and it is risky, to say the least, to promote agreements on both sides of the Atlantic to curb climate change when its success depends on a single country, China. If we add to this lack of diversification the fact that our Western diplomatic and security axis is not aligned with that of the Beijing government, the approach of this new crusade is as erratic as those of the Middle Ages.

Surprisingly, the inanity of the plan is already being revealed by the very organizations promoting it. Thus, the European Commission's

---

98 U.S. Energy Information Administration, "U.S. crude oil production will increase to new records in 2023 and 2024," January 25, 2023. https://www.eia.gov/todayinenergy/detail.php?id=55299

99 European Commission, "European Green Deal: Developing a sustainable blue economy in the European Union," May 17, 2021. https://ec.europa.eu/commission/presscorner/detail/en/ip_21_2341

100 The White House, "FACT SHEET: President Biden Sets 2030 Greenhouse Gas Pollution Reduction Target Aimed at Creating Good-Paying Union Jobs and Securing U.S. Leadership on Clean Energy Technologies," April 22, 2021. https://www.whitehouse.gov/briefing-room/statements-releases/2021/04/22/fact-sheet-president-biden-sets-2030-greenhouse-gas-pollution-reduction-target-aimed-at-creating-good-paying-union-jobs-and-securing-u-s-leadership-on-clean-energy-technologies//

report "Critical raw materials for strategic technologies and sectors in the EU"[101] identifies as very high the risk of shortages or cuts in the supply chains of rare earths[102] key to the renewable energy and electric mobility sectors. The disturbing report also contemplates how the demand for rare earths used in permanent magnets, for electric vehicles, digital technologies or wind generators will increase tenfold by 2050,[103] led by neodymium oxide, praseodymium, and dysprosium.

The politically set targets imply a consumption of critical metals unparalleled in history. The United States, for example, has officially announced the goal of achieving a carbon-free energy industry by 2035, and the main binding targets for the EU in 2030 include achieving a 55% reduction in greenhouse gas emissions compared to 1990 and reaching a 45% share of renewable energies in total gross final energy consumption. Wind energy and the electromobility sector are also key factors in the EU's roadmap for decarbonizing its economy, putting the circular economy on track, and achieving climate change objectives.

It is not surprising that there are not enough rare earths to go around as China's plans are no less ambitious than those of Western countries. The Middle Kingdom announced a goal of 25% electric vehicles by 2025 (compared to 25% in the U.S. by 2030) and the generation of 47% of its energy (24% wind and 23% solar) from renewable sources by 2060.[104] But the CPC is well aware of the scope of its claims and the physical implications at the feedstock level. National policies such as "Made in China 2025" are expected to have the unintended consequence of restricting supply to the rest of the world due to the prioritization of supply to China's own manufacturers.[105] While the

---

101 European Commission, Joint Research Centre, *Critical Raw materials for Strategic Technologies and Sectors in the EU: A Foresight Study* (Luxembourg: Publications Office of the European Union, 2020). https://rmis.jrc.ec.europa.eu/uploads/CRMs_for_Strategic_Technologies_and_Sectors_in_the_EU_2020.pdf

102 European Commission, *Critical Raw materials for Strategic Technologies and Sectors in the EU.*

103 Jamie Smyth, "To revive rare-earth industry, U.S. looks to the Mojave," *Los Angeles Times,* September 25, 2020. https://www.latimes.com/business/story/2020-09-25/rare-earths-california-mojave

104 Bruno Venditti, "Visualizing China Energy Transition in 5 Charts," *Visual Capitalist,* July 15, 2021, www.visualcapitalist.com.

105 Australian Strategic Minerals (ASM), "About ASM" (accessed May 23, 2021). https://asm-au.com/about-asm-home/

world waits in anticipation of the arrival of Chinese export quotas,[106] alarming figures show us our vulnerability at present. China produces among others more than 85% of the magnets that go into the wind turbines of its competitors and represents 70% of the world production for electric vehicles.

## A SILICON VALLEY SANS SILICON

China's dominance over the rare metals needed for the energy transition is such that in the words of Julian Kettle, senior vice president of metals research at Wood Mackenzie, "in the critical commodity restaurant, China is eating its dessert while the rest of the world is reading the menu."[107] Even so, there are parts of the West that are conveniently unaware of China's existence as a diner.

In August 2022, I was on a group working visit to Silicon Valley. Our reception was led by the mayor of Palo Alto who showed us their energy transition project, which makes them one of the first municipalities in the world to use only renewable energy sources. I took the opportunity to ask him his opinion on the hidden dependence of these renewable energy sources (solar, wind and battery storage) on China. His answer showed that he was aware of the problem and although he indicated his willingness to work towards solving it, looking for local suppliers and materials coming from the national territory, he also admitted that it is not feasible to develop a project like his by completely escaping the Chinese supply chains. He added that the solutions to such a problem cannot be local, lying with the mayor's office of a municipality, but must be state or national.

The reality is that Batou, in China's Inner Mongolia region, is a rare earth valley with a complete supply chain feeding factories in Shenzhen and the Pearl River Delta, China's technology rivals that of Silicon Valley. But paradoxically, the U.S. Silicon Valley is a valley without a major domestic supplier of either rare earths or silicon metal.

---

106 U.S. Congressional Research Service, Insight: "China Issues New Export Control Law and Related Policies," October 26, 2020. https://sgp.fas.org/crs/row/IN11524.pdf

107 Gavin Thompson, "Can the rest of the world repel China's magnetic pull over rare earth metals?" (opinion), Wood Mackenzie, May 19, 2022. https://www.woodmac.com/news/can-the-rest-of-the-world-repel-chinas-magnetic-pull-over-rare-earth-metals/

70% of this metal is manufactured in China.[108] The green energy project of the municipality of Palo Alto cannot escape the Asian giant's supply. The latter's dominance is evidenced by global production figures of 80% of solar panels,[109] 80% of lithium batteries,[110] and 90% of magnets for wind turbines. Silicon Valley does not have a healthy resource foundation, which should be formed by the raw materials that sustain its economy and its way of life.

## DEMATERIALIZATION, FRUGALITY, EFFICIENCY, DEMOCRATIZATION OF RESOURCES OR ... CONSUMPTION!

The energy transformation is occurring at a time when global demand for energy continues to grow by leaps and bounds and the planet is being electrified, digitized, and automated. Planet Earth will grow from being home to 7.6 billion citizens today to 8.6 billion by 2030 and 9.8 billion by 2050. This dizzying population change is accompanied by an increase in the middle class of the Global South, which, although possessing low purchasing power, does not renounce its energy needs and aspires to a highly technological Western lifestyle—a lifestyle with invisible energy predators that grow fat year after year, feeding on each of our e-mail attachments that cross the oceans and consume as much energy as a low-energy light bulb for an hour. The massive storage of our data in server farms consumes as much as entire cities. What about the invisible arteries of global communication which are submarine cables thousands of kilometers long or the increasingly abundant constellations of satellites? Some sources attribute 20% of the $CO_2$ produced on earth to the use of the internet.

Isabel knows firsthand the finiteness of resources and their repercussions, and comments with some frustration that "Western leaders interpret the fight against climate change more as an energy transition

108 Statista, "Production volume of silicon in China from 2010 to 2022" (consulted in September 2022).

109 Emily Chow, "China's solar glass shortage to drag on panel output into 2021," *Reuters,* December 3, 2020. https://www.reuters.com/article/china-solar-glass-idAFL1N2IJ0E2

110 Miguel Ángel Moreno, "China controls almost 80% of lithium supply, while Western countries have been 'tremendously slow,' which could make it impossible to meet electrification targets," April 11, 2022. https://www.businessinsider.es/china-va-ganando-carrera-litio-controla-80-suministro-1043057

than as a quest for energy efficiency." She complains about the lack of frugality. According to her, "energy frugality is a difficult concept to expand and enhance. Our organizations and political systems are oriented to encourage voracious consumption and increase production annually to infinity and beyond, in the pursuit of the chimera of eternal growth. The first world is betting heavily on the renewable energy card to win the game. But the minerals required are not renewable." When I ask her if she thinks that perhaps the capitalist world should show developing countries that path of abstinence and restraint, her answer leaves no room for doubt:

> Sharing to optimize consumption does not sound good to us, it sounds communist or utopian. Buying second-hand clothes, for example, recycling their use is unfortunately not something frequent. Creating more sounds better, it sounds like capitalism. Our solution always seems to be to produce something new, or more and better. Every day we also take for granted the programmed obsolescence and the expiration of all objects of daily use. We assume as normal our need for two cars per family and three personal computers. As if this were not enough, their industrial designs are also not designed to be easily recycled after use. There is also a lack of awareness among the population to reduce meat consumption.

There are many scientists who agree with Isabel's message, such as Vaclav Smil, one of Bill Gates' favorite authors. This Distinguished Professor Emeritus of the University of Manitoba, Canada, has spoken out extensively on the topic. In his book entitled *Building the Modern World*, he tries to make readers understand the necessity of dematerializing our culture. He cites, for example, that there is no point in producing more efficient electric motors, equipped with rare earths, if we manufacture ever larger and heavier vehicles. But there are many other measures that should accompany the efficient design of automobiles. The compulsory installation of heating systems that use air pumps, or the development of specific housing construction regulations would improve energy efficiency. One of the most significant examples is water. According to the U.S. Environmental Protection

Agency[111] (EPA) as a whole, drinking water and wastewater systems account for approximately 2% of the country's energy consumption. This amounts to more than 45 million tons of greenhouse gases per year. By incorporating energy efficiency practices into their water and wastewater plants, municipalities and utilities can reduce energy consumption by 15% to 30%. Water pumps whose electric motors are equipped with rare earths as well as heat pumps could increase efficiency, but these measures seem to have been put on the back burner.

## AN INSATIABLE METABOLISM

Nevertheless, the reduction of energy expenditure per individual and energy expenditure per Gross Domestic Product (GDP) is essential, especially if we consider that China and India already have almost 1.4 billion inhabitants each. Developing countries aspire to Western standards of quality of life and therefore to equivalent energy expenditure, but what should be emphasized is the concomitant understanding that the road ahead should point to Western countries' energy consumption reduction to narrow this gap. But who relates the metabolism of our countries to GDP? That is, how much minerals do we consume, how much waste do we generate and how much energy do we consume in relation to GDP? Although until recently we were bereft of this type of account, the first ones are already beginning to see the light and to make their way through the media to impact on the conscience of the citizens. Visualcapitalist.com published in 2023[112] that the average American consumes more than 17,000 kg (39,000 pounds) annually of minerals and fossil fuels. Although copper, for example, only represented 6 kg (13 lb.) of the total, according to Mario, geologist at Strategic Minerals Spain, "Anyone who has been in contact with mining knows that it takes many kilos of ore to obtain one kilo of the product; in the case of copper, more than 1000 kg of rock to generate one kilo. In the case of rare metals such as rare earth metals, that amount is much, much higher. It also depends on the efficiency of the

---

111 U.S. Environmental Protection Agency (EPA), "Energy Efficiency for Water Utilities" (accessed January 30, 2023). https://www.epa.gov/sustainable-water-infrastructure/energy-efficiency-water-utilities

112 Bruno Venditti and Sam Parker (graphics), "Visualizing U.S. Consumption of Fuel and Materials per Capita," *Visual Capitalist,* January 27, 2023. https://www.visualcapitalist.com/visualizing-u-s-consumption-of-fuel-and-materials-per-capita/

process and the mining company. " But does anyone consider that we should set aside part of the GDP revenue to compensate for the loss of earth wealth. That sort of amortization is not contemplated, but if it were, we might find ourselves paying taxes for the restitution of the damage to nature.

In search of more scientific opinions that confirm or disprove the incongruity of the approach of this crusade, which in addition to being unfeasible at a global level increases our vulnerabilities and dependencies, I turn to my collaborator Teresa Lorens. This geologist is one of the leading authorities in the field of rare metals in Spain. She also has the advantage of knowing both the public and private sides of the coin. Before working for the Spanish Geological and Mining Institute, she worked for Strategic Minerals Spain. Some of the elements that her former company exploited and commercialized will very possibly become part of the new list of critical material resources of the Spanish government.

I have been in contact with Teresa for more than three years and she has helped me along the long road of research to the publication of this book. We both commented on the proposed climate models of the International Energy Agency (IEA)[113] to keep the temperature increase below 1.5° C. All of them imply an unbridled consumption of variable renewable energies (wind and solar) to generate electricity. Starting from an average share of just under 10% today, the aim is to reach 40–70% by 2050 and even more in some regions. This New Zero Scenario also includes 1.6 billion electric cars by 2050, while there are only 1.46 billion cars in the world today.[114]

Teresa's opinion is along the same lines as that of her colleagues: "This roadmap is more a wish than a plausible reality," she points out. She finds it surprising that, according to the IEA itself, the average critical materials required will increase more than fivefold. "Where is the magic wand?" she exclaims. She goes on to state that

> Our Western politicians have overlooked the importance of designing the necessary resource exploitation cycles

113 IEA, "World Energy Outlook 2021, Executive Summary." https://www.iea.org/reports/world-energy-outlook-2021/executive-summary

114 Hedges and Company, "How many Cars are there in the World in 2023?," https://hedgescompany.com/blog/2021/06/how-many-cars-are-there-in-the-world/

to coincide with the energy transition, and the necessary collaboration between the energy and mining sectors is currently almost non-existent. The dialogue between the political leaders driving the energy transition and scientists has not been sufficient to meet in an acceptable reality.

Experts agree: science has not been sufficiently (or more accurately, uniformly) involved in the campaign plan against climate change. As a result, the production rates of rare earths, mainly neodymium and dysprosium, as well as other required metals, are not keeping pace. Several of the studies[115] devoted to calculating the materials that will be in short supply to meet this International Energy Agency scenario agree in adding to the rare earths other critical materials needed to make the scenario viable, mainly indium, copper, lithium, cobalt, selenium, and tellurium, although some studies extend the list further. Unsurprising, if we account for the composition of the simple 3-megawatt/hour wind turbine that populates our landscapes. According to data from the European Commission itself, the "bill" for the materials required for its production amounts to 335 tons of steel, 1200 tons of concrete, 3 tons of aluminum, 4.7 tons of copper and two tons of rare earths and zinc combined.

## A SHORTAGE FORETOLD

Forecasts predict that overall demand for rare earths will double between now and 2030 and will increase sevenfold by 2050. The long-term demand can perhaps be satisfied if we have cheap energy to make its extraction profitable and if the populations grant their "social license." Teresa tells me that, "Mining companies count on having to respond to hundreds or thousands of appeals filed by environmental companies within a few months in order to get the license to operate a mine" and continues, "It is a huge job. These complaints, even if they do not come to fruition, imply a bureaucratic attack against the companies from which it is difficult to emerge well."

115 Takuma Watari, Benjamin C. McLellan, Damien Giurco, Elsa Dominish, Eiji Yamasue, and Keisuke Nansai, "Total material requirement for the global energy transition to 2050: A focus on transport and electricity," *Resources, Conservation and Recycling* 148 (September 2019): 91–103. https://www.sciencedirect.com/science/article/pii/S0921344919302290

As Teresa points out, "In the short term the challenge is infeasible, especially if we want to obtain heavy rare earths such as dysprosium, which are even scarcer." As she explains to me "To the lack of reaction capacity of a forgotten supply chain, almost non-existent outside China, we have to add the lack of operational mines or mines that are expected to be exploited before that date. The production/reserves ratio is not growing at the required rate worldwide. In Spain, despite being rich in lithium and rare earths, we have not yet managed to extract a single gram. The same happens in most European countries." She cites the example of the lithium mine in Salamanca, where she is from, "Lithium was extracted from La Fregeneda for ceramic uses, but its exploitation ended in 2011. We have been twelve years without extracting this element despite the rich deposits in Spain."

After listening to these opinions and before we suffer the first effects of an energy transition hampered by lack of materials, surely choosing the energy frugality proposed by some scientists such as Isabel or Vaclav and organizing it at the state level may be preferable to a forced energy fast resulting from an outdated energy transition plan. Why wait for the first consequences to manifest themselves, perhaps in the form of electricity and fuel price peaks, unbearable for companies and citizens, or the effects of climate change? The war in Ukraine has served initially as a smokescreen to hide an energy crisis. When the wolf of the energy shortage was already showing its ears, many media wrongly blamed it exclusively on the effects of this conflict.

The underlying problem is that in this instance, it will not be enough to let the market self-regulate. Global energy supply and demand no longer go hand in hand but are in the hands of China's state-directed economy when it comes to renewable energies. Heretofore, the reasoning went like this: In a free market economy, an increase in demand for a mineral, metal, or hydrocarbon of fossil origin without an equivalent increase in supply leads to an increase in prices. This leads to an increase in production, but also to an increase in exploration and the development of new methods of exploitation. One example is crude oil, whose international demand and rising market prices, and thus the breakeven price, have encouraged extraction technologies such as fracking. The increase in demand and in the price of crude oil led to an increase in exploitable crude oil reserves and, therefore, in supply. But while the demand for rare earths will undoubtedly be a driver for industry in the coming years, as we have seen, given the special features of its supply (i.e., domination by a state that is not operating according to capitalist norms), Western capitalism will not meet demand in time and Western companies will suffer the impact of its scarcity. As the World Bank itself cites in its document, Mineral Intensity for the Energy Transition, "Low-carbon technology requirements, and therefore demand for relevant minerals and metals, is increasing faster the closer the world gets to achieving the 2015 Paris Climate Agreement commitment to avoid a 2°C global temperature rise."

The growth of wind energy production to contain climate change is increasing at an extremely rapid pace as shown in its possible Wind Power Generation Scenarios by the International Energy Agency. As we have seen, the main demand for rare earths is focused on neodymium and dysprosium to produce permanent magnets that equip wind turbine motors. During 2020, global demand was boosted by a record 93 gigawatts of wind power installed that same year, representing a year-over-year increase of 54%. The leading countries were China with 98% growth and the United States with 78%.

## THE ELECTRIC VEHICLE'S JOURNEY TO NOWHERE

Sales of electric passenger vehicles were not far behind. Despite the effects of COVID-19 on the economy and with overall new car registrations falling, global electric car sales rose 70% to a record 4.6% of total market share in 2020. About 3 million new electric cars were registered in the world that year. For the first time, Europe led with 1.4 million new registrations, overtaking China with 1.2 million.[116] Since then, the trend has continued and although it seems to point towards the moon, it is leading us instead to the precipice. Accompanying the trend, global demand for neodymium boron ferrous alloy (NdFeB) in electric vehicle traction motors increased by 31% between 2020 and 2021 and 39% between 2021 and 2022.[117]

---

116 International Energy Agency (IEA), "Global EV Outlook 2021: Trends and developments in electric vehicle markets." https://www.iea.org/reports/global-ev-outlook-2021/trends-and-developments-in-electric-vehicle-markets

117 M. Garside, "Demand for neodymium-iron-boron (NdfeB) permanent magnets worldwide from 2018 to 2022," *Statista,* October 19, 2021. https://www.

If the industry reacts in time before rare earth scarcity manifests, it could replace these motors with older and less efficient induction motors. Still, that would mean transforming a rare earths problem into a copper problem, accelerating the demise of one of the main endangered metals,[118] of which China also controls a large refining share, with 42%[119] of the world total. Batteries would also have to be more powerful and of higher capacity, increasing their weight and the amount of lithium required. More than 50% of the lithium is also refined in China. Another added problem is the price of these two metals which, from 2000 until today, has seen a five-fold increase.[120] This upward trend may continue as demand grows and supplies become scarcer. Without an adequate recycling rate, the electric vehicle trajectory is a journey to nowhere. It is in no one's interest to deplete the planet's mineral resources by generating competition or wars over resources. Lithium shows us the dead end of the electric vehicle, without massive recycling. Its demand has only just taken off. As the EU's competence center for forecasting warns, the global transition to a low-carbon economy will require global production of some metals to increase at least twelve-fold by 2050. In addition to lithium, demand for the rare earths neodymium, terbium, dysprosium and praseodymium, and for cobalt, graphite and indium, stand out. Never throughout history has there been such a massive and general increase in demand for the rare metals.[121] The EU has announced a ban on the manufacture of combustion vehicles from 2035 onwards, but without an equivalent rate of recycling of these metals we will be witnessing a slow-motion catastrophe from which only the hydrogen vehicle could pull us out. If we continue at this rate, the African cemeteries of materials, into

---

statista.com/statistics/1047263/neodymium-iron-boron-permanent-magnet-demand-worldwide/

118 Vaclav Smil, *Making the Modern World: Materials and Dematerialization* (Wiley, 2013), 162–163.

119 Statista, "Distribution of refined copper consumption worldwide in 2021, by region." https://www.statista.com/statistics/693466/distribution-of-global-refined-copper-consumption-by-region/

120 Macrotrends, "Copper Prices - 45 Year Historical Chart" (accessed Sept. 2022). https://www.macrotrends.net/1476/copper-prices-historical-chart-data

121 European Commission, Competence Centre on Foresight, "Developments and Forecasts of Aggravating Resource Scarcity," October 1, 2018 (accessed January 2023). https://knowledge4policy.ec.europa.eu/foresight/topic/aggravating-resource-scarcity/more-developments-relevant-aggravating-resource-scarcity_en

which we dump our industrial waste laden with rare metals, could become veritable gold mines.

The Beijing government, aware of the planet's natural limits and its own processing capacity, is already announcing the prospect of a million hydrogen vehicles on the road by 2035. At the same time, it is encouraging research and development of technologies that make hydrogen production cheaper. The Japanese are upping the ante with a forecast of 800,000 vehicles running on hydrogen even earlier—in 2030. This alternative is very attractive. A Toyota vehicle with a hydrogen fuel cell can be recharged in a hydrogen tank in 3 to 4 minutes, providing a range of 600 kilometers with only 4 liters of hydrogen. Meanwhile, a Tesla electric vehicle needs a 500 kg battery to provide 400 km of autonomy and takes more than 15 minutes to refuel using a high-voltage charger. Hydrogen also avoids the electromagnetic radiation that is produced in an electric refueling of such high intensity. But before scaling up any kind of technology, it is necessary to ensure the supply of the required materials.

The situation is reminiscent of the early 21st century, when the British Empire was progressively replacing its coal-fueled ships with oil-fueled ships of greater speed and range. The decision to implement this new technology was driven by the Chief Admiral of the British Navy, Winston Churchill, and was not taken without a detailed study of the advantages and risks. Great Britain was sitting on large coal reserves but lacked oil. The commission set up for the purpose confirmed the benefits of oil, but despite determining that abundant oil reserves existed worldwide, urged that peacetime storage capacity be built up to ensure sufficiency in wartime. The British government, aware of the strategic risk of not having an assured flow of crude oil, invested directly in Anglo-Persian Oil, now BP (British Petroleum). After acquiring 51% of its shares, it negotiated a secret contract to supply oil to the Admiralty for 20 years on attractive terms.[122] Shortly thereafter, oil also helped transition traditional cavalry to tanks and aircraft.

Today, the need for rare metals is four times higher in an electric vehicle than in an internal combustion vehicle. It is not just that the

---

122 Erik J. Dahl, "Naval innovation: from coal to oil," *Joint Force Quarterly* (December 22, 2000), retrieved January 2023 from *The Free Library*. https://www.thefreelibrary.com/Naval+innovation%3a+from+coal+to+oil.+(Cover+Story).-a080305799

West lacks a guaranteed supply—it has a guaranteed shortage. If the decision to implement electric vehicles in the West was taken in order to curb climate change, governments should also have previously ensured their supply of the requisite resources. If Churchill were to raise his head, he would tear his hair and cry out loud. He would probably then ask for the reports of the government commission set up to study the feasibility of adopting electric vehicles and demand accountability.

## SOLAR PANELS

As for solar panels, rare earths are currently not strictly necessary in solar power generation and can be substituted. However, the use of Chinese rare earths metals in small doses in every solar panel, acting as "metallic vitamins" makes it possible to improve their quality and efficiency. It is also the novelty of these metallic elements and their associated revolutionary applications that make having a secure or proprietary supply chain essential. Thus, new experiments show the possibility of extending the performance of solar cells[123] using ytterbium, which can absorb infrared light and then send it to erbium, which returns it as visible green light. But the rare earths erbium and ytterbium fall into the heavy earths category and China retains a literal total monopoly on their manufacture. China is also the largest producer of the gallium (under China's export ban) and tellurium used in solar panels. Although the main element for their production, silicon, is not monopolized by China, the refined polysilicon metal is. As a result, according to data from the International Energy Agency, more than 60% of solar panels are built in China.

In the case of rare earths, the time needed to develop national supply chains and the unwillingness of many companies to maintain "war reserves" in their warehouses will soon leave them with unsatisfied demand, as predicted not only by the European Commission but

---

123 A. Fakhim Lamrani, "Rare-earth-doped TiO2 rutile as a promising ferromagnetic alloy for visible light absorption in solar cells: first principal insights," *RSC Advances,* 2020, 10, 35505–35515 (September 25, 2020). https://pubs.rsc.org/en/content/articlehtml/2020/ra/d0ra05725h

Glenn Roberts, Jr., "Nanoparticle Breakthrough Could Capture Unseen Light for Solar Energy Conversion," April 23, 2018 (Accessed January 25, 2021). https://newscenter.lbl.gov/2018/04/23/nanoparticle-breakthrough-solar-energy-conversion/

also by a growing number of experts and scientists whose voices have not been heard or wanted to be heard until now.

## GEOPOLITICAL DIMENSIONS OF THE CRUSADE AGAINST CLIMATE CHANGE

Humanity will not be victorious in its fight against climate change without assistance from developing countries. Western countries cannot purify their cities in isolation. It is possible that we will purge our consciences and that the effort will serve as penance. In the end, it is the first world that has so far been guilty of global warming. But its environmental sins will not disappear without the help of the Third World. Unfortunately, many of these countries do not have the economic capacity to finance such a radical energy transition. For them, it means moving from wood as an energy source to renewables or nuclear without going through coal and oil. Who will pay for their energy transition?

In November 2022, the COP27 climate change summit in Egypt and the G20 summit in Indonesia were held in parallel. Shortly before its closure, a group of Western countries announced the granting of 20 billion in financing to one of the host countries, Indonesia.[124] The credit was intended to help the nation switch from coal as a primary energy source to renewables. This action may shed light on what lies ahead in the near future. Indonesia is a global producer of green metals such as nickel, copper, and tin, but it does not have the capacity to produce or manufacture wind turbines, solar panels, batteries or electric vehicles. This Western credit will not be used to develop their renewable energy industry. It will serve, under the convenient term of "strategic alliance," to favor a relationship in which the lending countries' manufacturers provide the developing countries with their green energy source products. Indonesia will be limited to providing the required production metals from its own mines and to pay with the credit received to Western companies. It may be that Chinese companies could offer better terms, if Indonesia decides to deviate from its current "strategic alliance," as it seems they may well do,

124 Cecilia Jamasmie, "Wealthiest nations offer Indonesia $20 billion to wean off coal," *Mining.com,* November 15, 2022. https://www.mining.com/wealthiest-nations-offer-indonesia-20-billion-to-wean-it-off-coal/

given their interest in BRICS membership. Otherwise, it appears that, without their own financing, the developing countries do not have a very promising range of options before them. Their economies will not develop thanks to the energy transition. Most of them will be forced to sell their limited resources at low prices and go into debt to buy finished green technology products.

A number of uncertainties are looming on their horizon: Will they voluntarily accede to World Bank and International Monetary Fund loans while complying with their conditions and loading up on foreign debt? Will they fall into a trap in the form of a debt spiral that will leave them sitting in the abyss of state bankruptcy and galloping inflation, or will they resort to the quicker and apparently cheaper loans from China, without conditionalities but with "counterparts" as the option to recover the unpaid depts with the operation rights or even claim ownership of some critical infrastructures? Will our Western companies be the ones to profit from mining in their countries and from all the contracts for the purchase of solar panels, wind turbines, electricity grids and infrastructure? Or will China take the initiative, still profit, and enjoy the geopolitical shift?

In the case of Indonesia, the financing package was channeled through the Partnership for Just Energy Transition, backed solely by several wealthy Western countries. This is the second package it awarded. The first was an $8.5 billion deal signed with South Africa at COP26. Talks are also underway with Vietnam, India and Senegal to reach similar agreements.

The fight against climate change and the required energy transition are reshaping the world geopolitical map and are shaping it with new economic-energy alliances. African and other developing countries could become a new breadbasket for the mineral raw materials needed for the energy transition. But the claim that these countries can make the energy transition themselves at the necessary pace is implausible. Indeed, the Indonesian government itself estimates that it needs another $580 billion to complete its energy transition by 2050.

While Malaysia turns to the West, many other developing countries opt for the Chinese alternative and look to the Asian giant for financing. Isabel Pino is a witness to the mining counter-offers that the Beijing government is pushing. She has been caught up in a program in which the EU is desperately trying to get the metals needed to fuel its Green Deal. In this case it is a strategic alliance with Chile. Isabel is very clear: "The EU is trying to establish a win-win relationship with Chile.[125] We provide technology, and they provide minerals." However, Isabel does not attribute the same benevolence to Chinese state-owned companies in Chile. "China does the cartography for Chile. A cartography that in many states is secret. This is their gateway to Chilean resources and the establishment of a link that goes beyond the purely commercial." She points out, "Calama, which is one of the largest mining cities on the planet, with exclusive dedication to this activity, has been filled with Chinese. There are more and more of them. You don't know what they do because they don't tell you, but their presence is increasing incredibly."

The city of Calama is the operations center for the exploitation of the Chuquicamata mine in the Antofagasta region. This mine, previously exploited by the Spanish, and even before Christopher Columbus landed in America, is the largest open pit mine in the world. A state-owned company, CODELCO, extracts gold, copper, and molybdenum from its ores, ever since copper mining was nationalized in Chile in 1971 by the dictator Augusto Pinochet. Minerals have always played a fundamental role not only in Chile's economy but also in its security. A Chilean Army officer who prefers not to reveal his name recently told me that, "My army has been partially financed for more than 40 years from part of the profits obtained from national copper sales. Pinochet created a secret law that ensured this financing. If China gets into the largest Chilean copper mine and the Chilean army is financed by this copper, to what extent does the Beijing government now have influence on the Chilean army and on the security of the country?" The Communist Party of China's lack of transparency in its dealings leaves the answers in the realm of speculation.

But according to Isabel, "Chile is not the only country. In Angola, Spain is doing a third of the geological mapping, but the rest is done by the Chinese and there are many other similar examples." The world is surreptitiously polarizing, and we are on the verge of a new cold war between China and its growing number of allies and the U.S.-led West, in which the economy has become just another instrument of national

125 "EU and Chile sign partnership on raw materials," *DW*, July 18, 2023, https://amp.dw.com/es/cumbre-ue-celac-la-ue-y-chile-firman-asociaci%C3%B3n-sobre-materias-primas/a-66274519

power. Africa is the continent where this competition for resources is best staged, often played out on the basis of the checkbook. The number of African countries that have resorted to Chinese debt for financing in recent decades has grown at an accelerated rate. Angola, for example, has 40% of its debt in the hands of the Asian giant.[126] China has become the largest bilateral lender in Africa, granting 1141 loans between 2000 and 2019, holding 20% of the continent's total public debt.[127] While China eclipsed the U.S. as Africa's largest trading partner, the International Monetary Fund warned of the risk of 18 African countries[128] defaulting on their debts. This number has doubled in just five years as China has become what the West regards as a "cheating lender" with hidden risks associated with their loans. In reality, only Beijing knows the extent of these risks because the terms of these loans are not transparent. In fact, since 2015, all loans granted by China in Africa have been subject to secret or confidentiality clauses.[129]

In what is known as a debt trap, China offers to build and finance new key infrastructure for governments in developing countries, often with low levels of governance, high levels of corruption and little chance of repaying the loan. China does so knowing that the chances of default are high. Presumably the intent is to take over the use of these facilities and to buy the political will of their leaders and representatives in international organizations, as arguably has already been the practice of some Western countries. I personally had the opportunity to witness the actions of the Beijing government through its Belt and Road initiative, through which it seizes so many critical materials and infrastructure, not only in South America but also in Africa, among others. Three years of flying missions over Djibouti have allowed me to get an aerial perspective of the reality behind the

---

126 Prinesha Naidoo, "Angola Is Accelerating Plans to Pay Down Its Debt," *Bloomberg,* October 13, 2022. https://www.bloomberg.com/news/articles/2022-10-13/angola-is-accelerating-plans-to-pay-down-its-debt?leadSource=uverify%20wall.

127 Global Development Policy Centre, "Chinese Loans to Africa Database." https://www.bu.edu/gdp/chinese-loans-to-africa-database/

128 "Reality Check: Is China burdening Africa with debt?," *BBC News,* November 5, 2018. https://www.bbc.com/news/world-africa-45916060

129 Zainab Usman, "What Do We Know About Chinese Lending in Africa?," Carnegie Endowment for International Peace, June 2, 2021. https://carnegieendowment.org/2021/06/02/what-do-we-know-about-chinese-lending-in-africa-pub-84648

acronym OBOR (One Belt One Road), the official name of this Chinese initiative. Everything I observed from above in my aircraft day after day made sense later on the ground, after landing and arriving at the Kempinski hotel. In Djibouti it is said that "everything happens at the Kempinski Hotel." This hotel is owned by the president of the country and is used both for the highest-level meetings and celebrations and to accommodate the personnel of various armies. It is a matter of security. Along with the French, American, Spanish, Italian, Japanese and Chinese military bases, it is the place with the highest level of security in the country. Although already secure in itself, the foreign military presence and the ban and effective control on the civilian possession of weapons make this strategic enclave one of the safest on the East African coast. So much so that the U.S. has in Djibouti the military base that houses its African Command (AFRICOM). Japan opened its first military detachment there since the Second World War, and China its first base outside its territory.

This nation is a crossroad that serves as an observatory to, with some certainty, appreciate the modus operandi of the Chinese government in Africa. China does not make noise, it advances stealthily, but at a speed that ridicules that of Western states. On one day, one hears in the Kempinsky hotel bar that China plans to build a port of its own in Djibouti, independent of the state and to be shared by all other nations. After taking off two weeks later, you see the first construction work at the chosen site. Discussing it with a colleague we asked ourselves, "Where is China going to get all the manpower, machinery and materials required to build this port in a country with hardly any infrastructure and where there is a shortage of qualified personnel?" But the answer is not long in coming when from the air we observe how Chinese ships arrive from the Asian giant transporting everything required. China builds with its personnel, with its steel, with its cement and with its cranes and excavator shovels. It does so with such independence that there can be no delays attributable to third parties. They work fast and without disturbing the local authorities, China adapts to the rules of its hosts.

When I later heard in the Kempisnky is that China was not only planning to develop its own port, but that it, too, was going to have a naval base, I understood the presence of Chinese military personnel in the hotel. But the rumors did not stop there. They will also build a railway connecting Addis Ababa, the capital of Ethiopia with their own port . . . and the labor force of the Beijing government's construction companies is drawn from convicts who have had to choose between prison in China or work in Africa. Although I could not verify this last comment, there are sources that corroborate similar situations in other parts of Africa such as in Angola[130] or Algeria, for example.

Having made flight after flight, over a period of three years, I feel like a spectator of one of those old cinematographic short films in which the slides follow one another rapidly trying to reproduce the movement—a movement that never stops. By 2017, barely three years after hearing the first rumors, China already had a naval base capable of hosting its aircraft carriers. Work has also been completed on its exclusive civilian port, of which it owns 23.5%, the Doraleh Multipurpose Port, much more modern than the traditional port of Djibouti. Located only two kilometers from the naval base, this port is already connected to a railway that connects it to Ethiopia's capital, Addis Ababa. In addition to its container and crude oil cargo terminals, it has a free trade zone built and financed, of course, also by China. The more than 800 kilometers of railway track connecting Addis Ababa to the Chinese port make this railway project China's largest infrastructure investment in Africa. China's conquest of Djibouti is progressing by the stroke of a checkbook and bricks. The construction work was carried out by subsidiaries of the China Railway Construction Corporation and the China State Construction Engineering Corporation, with financing from the Export-Import Bank of China.[131] The military component of this new Dubai, this new Hub in Africa, also materializes, of course, in the Kempinski Hotel, which was temporally flooded with military personnel from the People's Liberation Army. Their troops occupied practically an entire floor of the monumental hotel before moving to the naval base.

---

130 Centre for Chinese Studies, Stellenbosch University, *China's Interest and Activity in Africa's Construction and Infrastructure Sectors* (November 2006), 82. https://www.icafrica.org/fileadmin/documents/Knowledge/DFID/China%E2%80%99s%20Interest%20and%20Activity%20in%20Africa%E2%80%99s%20Infrastructure%20and%20Construction%20Sectors.pdf

131 David Styan, "Doraleh Multipurpose Port (I)," *The People's Map of Global China,* March 4, 2022. https://thepeoplesmap.net/project/doraleh-multipurpose-port-phase-i/

Since then, the Asian giant's presence in the country has continued to grow at a pace in step with loans to the government. Among its "self-financed" construction projects with loans to the Djibouti government: a new gas pipeline, schools, road renovations, the building of the Ministry of Foreign Affairs—the list goes on—and in front of the Kempinski now stands the splendorous Chinese embassy. The Djibouti government's warnings of default on Chinese foreign debt at the end of 2022 are accompanied by the latest move by the Beijing government in its country: the construction of a base for the launching of satellites and space rockets. With 70% of the country's debt in Chinese hands, its sovereignty is threatened. The same is happening in regions rich in critical and strategic minerals such as Congo or Angola, for example.

But the repercussions of non-payment to the World Bank are not the same as the consequences of non-payment to the Chinese government. When China sends the debt collector, it does so with the intention of keeping the infrastructure that has been built Djibouti could follow the example from Sri Lanka: China loaned Sri Lanka $1.26 billion to finance the Hambantota port from 2007 to 2014. As Sri Lanka's debts mounted, China's state-run firm China Merchants Port Holdings took over management of the port under a 99-year lease for $1.12 billion, which Sri Lanka used to strengthen its foreign reserves. As a result, in August 2022, a Chinese missile-tracking vessel was allowed to dock despite objections from the United States and India.

The subjugating potential of China's debt in the political and diplomatic sphere could result in an implosion of the functioning of the classic international organizations created by the West and which have so far favored it. This fact was evident in the UN vote to condemn the war in Ukraine in which most of the countries that are aligning with China cast a neutral vote.

But the U.S. does not give in so easily and despite the slowness of the democratic processes compared to the Chinese state-run system, it takes certain initiatives. At the beginning of 2023, for example, it signed an agreement with Zambia and Congo for the extraction and processing of the metals needed for the batteries of electric vehicles.[132]

---

132 UNECA, "Trade ties: Zambia and DRC sign cooperation Agreement to manufacture electric batteries, create jobs," *Africa Renewal: May 2022.* https://www.un.org/africarenewal/magazine/issue/may-2022.

Between them, the two countries possess 80% of the materials needed to manufacture them, including cobalt, lithium, copper and rare earths. The U.S. will seek to develop the country with jobs not only in the mines but also in new refining plants.

While African leaders are debating between corruption or real development of their countries, between long-term gain or immediate profit, what is clear is that if the West lets China finance the energy transition in developing countries, China's projection and influence in these countries will be multiplied. China would gain an even more advantageous position to exploit the mineral resources that make this transition possible, while at the same time, through its new economic-energy alliances, it would redraw the geopolitical map, gradually turning it shades of red.

## THE EUROPEAN UNION'S DANGEROUS ENERGY FRIENDSHIPS

Africa is not the only continent experiencing the shocks produced by the tectonic plate movements of this crusade against climate change; the historic foundations of the European Union are likewise shaking. Since 1952, the European Union, then represented by its embryonic European Coal and Steel Community,[133] has been enormously successful in its fundamental quest for collective peace and prosperity by enhancing economic cooperation within a single market. While its international approach has enabled the bloc to compete with other superpowers, it has not offered it sufficient protection against some of the negative consequences of globalization in a modern era defined by outsourcing, cost-based decision making and economic benefits, but not security.

The security issue ostensibly posed by the EU's dependence on Russian energy highlighted most clearly by the war in Ukraine has demonstrated the narrowing gap between economic and security policy, and the very fraught situation in which Europe has been placed as concerns its loyalties and economic interests. We have witnessed the profound extent of the effects associated with the "militarization" of

133 "Treaty establishing the European Coal and Steel Community and related instruments (ECSC treaty) - Contents," Publications Office of the European Union, April 18, 1951. https://op.europa.eu/en/publication-detail/-/publication/353a22f9-8e69-4dd9-b1cf-db402253e897

critical resources and supply chains. But as difficult a position as the EU has endured due to its severing of connections with Russia, today its possible dependence on a market for critical materials in the hands of China, led by its rare earths,[134] poses an even more dangerous challenge to its existing relationships. Its economic implications are far more profound and long-lasting, and the EU has even less opportunity to disengage.

After the Russian invasion, alarm bells rang and in a desperate race to get rid of their dependence on Russian fossil fuels, some European countries were exchanging one energy dependence for another. Several of them had turned a deaf ear to the European Commission's source diversification guideline, reflected in its 2015 "Energy Union," and believed they saw a double salvation in renewable energies. Inexhaustible energy from the sun and wind and independence from Russia was the siren call. Energy security was once again in question and relegated to economic objectives. Although theoretically the security strategies of each NATO member nation are periodically harmonized in its Strategic Concept, the energy security strategies of some member nations seem to look the other way. In this case before the war some looked towards Russia despite regarding it as their main strategic enemy. Now they are looking towards China. Put bluntly, some EU members were previously benefiting from a political neutrality with Russia that now extends in the direction of China. Globalization allows it (so long as it lasts), but it may not be long until paradoxically, the guarantor of this globalization, the USA, is engaged in an open and declared trade war against China.

This strategic-economic incongruity was led by the largest European economic power, Germany. A 49% dependence on Russia[135] in its gas imports and excellent relations with China had been appraised by Angela Merkel herself. Thus, the German Chancellor in 2018 was

---

134 Brendan P. Diazma and Juan Manuel Chomón Pérez, "The EU's Vanishing Dream of Energy Security," *European Security & Defence,* October 10, 2022. https://euro-sd.com/2022/10/articles/exclusive/27508/the-eus-vanishing-dream-of-energy-security-how-a-desperate-shift-away-from-russian-energy-dependence-ushers-in-a-greater-challenge-for-the-european-union/

135 Statista, "Share of gas supply from Russia in Europe in 2020, by selected country" (accessed April 13, 2022). https://www.statista.com/statistics/1201743/russian-gas-dependence-in-europe-by-country/

in charge of closing trade agreements in her visit to Xi Jinping,[136] for some of the main German flag companies, such as Volkswagen, BASF or Siemens. Despite U.S. wishes, Germany was also pushing for the development of the NordStream II pipeline that would double the capacity of gas coming from Russia to Germany. This new pipeline was intended to undo a certain economic co-dependence between Ukraine[137] and Russia, generated by the Soyuz and Bratsvo (fraternity) pipelines. These served as the main arteries through which Russia brings gas to Europe, which increased Ukrainian vulnerability and would reduce its gas revenues.

European countries seemed to be forgetting a fundamental historical lesson. It was the collapse of the USSR and the existence of U.S. world hegemony that fostered the development of globalization.[138] Most of the standard structures of globalization such as the World Trade Organization, the International Monetary Fund, the World Bank, the Organization for Economic Cooperation and Development in Europe, or even the UN are organizations that were strongly driven by the United States. This leviathan offered protection to its allies and a period of relative peace. Its supremacy has sponsored globalization.

Now that the Western world has engaged by proxy in the Ukraine war on the borders of the EU and finds its weapons arsenals severely depleted, defense budgets are increasing, but its energy security remains compromised. Europe is at an energy crossroads. The decisions it makes in the coming years may lead it to face the existential dilemma of giving up access to Chinese rare earths. That would mean drastically halting its plans to implement and exploit renewables as a major source of power generation. The consequence could be a further crippling blow to its industry....

---

136 Thomas Escritt and Michelle Martin, "China and Germany sign multiple agreements and pledge to pursue free trade," *Reuters,* July 9, 2018. https://www.reuters.com/article/mercados-china-alemania-li-idLTAL1N1U50YL

137 Norberto Paredes, "The controversial Nord Stream 2 gas pipeline from Russia to Germany (and what role it may play in Europe's energy crisis)," October 8, 2021. https://www.bbc.com/mundo/noticias-internacional-58817851

138 Mark Sheetz, *GCSP Policy Brief No. 15: US Hegemony and Globalization,* Geneva Centre for Security Policy, December 6, 2006. https://www.files.ethz.ch/isn/92833/Brief-15.pdf

## AT THE ENERGY CROSSROADS

In April 2022 the EU Parliament demanded a complete halt to the purchase of what it termed Russian "blood gas"[139] and the European Commission announced the increase of U.S. liquefied gas imports by 15 bcm (billion cubic meters) by 2022 and the creation of the Energy Security Task Force.[140] However, buying liquefied gas from the U.S. means buying gas extracted by fracking (hydraulic fracturing), a technique disdained by most EU countries in their territories.[141] Fracking wells are major emitters of methane, the second most significant gas contributing to global warming, as well as being associated with the contamination of subway aquifers, earthquakes and other environmental damage.[142] This technique therefore goes against the global objectives set at the 2015 Paris summit to halt climate change and against European energy security objectives.

Therefore, in the attempt to reduce energy dependence on Russia beyond Liquefied Natural Gas (LNG) in the short to medium term and to continue the crusade against climate change, there are only two viable options available today on a large scale:[143] nuclear power, and renewable energies.[144]

---

139 European Parliament, "EP calls for a total embargo on Russian oil, coal, nuclear fuel and gas," April 7, 2022. https://www.europarl.europa.eu/news/es/press-room/20220401IPR26524/el-pe-pide-un-embargo-total-al-petroleo-carbon-combustible-nuclear-y-gas-rusos

140 European Commission, "Joint Statement between the European Commission and the United States on European Energy Security," March 25, 2022. https://ec.europa.eu/commission/presscorner/detail/en/STATEMENT_22_2041

141 Juan Diego Sández Arana, "Hydraulic fracturing in the European Union: state of play," November 3, 2014. https://www.ieee.es/Galerias/fichero/docs_marco/2014/DIEEEM18-2014_FracturacionHIdraulica_SandezArana.pdf

142 Susan L. Brantley and Anna Meyendorff, "The Facts on Fracking," *The New York Times,* March 13, 2013. http://www.nwsofa.org/wp-content/uploads/2013/11/New-York-Times-The-Facts-on-Fracking-1.pdf.

143 On February 2, 2022, the European Commission adopted a Supplementary Climate Delegated Act (the "CCDA") that lists specific nuclear and gas activities as "environmentally sustainable" for the purposes of the EU Taxonomy Regulation, subject to strict criteria.

144 International Energy Association (IEA), *A 10-Point Plan to Reduce the European Union's Reliance on Russian Natural Gas,* March 2022. https://www.iea.org/reports/a-10-point-plan-to-reduce-the-european-unions-reliance-on-russian-natural-gas

However, nuclear power has come under sustained criticism from environmental groups in different EU countries. Their opinion has been reflected in the programs of political parties, and in their decisions. As a result, countries such as Germany and Spain have virtually abandoned their nuclear programs.[145] The initial source of this strong discredit is its association with military uses, the genocide of Hiroshima and Nagasaki. The subsequent accidents at Chernobyl, Three Mile Island and Fukushima, together with films such as "The China Syndrome" have served to discredit one of the energies that has in actuality so far caused the fewest deaths per terawatt-hour produced.

Unfortunately, our image of nuclear technology has remained stuck in the 1980s, which is when most of the anti-nuclear movements started their campaigns. While the big oil companies have carried out greenwashing advertising campaigns, the governments that own the nuclear power plants have not done the same with their plants. No one has shown the evolution and advantages of nuclear energy to the public, nor have they been bombarded with pro-nuclear power propaganda. Today there are reactors that are much safer than those manufactured 30 or 40 years ago, some of which are still in service. One example is the new Chinese reactor built in the Gobi Desert, China. This Molten Salt Reactor[146] needs neither pressurization nor water and the thorium isotope used as fuel loses its radiologically harmful effects in only 300 years instead of the nearly 10,000 years of traditional uranium. Moreover, thorium is much more abundant than uranium in the earth's crust and is not yet in widespread use. This metal is today little more than a waste material derived from obtaining other metallic elements, among them rare earths.[147]

On the other hand, a nuclear power plant usually takes at least 5 to 7 years to build in many Western countries. But considering the

---

145 Kerstine Appunn, "Q&A: Why is Germany phasing out nuclear power - and why now?," *Clean Energy Wire,* April 14, 2023. https://www.cleanenergywire.org/news/qa-why-germany-phasing-out-nuclear-power-and-why-now.

146 Eric van Vaerenbergh, "China shows us the path to the nuclear future," *European Scientist,* October 12, 2021. https://www.europeanscientist.com/en/features/china-shows-us-the-path-to-the-nuclear-future/

147 Magdi Ragheb and Lefteri Tsoukalas, *Global and USA Thorium and Rare Earth Elements Resources,* presented at the 2 nd Thorium Energy Alliance Conference, The Future Thorium Energy Economy, March 29–30, 2010. https://thoriumenergyalliance.com/wp-content/uploads/2020/02/Global-and-USA-Thorium-and-Rare-Earth-Elements-Resources.pdf

disinvestment in this sector in general in the West, underinvestment in its supply chains and the lack of qualified technicians, the construction of a new power plant in Europe takes up to 10 or 12 years. In contrast, their Chinese counterparts are completed in only 3 years. Although nuclear power plants subsequently provide continuous and stable energy for 40 years, the payback, the profitable phase of the project, does not begin until several years after the electoral term in which it was initiated. In a Europe where populist governments are on the rise, the construction of new nuclear power plants does not bring the required immediacy of results to the political message. Many voters are more satisfied to see their electricity bills decrease, thanks to the installation of renewables that have become cheaper, than having governments pursue strategic autonomy based on a defamed nuclear energy. Thus, politicians, following the motto "first to arrive, first to be served," excuse themselves from pursuing nuclear power by pointing to the fact that the lack of materials, despite being just around the corner, has not yet arrived.

Contradictorily, as the life extension of nuclear power plants, up to 60 years in some cases, is indeed profitable in the short term, when European governments are really beset by the problem of energy security, they resort to extending their life still further. Compared to the models available today, these plants are antediluvian, but since their initial investment has already been amortized, they generate electricity at megawatt-hour prices like those of renewables. As in the case of shortages caused by the Ukrainian war, prohibitive gas costs are thus alleviated. But at the crossroads between nuclear, gas and renewables, many European countries are dangerously deciding to go down the road of renewable energies without considering the backup of nuclear energy, which makes them fragile when it comes to dealing with China.

Countries such as Germany and Spain, after an initial renunciation of their nuclear programs, already produce more than 40% of their energy from renewable energies. No wonder that reports such as those of the Norwegian consulting firm Rystad pointed out in October 2022 that due to increases in the price of natural gas, operating a gas-fired thermal power plant for electricity generation is ten times more expensive than obtaining electricity from photovoltaic plants. Moreover, the report indicated that investment in renewables (solar and wind) at current electricity prices can be recovered in less than twelve months.[148]

Thus, for the first time in its history, Europe injected in 2021 more funds in the development of these renewable energies than in gas and oil extraction. Many European countries seeking to decarbonize their energy sources are distancing themselves from their allies, believing that in exchange they will also gain energy independence, which is nothing more than a mirage,[149] behind which lies the Asian giant.

## THE HIDDEN PRICE OF RENEWABLE ENERGIES

In the European energy restructuring resulting from Western sanctions imposed on Russia during the war in Ukraine, Germany is fleeing in panic from Russian fossil fuels and aims to achieve no less than 80% of its energy mix from clean energies by 2030. To achieve this target, revised to take account of the new geopolitical situation and moving away from Russia, it has enacted the Renewable Energy Sources Act, with a clause identifying clean energies as being in the interest of public safety.[150]

Germany aims to multiply its offshore wind power capacity by a factor of 3.7 by 2030 and then 8,6 by 2045. Until now, this energy represented only 4.3% of its energy mix. Germany has made a strong commitment to renewable energies, especially offshore wind power. What does not seem to bother the Berlin government is that the main elements that give life to offshore wind turbines are the permanent magnets of their motors, which also equip the engines of their electric vehicles, and which are full of rare earths.

Despite the expected cost of materials and issues related to their origin, the EU incomprehensibly upped its ante on renewables for the

---

148 Rystad Energy, "Renewable projects payback time drops to under a year in some places – capital investments shoot up," October 11, 2022. https://www.rystadenergy.com/news/renewable-projects-payback-time-drops-to-under-a-year-in-some-places-capital-inve

149 Rona Rita David, "Europe's Bet on Renewable Energy," *Energy Industry Review,* February 17, 2022. https://energyindustryreview.com/renewables/europes-bet-on-renewable-energy/

150 Electrek, "Germany raises its clean energy target from 65% to 80% by 2030," *World Energy Trade,* April 6, 2022, https://www.worldenergytrade.com/politica/europa/alemania-aumenta-su-objetivo-de-energia-limpia-del-65-al-80-para-2030

energy transition in May of 2022, and changed its announced 2030 targets.[151] Its new REPowerEU initiative entails a dramatic expansion of clean energy technology to a staggering 45% of the total energy mix by 2030, up from the already reckless initial forecast of 30%. With the intention of producing 30% wind energy by 2050, its dependence on Chinese rare earths now dwarfs that on Russian gas. China today produces more than 90% of the magnets that equip the electric motors of wind turbines and electric cars produced in the EU and the high-power batteries on which the EU's Green Deal depends entirely.[152] These data are not mentioned in the press releases and fact sheets of the Repower Europe program. This program also fails to mention that the last three attempts to open a rare earth mine on European territory, in Greenland (Denmark),[153] Sweden,[154] and Spain,[155] have been rejected at the national level and that, as a consequence, the EU does not have a single operational rare earth mine.

On mining issues, the EU's effectiveness pales in comparison to that of China. Between 2013 and 2017, the European Commission funded EURARE, a project for the "development of a sustainable exploitation plan for Europe's rare earth deposits," which ended up studying and investigating 76 different locations for mining in the bloc. But despite initial optimism, the project's recommendations have largely been shelved, as popular environmental concerns block any attempt to obtain mining licenses. While the EU is fighting protests, China is weaving a new energy market in line with a new world order in which it sits on the throne. European governments, dragged along

---

151 European Commission, "State of the Union: Commission raises climate ambition and proposes 55% cut in emissions by 2030," September 17, 2020. https://ec.europa.eu/commission/presscorner/detail/en/ip_20_1599

152 European Raw Materials Alliance (ERMA), "Ensuring access to the raw materials for the European Green Deal: A European Call for Action," September 30, 2021. https://erma.eu/european-call-for-action/

153 Charlie Duxbury, " EU's plan to source rare earths takes a hit in Greenland," *Politico,* May 25, 2021. https://www.politico.eu/article/rare-earth-mining-project-greenland-eu-radioactive-uranium/

154 Charlie Duxbury, "Sweden's ground zero for the EU's strategic materials plan," *Politico,* November 20, 2020. https://www.politico.eu/article/swedish-ground-zero-for-eu-strategic-materials-plan/

155 AFP, "Spain's rare earths pit greens against tech security -- and profit," *RFI news,* October 6, 2021. https://www.rfi.fr/en/business-and-tech/20211006-spain-s-rare-earths-pit-greens-against-tech-security-and-profit

by German leadership, seem to be willing to trip over the same stone twice and are once again forgetting the first requirement set by the EU regarding energy security: diversification.

Another EU program is the European Raw Material Alliance (ERMA), which is also trying to reduce dependence on Chinese rare earths, but without tangible success. In one of its latest initiatives ERMA publishes the "European Call for Action on Rare Earth Magnets and Motors" in which it states:

> So far, ERA has identified 14 projects—from mine to magnet—subject to potential funding (with an investment volume of 1.7 billion euros), which would form the foundations of a European rare earth industry capable of meeting 20% of EU demand by 2030.

In other words, the EU Commission already admits and assumes a minimum of 80% dependence on rare earths from abroad. Moreover, being realistic and taking into account the time lags associated with the opening of new mines in Europe (10–15 years) and construction of rare earth processing plants (6–8 years),[156] we can easily understand that the dependence of the EU (today mainly on China) for the supply of rare earths will remain complete in the coming years.

## MINING JEWELS IN EUROPE

Without active rare earths mines in Europe, the task of finding mining sources to feed the European Neo Performance Materials processing plant falls to its senior metallurgists. Some of them are men of the world, having traveled the globe visiting mines from Africa to North America to Australia and now to Europe. Their wide range of experience, vision, contacts, and judgment makes them key players within the company.

When I met one of them in Sillamäe, he explained to me that refining is highly dependent on the grade of rare earth oxide concentrate. Grades are everything in mining. The grade, as it is known in the mining environment, or the degree of concentration of the ore,

156 Teresa Llorens González, Geologist of Strategic Minerals Spain S.L., interview conducted on November 22, 2021.

is paramount because the lower the grade, the more total energy will be needed to finally get the metal. This total energy, necessary for mining and separation, is what sets the limits of its exploitation, its mining viability. As this expert explained, sometimes the tailings of an ore— the mining leftovers from the extraction of another metallic element—can be interestingly rich in certain rare metals. These tailings exist, for instance, in the mines owned and operated by Strategic Minerals Spain. These former tin mines had been closed for years, but today it is not just tin that is of interest, but also the by-products.

There may be treasures in Europe to be discovered, or rather to be publicly recognized as such. Perhaps it is not necessary to open new mines, but rather to properly exploit the existing and former ones. But it is fundamental for the viability of a mining project to assess the quality of the tailings, including what elements they contain and in what degree of concentration they are found.

Against all odds, in a continent where the mining of rare metals and even more so of rare earths has been banished, companies like Strategic Minerals Spain have obtained a mining concession to exploit tin, tantalum, niobium and rare earths and even take advantage of by-products such as feldspar. The EU has recognized these mines as an example of sustainability and circular economy in mining. The circular economy is a strategy that aims to reduce both the input of virgin materials and the production of waste, closing the "loops" or economic and ecological flows of resources. Nevertheless, this company does not have any tangible support beyond this mention. Amazingly the output of these mines in northwest Spain not only simultaneously contain all three of Neo's core products in Estonia (tantalum, niobium, and rare earths), but if properly supported, also represents the possibility of connecting the supply chain wholly within Europe. This would improve the company's reliability, remove its initial sourcing from geopolitical risks and arouse the interest of rare metals buyers who favor security over scratching for the last penny, or otherwise put, given commodity traders' profit orientation, prefer sanctions-free certainty over the jeopardy of trading in resources vulnerable to same. What is more, this new trade agreement could favor consideration for an EU aid grant.

When I arrived in Ourense, driving through the Galician mountains and chestnut forests, I could appreciate that well-meaning environmental groups want to protect paradises like this one. All of them should visit the facilities of this mine to observe that the tantalum capacitors of their computers or the rare earths that illuminate the screen or make their cell phones vibrate are compatible with these landscapes. Responsible mining exists; I am a witness. Several things struck me at the Pnouta mine. The first is how few personnel are required; everything is automated. The second is the incredible use of existing resources without damaging nature. For example, the mine does not use water from the village or from the river, even though it could as water is abundant. According to Mario, the company's geologist, "we reuse the rainwater that remains in some of the old tailings ponds that have not yet been remediated, filtering it beforehand with a filter press." Chestnut trees have been planted in the remediated ponds to respect the ecosystem of the area.

When Elena Terrón, head of human resources of the company, explains to me the beginnings of the company, I can understand her respectful and efficient philosophy. As she tells me, "Our first steps were to remediate the tailings ponds and dumps of an old mine that had been badly closed. We took advantage of a lot of material that had been discarded in these old, abandoned tin mines." Elena points out that, "In the 1980s, no attention was paid to by-products such as rare earths or tantalum. The electronics boom had not yet arrived. In many cases, the damage to nature was also not repaired when the mine was abandoned." It is difficult to level environmental accusations when a company starts by repairing the environment while providing jobs in the community. The local Galician accent flows among the staff at the facility; many are from the next town over. Some have even been trained by the company to recruit employees locally.

Even so, a high representative of the Galician Mining Chamber, commented to me in a later interview, that "Not all environmental groups are well-intentioned. Some hide their own interests." According to him, "Unfortunately some environmental groups become a tool to achieve other objectives." Curiosity makes me follow his words very carefully when, after asking him for an example, he states, "The envy in the towns is very bad. Some denounce the mining company on duty through the NGO because it has not bought the land and has bought it from the neighbor." He goes on to add more details. "In the villages everyone knows each other. We all know that here there is a fellow countryman who has opened a web page in which he systematically discredits all the mining companies. When I ask him what interest could anybody have in subsidizing such activities, his look in itself is already part of the answer and I see my naivety reflected in it. For some major producers of metals and supplies of our European companies, it is more profitable to kill mining by subsidizing some NGOs with a little money than to compete against them [the mines]."

Paco Polonio, PhD in Geology, technical director and one of the major shareholders of the company Strategic Minerals Spain believes that some of the NGOs that attack mining, with spurious interests, should be investigated. "Their economic activities and fund transfers should be investigated." But the true obstruction is rather at the regulatory level, where mining companies are confronted with strict environmental laws, which may not adequately take into account the importance of rare earths for national security.[157] If they also have to fight against NGOs with dubious funding and interests, then these companies urgently need the support of their states. Especially since we may be talking about the only European mine producing rare earth concentrate today. Elena Terrón speaks to me with sincerity when she says that "sometimes mining companies prefer not to denounce NGOs so as not to be in the limelight anymore"—a sad reality.

The issue may lie with the fact that while many NGOs are well-intentioned, they may lack scientific training. The opinions of several experts coincide; they point out that although many of these environmental groups defend recycling, they underestimate the pollution generated by the acids used in their processes, which exceed by several orders of magnitude those needed in mining to obtain the same amount of a metal. Most of them estimate that achieving a degree of recycling greater than 25% of some materials is extremely complicated. It is not very healthy or efficient to recycle rare earths from an iPhone or a hard drive.

Given the complex landscape surrounding rare earths, it is no coincidence that the world's existing rare earth refining centers outside China, with significant global production capacity, can be counted on one hand, and that new initiatives to create them in Canada, Brazil, Great Britain, Poland, Australia and the USA are without exception

157 Enrique Burkhalter, Project Manager for Quantum Mining's Matamulas rare earth mine. Personal interview conducted on November 23, 2021.

supported by the state. Even so, to be economically viable they need to have the rare earth concentrate to feed the factory and customers to whom to sell their end products, the rare earth metals, at a competitive market price. China is not willing to give up market share so easily and while it is increasing its production capacity and trying to gain global control of the mines, it continues to subsidize production and refining. While Europe and its Western allies may have competed under different rules—Chinese rules based on state support (subsidies, exemptions and tax breaks) often go against the developed Western standards reflected by the World Trade Organization—nevertheless, it now appears that the U.S. is ready to embrace industrial subsidies as we will see in the next chapters.

Meanwhile, in Europe, without stronger legislative support, the European Raw Materials Alliance (ERMA) launched by the European Commission in 2021, now unfortunately faces a fate similar to that of EURARE. Private investors are averse to risks such as changes in political regulations, the unpredictability of global markets and the high costs of developing an increasingly complex supply chain. Hopes are therefore now focused on the new EU Critical Raw Materials Act, which attempts to provide an answer to the ineffectiveness of current European initiatives, the aggravation produced by the U.S. Inflation Reduction Act and the absolute dependence on China. Aware of its importance, the President of the European Commission, Ursula von der Leyen, quoted when announcing its future publication that it will serve to "secure the new gas and oil at the heart of our economy ... lithium and rare earths will soon be more important than oil and gas."[158]

## THE EU VULNERABILITY

The EU response to Russia's invasion of Ukraine has in most respects been one of unprecedented resolve, reflected most notably in the total flight ban, coordinated economic sanctions, Sweden and Finland's NATO candidacy and, most recently, Denmark's accession to the Common Security and Defense Policy.[159] But it is hard to imag-

158 European Commission, "Critical Raw Materials Act: securing the new gas & oil at the heart of our economy | Blog of Commissioner Thierry Breton," September 14, 2022. https://ec.europa.eu/commission/presscorner/detail/en/STATEMENT_22_5523

159 Susanne Gargiulo and Reuters, "Russia's war on Ukraine prompts Denmark to vote to join EU shared defense policy," *CNN,* June 1, 2022. https://edition.cnn.

ine a similar response against a potential adversary whose isolation from the world would have wider and more devastating consequences: China.

In recent years, there have been instances where the EU has shown concern about China's actions by condemning human rights abuses against the Uyghur population,[160] decrying the "Belt and Road Initiative" alternatives for Africans,[161] and criticizing the recent election processes in Hong Kong,[162] but apart from some symbolic and soft exchange of sanctions, Europe has been careful not to do anything that could be seen as strongly antagonistic to its largest trading partner.[163]

As China watches the global response to Ukraine, it is no doubt considering options and timing with respect to China's own long-proclaimed promise to reunify Taiwan with the rest of the country.[164] However, President Biden's assertive statements in May[165] of 2022 and the subsequent controversial diplomatic visit by House Speaker Nancy Pelosi in August followed by numerous visits by U.S. Congresspeople and other officials demonstrated renewed U.S. determination to counter such objectives. Recently the EU seems to increasingly share the U.S. policy towards Taiwan, as is indicated by the recent visits to the island of Formosa by German Chancellor Scholz and above all by Commission President Ursula von der Leyen. Previously, when Lithuania opened a "Taiwan Representative Office"

---

com/2022/06/01/europe/denmark-eu-defense-policy-intl/index.html

160 European Parliament, "European Parliament resolution of 9 June 2022 on the human rights situation in Xinjiang, including the Xinjiang police files," June 9, 2022. https://www.europarl.europa.eu/doceo/document/TA-9-2022-0237_EN.html.

161 Jan van der Made, "Europe counters China's Belt and Road strategy with plans for €150 billion investment in Africa," *RFI,* February 11, 2022. https://www.rfi.fr/en/africa/20220211-europe-counters-china-s-belt-and-road-strategy-with-plans-for-%E2%82%AC150-billion-investment-in-africa

162 Josep Borrell Fontelles @JosepBorrellF, "Election of #ChiefExecutive violates democratic principles and political pluralism in #HongKong," Twitter post, May 8, 2022. https://twitter.com/JosepBorrellF/status/1523229796544958467

163 "China overtakes US as EU's biggest trading partner," BBC News, February 17, 2021. https://www.bbc.com/news/business-56093378

164 Brad Lendon, "Taiwan watches China as China and the world watch Ukraine," March 8, 2022. https://edition.cnn.com/2022/03/08/asia/taiwan-china-ukraine-russia-wu-intl-hnk/index.html

165 Tessa Wong, "Biden vows to defend Taiwan in apparent US policy shift," *BBC News,* May 23, 2022. https://www.bbc.com/news/world-asia-china-61548531

in 2021, China's response was swift;[166]it unofficially restricted trade relations with the tiny Baltic nation and exerted indirect economic pressure through the rest of the EU. And despite some condemnations of Beijing's discriminatory measures and offers of economic support to Lithuania, the overall response from the rest of the European bloc was largely noncommittal, following an increasingly common pattern of strategic ambiguity.

Like Vladimir Putin's periodic tests of EU resolve, dating back to his statements at the 2007 Munich conference,[167] China's attempts at economic coercion are arguably similar: comparatively small-scale tests that predict future actions on a larger scale. Despite EU sanctions and condemnation citing Russia's war with Georgia,[168] and its annexation of Crimea, Europe's lucrative energy deal with pre-Ukraine Russia continued to grow, further deterring Europe's use of available weapons in its foreign policy arsenal. Similarly, EU condemnation of China is still very limited by a deepening economic dependence.

While it can be argued that China's very dependence on the West as trading partners would limit its option to play the "rare earth card," perhaps limiting the ban on rare earth exports only to arms companies, that situation may not be permanent.[169] Moreover, while Beijing employs its own form of strategic ambiguity[170] in the Russia-Ukraine war, it is positioning itself well for a shift, pivot or rebalance to counter any possible future economic disruption or trade war. With the January 2022 launch of the Regional Comprehensive Economic Partnership[171] (RCEP)—the world's largest trade agreement—and

166 Matthew Reynolds and Matthew P. Goodman, "China's Economic Coercion: Lessons from Lithuania," Center for Strategic & International Studies (CSIS), May 6, 2022. https://www.csis.org/analysis/chinas-economic-coercion-lessons-lithuania

167 See "Putin's famous Munich Speech 2007," RussianPerspective, November 19, 2015, video, 30:46. https://www.youtube.com/watch?v=hQ58Yv6kP44

168 Peter Dickinson, "The 2008 Russo-Georgian War: Putin's green light," Atlantic Council, August 7, 2021. https://www.atlanticcouncil.org/blogs/ukrainealert/the-2008-russo-georgian-war-putins-green-light/

169 Jeff Pao, "China takes rare earth aim at Raytheon and Lockheed," *Asia Times,* February 22, 2022. https://asiatimes.com/2022/02/china-takes-rare-earth-aim-at-raytheon-and-lockheed/

170 Carla Freeman, "China's Ukraine Gambit: Beijing Plays Both Sides," United States Institute of Peace, April 14, 2022. https://www.usip.org/publications/2022/04/chinas-ukraine-gambit-beijing-plays-both-sides

171 Left out of the Indo-Pacific deal, China pushes toward the world's largest trade deal.

Beijing's "Made in China 2025" initiative, it may only be a matter of time before Xi Jinping, seeing his dependence on the bloc of liberal democracies reduced, feels comfortable taking more concrete steps to fulfill his foreign policy aspirations.

And even if the EU were to apply the lessons learned from Russia, when considering the rare earths market there is no realistic alternative to China's supply chain. Unlike with Russian oil and gas, there is no other partner for the EU (or the U.S.) to turn to in the event of trade disruption, as a result of the difficult and environmentally challenging infrastructure that China has been perfecting and patenting for decades while the rest of the world stood idly by.

The time has come to draw lessons from Ukraine conflict about our EU-Russia energy and trade relationship. The parallels with our relationship with China are obvious. We cannot make the same mistake. What would be the repercussions of China's invasion of Taiwan? What if China stops abruptly its economic activity with the island which represents 42%[172] of the total or carries out a full rare earths embargo paralyzing Taiwan activity? What if China enhances support for Russia in Ukraine conflict? Will the West continue to get critical materials under Chinese control, such as rare earths? Hopefully it shouldn't take a conflict in Taiwan for us to realize the fragility of our energy strategy reoriented to renewables. The first concern for China is . . . China! When its domestic demand for rare earths becomes so strong that it can hardly be met, its solidarity may well end where its borders end. China's dependence on the supply of rare earths is therefore contrary to the EU's strategic autonomy. Will the European Union continue to align its energy policy with its defense and foreign affairs policy and that of its allies—who as far as it concerns rare earths, face the same dilemma?

Buying electricity from French or British nuclear power may regretfully not be possible, as French have downgraded their nuclear power and Britain doesn't have any to spare. On the other hand, buying American rare earth metals are similarly dubious, dependent mainly on Mountain Pass or their Australian cousin company, Lynas. The safest way to start developing a European supply chain is for Europe

---

172 Evelyn Cheng, "Taiwan's trade with China is far bigger than its trade with the U.S.," *CNBC,* August 4, 2022. https://www.cnbc.com/2022/08/05/taiwans-trade-with-china-is-far-bigger-than-its-trade-with-the-us.html

to exploit its own mines and resources with the utmost environmental care. But for the sake of safety this option must be politically supported, especially for countries that want to complete the energy transition away from hydrocarbons without resorting to the nuclear option. But the current EU Green Deal and similar national energy policies based on more than 50% renewables, which lack urgent measures to secure rare earth supply chains, will lead us to exchange one energy dependency (Russia) for a similar one (China).

Caution when making decisions by the EU is essential and therefore the European Commission has cautiously evaluated the possibility of increasing the production of rare earths at the Sillamae processing plant in Estonia. In November 2022, Neo Performance Materials announced that the Estonian Government awarded the company a grant of €18.7 million under Europe's Just Transition Fund ("JTF"). Neo's grant is the first such award to a critical materials company in the EU under the JTF program.[173] The company will help fill European supply shortages of rare earth metals for the next few years and will expand the functions of the Sillamae mill. Improved recycling capacity, heavy rare earth separation and permanent magnet manufacturing are among Neo's objectives for its Estonian plant. The Canadian-based international company has a supply chain for rare earth metals outside China. The Sillamae factory ships its various separated rare earth concentrates to its factory in Thailand, where the metals and alloys are manufactured.[174]

But the initial supply of rare earth concentrate coming into Estonia comes from two countries, the United States and, unless it is struck with EU-U.S. sanctions, Russia.[175] However, we should not be too surprised by the partial dependence of this plant on Russian

173 Republic of Estonia Ministry of Economic Affairs and Communications and Neo Performance Materials, "Joint Communiqué In Supporting Expanding Valued-Added Rare Earth Product Manufacturing In Estonia," *Bloomberg,* November 17, 2021. https://www.bloomberg.com/press-releases/2021-11-17/joint-communiqu-in-support-of-expanding-valued-added-rare-earth-product-manufacturing-in-estonia

174 Republic of Estonia Ministry of Economic Affairs and Communications, and Neo Performance Materials, "Joint Communiqué in Support of Expanding Valued-Added Rare Earth Product Manufacturing in Estonia," November 17, 2021. https://www.neomaterials.com/joint-communique-in-support-of-expanding-valued-added-rare-earth-product-manufacturing-in-estonia/

175 Personal interview with Andrei Litvinjuk, operations manager, Neo Performance Materials, Sillamae, Estonia, October 20, 2021.

rare earth concentrate, although strategically it would be preferable for it to use that of the Spanish company Strategic Minerals Spain or another European one if available. Many European nuclear power plants use enriched uranium rods as nuclear fuel, coming from the Russian company Rosatom, which has never been targeted by EU or U.S. sanctions.

Trying to work on two tracks at the same time, the EU also announced in 2022 the creation of a new independent and EU-funded rare earth processing center in Poland. But the European Commission is aware of the deadlines to develop it (6–8 years) and of the urgency and importance of the problem. The excellent cost-opportunity ratio of relying on the Sillamae plant, grants the above-mentioned credit to the Canadian company Neo Performance Materials for the renovation and expansion of its refinery in Estonia. Neo still must ensure an adequate supply of ore concentrate to the refinery, but once a European country secures the production of metal powders and/or rare earth alloys, the bottleneck established by China can be broken much more easily. The time would then come, if required, to increase the production of permanent magnets by certain companies (e.g., Euromag[176] ) or other rare earth end products, in the interest of developing a fully vertically integrated supply chain.

## THE EU STRUGGLE TO OBTAIN MINERALS

The EU is hastily seeking to obtain its rare earth concentrates, driving an incongruous move towards renewables and electric vehicles that need its minerals, but sporting a self-inflicted wound vis a vis lack of domestic mines. By developing the concept of strategic cooperation, to establish an area of prosperity and stability and to tighten the links between EU and its partners, it is setting its sights primarily on the African continent and some South American countries. Let us hope that this strategic cooperation will not only be fruitful but also respectful of environmental and social standards and help to maintain or improve the governance of the countries that are the object of its ambitions, using Western standards. The result of this cooperation must do better than just to outsource our pollution and take advantage

176 Euromag, "Our Materials," consulted on December 8, 2022. https://www.euromag-magnets.com/en/materials/

of cheap labor and lax or almost non-existent environmental and labor regulations in some African countries, as has been the course of action to-date. It would not be fruitful to reinforce the growing kleptocratic market for African metals.

The EU has other, more drastic options to try and quench the fire for the time being. These include the creation of war reserves of rare earths, encouraging the substitution of these elements with domestic alternatives, subsidizing recycling methods that are not yet economically viable, and diversification by trying to create products that dispense with rare earths altogether. The most appropriate solution is perhaps the recovery and exploitation of mining by-products containing rare earths existing in mines already open in Europe, but all these measures need to be accompanied by more forceful government interventions than those developed so far. European governments cannot leave an energy security issue and their climate objectives to a free market driven by neoliberal globalization. In the absence of strong and sustained government support, it is unlikely that private industry will be able to overcome the challenges and develop a viable competitor to the Chinese rare earth monopoly—especially since it is up against a market artificially manipulated by China.

In a capitalist system, state intervention is seen as an intrusion, though it goes on all the time in capitalist countries, whether by favorable taxation, suppression of organized labor, etc. But in order to guarantee renewable energies, states have no choice but to politicize "green metals." This is nothing new. The supply of energy between countries has always had a political component and this time these materials are the enabling vehicle for this. The geopolitics of renewables is still young and immature, but there is no reason to leave energy security in the hands of China, even were relations with China to be positive. Beyond the aforementioned patches, the EU has two main and non-exclusive options: (1) aggressively promote and support the development of mines and processing facilities within the bloc; and/or (2) partner with like-minded allies outside Europe in order to more equitably share the burdens and responsibly develop this essential infrastructure.

Several IGME geologists whom I consulted believe that Sweden could be the salvation for the bloc. The Swedish government's 2023 televised announcement of a huge discovery of rare earths in Arctic

Sweden is possibly more an attempt by Sweden to reach out to the EU than a new discovery of rare earths. All agree that it is very difficult to find new deposits in Europe anymore. Everything is known and mapped; at best, quantities of material or extensions are redefined. It seems therefore that what changes are the governments and their stance for or against mining. The new government in Sweden may be more pro-mining than the previous one, especially as circumstances have also changed. Russia is a historical enemy of Sweden, and its government may have already realized that rare earths are also needed for weaponry and other aspects of security. In general, these views are reinforced by the existence of another rare earth mine in Sweden. In the opposite direction of the announced Kiruna mine, located above the Arctic Circle, is the Nora Karr mine. This mine lies 300 kilometers southwest of the capital, Stockholm. Owned by Leading Edge Materials, the mine is the only one in Europe with such highly prized heavy rare earths as dysprosium and terbium, but the mining concession has been on hold for years. Perhaps better political winds are now blowing for both mines. Not surprisingly, the only mine in the world mining heavy rare earths outside China is Australia's Brown-Hill mine and only then in very small quantities at its pilot plant project.[177] The demand for heavy rare earths has multiplied by several orders of magnitude over the last two decades. Many experts agree that four heavy rare earths, europium; dysprosium; terbium and yttrium, are among the elements for which shortages are likely to occur soon.

Taking advantage of my visit to the Strategic Minerals Spain company, I took the opportunity to ask Polonio, the technical director, about the subsidies. His answer is very honest in recognizing that "Subsidies without precautions are not the solution. If a mining company is subsidized and its rare earth concentrate is sold to China, we are giving the money away. What is needed is protection for our companies. Encourage the next step in the rare earth value chain to buy from the previous step within Europe. This is the only way we will be able to compete with Chinese products." Polonio's view ultimately translates into a similar application of the main measures of the American Inflation Reduction Act. In the absence of similar

177 Zhang Xun, China Metal Mining, "Medium and heavy rare earth projects outside China," June 15, 2020. http://www.tjtzm.com/English/new/2020-06-15/119.html

tax advantages in Europe, his company's portfolio also includes the ubiquitous Chinese customers.

According to Óscar Crespo, the company's operations director, "An example of how well-used subsidies can work is the subsidies that were applied to coal in Europe until 2018. Thanks to them, European coal-fired power plants were able to feed themselves without having to buy from abroad." Óscar recalls, "When the subsidies were withdrawn, the price of coal rose in Europe from 90 Euros per ton to around 550 Euros. With those prices that were not competitive, practically all the European mines closed."

Another option for Europe could be Turkiye, which in July 2022 announced the discovery of an apparently colossal treasure, the world's second largest reserve of rare earths. Despite an often-tense relationship with the West, Turkiye remains a member of NATO and these critical deposits could prove to be an important strategic asset for the alliance. The spectacular internationally released announcement of the size of the discovery hints more at Turkiye's willingness to seek international partners to develop this industry than at the reality, which is that this bastnasite deposit has yet to be geologically speaking correctly explored and its value well defined. This deposit would be familiar to agencies in this sector and national geological services of western countries such as Britain and America, when referred to by the name of Kizilçaören.[178] Ultimately, in the mining world everything depends on the grade. Grade is king, and the viability of mining will depend on what elements are ultimately found in the deposit and in what grade or concentration. High lanthanum and cerium richness, for example, would be of little value because of the worldwide abundance of these elements.[179]

## EUROPE HAS MET ITS ENEMY: ITSELF

Through EURARE and ERMA, the European Commission has supported the procurement of highly coveted rare earths, but the complex nature of the legislative process makes it extremely difficult to

---

178 United States Geological Survey, "Mineral Resources/Online Spatial Data/ Rare earth element mines, deposits, and occurrences/Kizilçaören," https://mrdata.usgs.gov/ree/show-ree.php?rec_id=44, accessed on Nov. 2022.

179 Baraniuk C., "Turkey Probably Hasn't Found the Rare Earth Metals It Says It Has," Jul. 2022, https://www.wired.com/story/turkey-rare-earth-metals/.

transform opinions and recommendations into directives and regulations. With its semi-federal and somewhat unstable political status, the EU is challenged to achieve the consensus necessary to form strategic partnerships outside the bloc and to pass regulations that do not erode the sovereignty of member states. As both the global pandemic and Russian aggression in Ukraine have recently demonstrated, the EU is improving its ability to react more quickly and decisively to a crisis.

But compared to Europe's politically driven response to its perceived threat in relation to oil and gas, the threat of China's monopoly on rare earths is widely underestimated or conveniently ignored in most of Europe. If the development of the rare earth supply chain is not prioritized, the EU's rapid move towards clean energy solutions will trade a nearly 30% dependence on Russian oil and gas for a much greater and much more damaging dependence on China. And because of the growing interconnection between economic and security policy, EU inaction risks jeopardizing not only its energy independence goals, but also perception of its support for democratic values abroad and its ability to maintain strategic autonomy among the world's superpowers.

Finally, it seems that in the West, we have met our enemy and it is ourselves. Once again it seems capitalism must be saved from itself. To get out of this impasse which the EU has voluntarily got itself into, we must harken back to its origins. When the French Foreign Minister, Robert Schuman, initially proposed the European Coal and Steel Community in 1950, the purpose was to pool resources and eliminate a competition for critical materials that, until then, had already twice fueled catastrophic world wars. In Schuman's own words, this unity of effort would make war between rivals "not only unthinkable, but materially impossible."[180] It demanded some short-term national costs and sacrifices, but, as one of the founding actions of the EU, this action can be held at least partially responsible for the bloc's subsequent historic period of stability. Given the current challenges to European solidarity—both internal and external—it is time for the EU to consider a similar, unifying effort with the same goal and potential to foster peace and long-term sustainability.

---

180 European Union, "Schuman declaration May 1950," May 9, 1950. https://european-union.europa.eu/principles-countries-history/history-eu/1945-59/schuman-declaration-may-1950_en

The constructivist solutions that have ensured peace in Europe for so many years came at a time of collective consciousness resulting from the devastation of the Second World War. Today their memory is so distant, several generations behind us, that trying to apply the same formula on a global scale, with a world immersed in the trend towards de-globalization and adding major powers' opposing ideologies to the equation, seems complicated. However, as we will see below, the ceding of powers to a new and neutral supranational entity to control resources is also a valid (albeit idealistic) option to jointly combat global warming. Faced with the precipice of climate change, countries have not only an individual but a collective responsibility. It is not enough to obtain the materials to meet their national decarbonization targets, but they must coordinate so that they can all make their energy transition.

## WHO'S WATCHING THE STORE?

An era of relative peace was dawning in the world after the fall of the USSR, with a decrease in the number of inter-state conflicts and the resulting casualties. Many Western governments saw their role as guarantors of security losing relevance. However, threats such as COVID show us that states continue to play a fundamental role and that our security cannot be guaranteed without them. Western governments are invested with their new role of guaranteeing human security in all fields, such as food security, health security, energy security, etc. But governments are newcomers to these scenarios and the security structures inherited from their past are not prepared to face these new threats with full guarantees.

Who is in charge of guaranteeing the supply of rare metals? Or, for example, antibiotics? Many are subject to an overwhelming Chinese monopoly. The defense ministries of Western countries are used to dealing with "hard power" threats, i.e., classic military threats, and the interior ministries with crime and criminality within their borders. Even so, they are forced to expand their domains and areas of action by developing "space forces" for the new space domain, or cyber armies or cyber police for the cyber domain. However, these ministries are only neophytes in some domains of human security and are often not integrated into existing structures. On the other hand, ministries of industry or energy focus on stability, progress, development and growth of the economy. Human security slips through the fingers of governments like sand. For the time being, countries are generally content with actions or laws that encourage and incentivize private entities to create some security level, as is the case with the supply chains.

In the USA, the main endeavors are reflected in the Rare Earths Offshoring Act ("ORE Act"), and the U.S. Critical Minerals Exploration and Innovation Act of 2020. But in case anyone was left in any doubt as to the security dimensions of this problem, the Trump administration did not hesitate to invoke Title III of the Defense Production Act, to "strengthen core capabilities of essential domestic industry and the critical defense workforce in the aviation, rare earth materials, and electronics industries." The Biden administration also used it to ensure energy security and encouraged the development of solar panels, freeing imports of the necessary materials from taxes, to combat the monopoly of the Chinese market.

These new U.S. laws show the attempts of the most powerful nation in the world to exercise the fundamental principle of its existence, its *leitmotiv*, which, like that of every state, is to provide security to its citizens. This time, the laws attempt to guarantee security in arenas outside of those traditionally considered security concerns. If the crusade against climate change has been poorly planned, it is due to the lack of a commission to assess the implications for human security both nationally and globally of implementing changes in resource access and use. This would involve scientists (geologists, economists, chemical engineers, etc.) and experts in international relations and security working together with the same priority: human, national and international security.

The stakes are high. Climate change triggers and enhances threats such as natural disasters, rising sea levels, droughts, and famines, etc. If these threats materialize, it is anticipated this will provoke waves of migration, conflicts over resources, increased criminality, destabilization of governments, and so forth. States are aware of the challenge and of their important role in protecting us from the threat and mitigating the risks, but they lack experience in these arenas of human security compared to classic threats and the traditional concept of national security.

It is no longer just a question of whether to leave our energy security in China's hands, but also whether Western policymakers are properly advised. We are trying to carry out an organized, large-scale, top-down energy transition for the first time in history, and it is the world's political leaders who are leading the way. But unlike the interventionist economic model of the Beijing government, our free-market capitalist system does not handle government interference well. The distortions that are created are unacceptable to private enterprises and corporations, because private capital and investments are not used to responding to such instructions. In addition, Europe intends to carry it out in record time compared to the other energy transitions we have experienced in history. Time is pressing, yes, but that should not be the reason for rushing into a climate crusade without the necessary scientific advice.

As it is currently shaping up, the green energy transition has a dark future. Today, many critical minerals such as rare earths should be treated in the same way as fossil fuels because their stocks are limited. If recycling does not cease to be a utopic promise and overcomes its limitations, some metals should soon be considered as endangered species. Some scientific journals such as the French *l'Usine Nouvelle*, created in 1891 and with a great reputation in the industrial world, have already been announcing for more than a decade the future shortage of critical metals. For example, in 2017 this now digitized magazine pointed out that even without an increase in the current rate of consumption, copper and silver will remain exploitable worldwide for less than 21 years, and even less time for other metals such as antimony, tin, lead, gold, zinc and strontium. The magazine points out that we will no longer have economically viable reserves of a total of 17 metals before the end of this century.[181] Humanity will soon reach its growth limits if it maintains a lifestyle that is unsustainable for the 11.2 billion population projected for the year 2100.

In response to the initial failure of this crusade, some countries affected by environmental catastrophes are now demanding justice—specifically, climate justice. These nations are seeking compensation from the main causes of climate change. A good example is Pakistan

181 Myrtille Delamarche, "De surprenantes matières critiques," *L'Usine Nouvelle,* July 10, 2017. https://www.usinenouvelle.com/article/infographie-de-surprenantes-matieres-critiques.N563822

whose floods left more than 10% of its territory covered with water. The new fund created to compensate for losses and damages caused by climate change should be fed mainly by nations such as the U.S. This nation has been responsible for the emission of about 20% of the greenhouse gases produced historically. The volume rises when alluding to the possibility that without "fair contributions" to the fund, developing countries like Pakistan might be tempted to default on their foreign debt in retaliation.

Perhaps the time has come to stop and rethink the crusade. It may be that if we approach the issue from the perspective of security, real respect for the environment and the democratization of resources, and not from a solely economic approach, we will succeed in launching a more informed campaign plan. But in order to do so, it is essential to know the dark side of this crusade as it has been designed.

# 5. THE DARK SIDE OF THE CLIMATE CRUSADE

## THE MAGIC OF HYDROGEN

In trying to escape fossil fuels and the effects of climate change, humanity is looking up. Just above our heads is hydrogen. It is the most abundant element in the universe and its content in the atmosphere makes it almost inexhaustible. Looking even further up there is the sun that bathes us every day with its energy. But before we launch ourselves in pursuit of the energy manna of our era, we would do well to look down to the ground, to our feet, and start digging. Without mining, neither the production of hydrogen nor the harnessing of solar energy would be possible. The difficult thing will be to avoid changing the pollution paradigm from the atmosphere to the earth, to not go from $CO_2$ derived from fossil fuels to the pollution of mined areas and surrounding water resources by acids and heavy metals.

Our society looks to hydrogen as the great ultimate energy hope, even though it is essentially a method of energy storage and transport. Hydrogen is unlimited and can be obtained almost inexhaustibly from both air and seawater. But from the outset, we are warned of the existence of various types of hydrogen depending on its origin. The degree to which the procurement source is harmful to the environment is what classifies it as gray, blue, green, or pink hydrogen. The darker the color, the more harmful it is to the earth. In the case of the golden hydrogen, its color represents an imminent gold (hydrogen) rush and a promise of high value for humanity. This kind of hydrogen is generated naturally in the Earth's crust. Hydrogen gas fields can be formed by a range of internal Earth processes. If these reservoirs can be traced and the gold hydrogen extracted in a clean and safe way, then it will be a highly sustainable and acceptable form of green energy.

Black hydrogen (obtained from burning oil) is the most harmful. Gray is in second place. Here, coal burning is the energy source used to separate H2 molecules. The hydrogen most widely used today is blue, made from natural gas—and is therefore still a fossil energy source. Natural gas is basically methane, a greenhouse gas in itself, but it also produces carbon dioxide when burned. Green hydrogen, which aspires to be the true manna, comes from water. The energy for the separation of its molecules by electrolysis is obtained by renewable energies that are unfortunately always mistakenly labeled as green. Producing green hydrogen with renewable hydropower is part of the present recipe for saving the earth.

While waiting for the energy salvation of hydrogen, Western society has developed an obsessive-compulsive disorder. Its panic about climate change has led it to create a ritual that it repeats as often as necessary to ward off its fears: install solar panels and wind turbines. The danger is that, in contrast to hydrogen, renewable energies (wind and solar) are always considered clean and associated with the color green, despite the fact that mining is required to obtain elements necessary for solar panel and turbine production. Hydrogen obtained from wind turbines or solar panels, whose elements have left behind a lot of pollution, could more accurately be categorized as brown hydrogen. After all, there is no such thing as black or gray renewable energy in our minds.

The analysis to determine the benign or malignant origin and production methods of their required "green metals" is not carried out rigorously and does not take the entire process into account. Very few citizens in the West are aware of the environmental impact of the production of solar panels, wind turbines, batteries, or electric motors. The remoteness of Chinese factories seems to keep them safe from the pollution generated there—or rather, from an awareness of it. This time, Don Quixote is right. When we see one of our new windmills, we should actually be seeing evil gray giants full of materials coming from fossil mining and manufactured thanks to electricity coming from coal. Even without knowing their origin no one wants them near their homes. They are noisy and break the landscape. So, we banish them and send them out to sea, far from our shores. This exile necessitates even more rare earths use per turbine, which must be just as powerful, albeit easier to maintain and lighter. The higher the population density of a country, the more likely it is that the wind giants will have to move out to sea.

However, to obtain and use on a large scale the so-called pink hydrogen (also called red) by means of nuclear energy, as Japan intends, would allow us to escape global warming for several centuries. Taking into account the high safety and low waste produced by the last nuclear reactor generations, perhaps *pink* hydrogen is actually the preferable version?

## THE HIDDEN COSTS OF SOLAR ENERGY

Solar energy, besides being the cheapest of renewable energies, usually easily escapes classification as a pollutant. However, like green hydrogen, it is also a good example of the fossil world in which these supposedly renewable technologies operate.

As a U.S. official from the NATO Center of Excellence for Energy Security explained to me on a visit to their facilities in Vilnius, Lithuania, in March 2022, "the production of solar panels has a huge carbon dioxide footprint and pollution associated with it that is not being taken into account." The International Energy Association itself points out that many authors, by prior agreement, do not take into account the $CO_2$ emissions produced to obtain either the charcoal or the wood pellets used to feed the smelting furnaces that transform quartz into metallic silicon at high temperatures. As I am told by the Energy Security Center and corroborated by their publications, the $CO_2$ emitted by the coal-fired power plants that provide electricity to the refineries to continue the process of purifying the silicon into high-grade metallic polysilicon is not taken into account in the calculations either. Finally, they also do not consider the emissions produced in the transportation of all the materials involved in the process before they reach the Chinese factories.[182] In a very feasible example, charcoal and wood pallets could come from the Brazilian Amazon, quartz from the U.S. Cerrejón mines in Columbia, and coal from China itself. Mining is not a renewable activity and in general decarbonization, as it stands, is itself a source of greenhouse gas emissions.

The gigantic and archaic metallurgical smelting furnaces used to obtain metallic silicon have not evolved much in the last 100 years.

---

182 International Energy Agency (IEA), *$CO_2$ Emissions from Fuel Combustion:* Data Base Documentation (2020 Edition). https://iea.blob.core.windows.net/assets/474cf91a-636b-4fde-b416-56064e0c7042/WorldCO2_Documentation.pdf

They still use three large rods, carbon electrodes, up to one meter in diameter and between 10 and 20 meters high. Their fuel is still a mixture of charcoal, coal, and wood pellets, which are mixed with the quartz from which the silicon is extracted to obtain the metallic silicon. These installations are a source of pollution in the form of sulfur dioxide, carbon monoxide, hydrogen chloride and nitric oxide.[183]

Continuing downstream, the process remains as highly polluting as it is unknown, as the coal-fired power plants that provide the electricity to produce the high-purity metallic polysilicon are major emitters of $CO_2$. This metallic polysilicon is used by almost all existing solar panel models. The production of polysilicon rods requires a continuous and uninterrupted flow of electricity, 24/7, and consumes a minimum of 175 megawatt hours per ton of polysilicon. In China, each polysilicon metal refinery is typically located next to a carbon plant that provides the necessary electricity at low cost. Kilns powered by electricity from renewable energies, such as those in Norway, are rare gems in the world.

To get an idea of the pollution associated with a single polysilicon plant, which can consume 400 megawatts, it is sufficient to note that this electricity could only be used to power around 300,000 homes. But the pollution generated does not stop there, because in order to subsequently obtain single crystal solar cells, known as mono-photovoltaics, the purification process is doped by adding rare earths, in minute quantities, which make it possible to obtain the desired conductivity conditions.[184] And, as we shall see, extracting rare earths is a dirty business, often associated with high pollution.

If we finally wanted to apply the concept of a circular and sustainable economy for photovoltaic energy, we would have to think about recycling the thousands of solar panels that are currently being installed. But because of the complex and irreversible transformations that take place during their production, the recycling of the elements that make up the solar panels is very limited, as is the recycling of the

183 New York State Department of Environmental Conservation – Facility DEC ID: 9291100078 PERMIT Under the Environmental Conservation Law (ECL) Permit Issued To: GLOBE METALLURGICAL INC Permit Type: Air Title V Facility Permit ID: 9-2911-00078/00009 Effective Date: 04/21/2016 Expiration Date: 04/20/2021 http://www.dec.ny.gov/dardata/boss/afs/permits/929110007800009_r3.pdf–

184 NATO Energy Security Centre of Excellence, *Energy Highlights,* November 16, 2021, 29–31.

DC-to-AC transformers, charge controllers and other elements that accompany the solar panels during their installation. [185]

Tian Min, general manager of Nanjing Fangrun Materials, a Chinese recycling company in Jiangsu province that collects the recalled solar panels, claimed that the solar energy industry was a ticking time bomb. "It will explode with force in two to three decades and wreck the environment, if the estimate is correct."[186]

Regardless of the good intentions of our politicians and environmental protection groups, the laws enacted, and the investments made, the reality is that not a single watt of energy is produced in the world without significant expenditure of raw materials and fossil fuels. The process of manufacturing the fastest growing renewable energy is not a renewable process, and its hidden costs are not accounted for.

Social awareness of environmental damage has been growing in recent decades, and as a result the people of many countries are demanding actions and policies from their governments to preserve and protect ecosystems. If these same citizens were sufficiently aware of the damage inflicted on the earth by irresponsible mining, the working conditions under which it is carried out in some countries, and the carbon footprint and pollution produced by refining processes, they would also call on their leaders to act against it. Consequently, the initial reaction of Western leaders could involve further bans and restrictions on both the importation of these metals, and on the way in which Western companies conduct mining, processing of the minerals and manufacture of solar panels and wind turbines, both in third countries and in the West. Inadvertently, the anticipated shortage of rare earths and other "green metals" could be further exacerbated.

## RARE EARTHS, A DIRTY BUSINESS

In the West, we want to have our cake and eat it too. We expect the ingredients to appear immaculately, as if by magic, and the cakes to appear already baked. Governments mandate a rapid transition to

---

185 Thomas A. Troszac, "The hidden costs of solar photovoltaic power," *Energy Highlights,* no. 16 (NATO Energy Security Centre of Excellence, 2021): 30.

186 Stephen Chen, "China's aging solar panels are going to be a big environmental problem," *South China Morning Post,* July 30, 2017. https://www.scmp.com/news/china/society/article/2104162/chinas-ageing-solar-panels-are-going-be-big-environmental-problem

renewables and electric vehicles but are reluctant to pay the real price. The mining and processing of rare earths is a dirty business that, if not carried out with due precautions, is aggressively damaging to the environment and can have dire consequences for humans involved in the processes or living in the vicinity. The West, in general, wants nothing to do with these businesses. The degree of intentionality being unclear, it is difficult to know whether they have been abandoned, stolen or outsourced.

There are three main minerals from which rare earth elements are currently extracted, bastnasite, monazite and xenotime, although they are not the only ones. The processes for obtaining and processing these minerals depend on which of the 17 rare earth elements the mineral contains.[187] These minerals are usually extracted by digging large open-pit mines of up to 50 square kilometers, using dynamite. This can lead to the displacement of local indigenous communities and the destruction of the surrounding ecosystem. An example of this displacement of native populations resulted from the signing in February 2020 by Brazilian President Bolsonaro of an authorization for mining activities in indigenous areas of the Amazon.[188] There are also some deposits where the minerals containing rare earths are not extracted, with the process skipping this phase and proceeding directly to in situ leaching. In other words, large surfaces are sprayed with acid solutions and solvents, which pass through the rock. The entire process uses not only large quantities of acid, solvents and alkaline solutions, but also enormous quantities of water, the massive use of which can lead to water scarcity for local populations. Government-sponsored mining companies, by restricting water access for local populations, can lead to unrest and conflict over water resources. Drought-prone countries, such as South Africa, have witnessed an increase in conflicts over the lack of their water supply.[189] For years, South African industry,

187 Reboredo R. Prego, "What do we know about rare earths?," Centro Superior de Investigaciones Cientificas, Ministerio de Ciencia, Innovación y Universidades, Madrid, 2019.

188 J. Siqueira-Gay, B. Soares-Filho, L. E. Sanchez, A. Oviedo, and L. J. Sonter, "Proposed legislation to exploit Brazil's indigenous lands will threaten Amazon forests and their valuable ecosystem services," *One Earth,* 3 (2020), 356.

189 Michel Penke, "Toxic and radioactive: The damage from mining rare elements," *DW,* April 13, 2021. https://www.dw.com/en/toxic-and-radioactive-the-damage-from-mining-rare-elements/a-57148185

government and public opinion have debated—without reaching a clear agreement—whether companies should have privileged access to water and to what extent the population should be allowed to suffer shortages.

On the other hand, without careful mineral extraction which requires extensive use of water, the soil acidifies and becomes toxic and non-viable for agriculture, destroying fauna and flora. The affected area extends far beyond the mine. It is estimated that for every ton of rare earths, about 2,000 tons of toxic waste are produced. This toxic waste is collected in huge tailings ponds and their toxic and acidic waters sometimes seep into underground aquifers, contaminating much larger areas that sometimes connect to surrounding rivers. Once the toxic products and residual metals have been distributed through the air, soil and water, they are very difficult to remove. This form of extraction results in the destruction and contamination of the natural water system. Unique plants and animals lose access to groundwater and watering places.[190]

In the case of illegal mining, such as the abundant mining carried out in Myanmar near the border with China, it consists of directly "burning" the ionic clay soil by pouring ammonium sulfate to extract the rare earths. In many cases, seepage into the subsoil occurs.

When we move downstream in the supply chain, towards the separation and processing stages of rare earths, things do not improve. The two main techniques used to separate the elements[191] add to the damage, with the production of radioactive waste (uranium and thorium), as well highly toxic elements (arsenic and fluoride, for example) to which both workers and the inhabitants of the area are exposed. If thorium and uranium have been dissolved, the waste then becomes a wastewater management problem. These factors are associated with the development of cancers, such as bone and skin cancer, malformation of fetuses, damage to the central nervous system, cardiovascular disease, and respiratory problems.[192] In China's Baotou region of Inner

190 Michel Penke, "Toxic and radioactive."

191 "Cracking or roasting" using acid, alkaline or hot solutions, leaching with a series of solvents or chemical precipitation and evaporation to separate the rare earths and "froth flotation": coating the ore with water-repelling chemicals that adhere to the rare earth minerals and trap air particles, causing the rare earths to float on top of a solution.

192 Michael Standaert, "China Wrestles with the Toxic Aftermath of Rare Earth

Mongolia, the world's largest iron ore and secondarily rare earth mining site, surrounding farms and nearby villages have been poisoned, causing thousands of people to leave the area.[193]

But sometimes the casualties of illegal mining do not occur indirectly because of the contamination but directly on site. This is what a Burkina Faso Army engineer officer I had the opportunity to interview told me. This commander told me that "in his country, illegal mining is not prosecuted, they turn a blind eye. But unfortunately, people die every year. The problems come with the rain. Many times, illegal mines are narrow holes to access gold, bauxite or manganese. These thin tunnels, which sometimes have a good slope, fill with water and the miners die. Sometimes they are children." When I ask him why mining exploitation is not regularized in his country his answer leaves no room for doubt, "Our own minister of mines is in the middle of a judicial process for selling illegally outside the state circuit." He adds "The corrupt are favored by the lack of clear laws and willingness to reinforce them."

But pollution from mining critical metals does not stop at the mines. The smelting of rare earth elements to obtain their metals contributes to air pollution mainly through emissions of four gases: carbon dioxide, sulfur dioxide, nitrogen oxides and waste gases containing fluorine and heavy metals. Some of these come simply from the consumption of electricity or fossil fuels and others from smelting. These gases contribute directly to global warming and acidification.

If we are to calculate the true environmental cost, we must consider all the environmental damage produced in a comprehensive manner. We must also add the impact of road construction and its use by vehicles dedicated to transport between the mine and the processing and storage centers, as well as the use of fossil fuels to generate electricity in the mining facilities through generators or to power the vehicles used in the mine. Here, once again, the extraction of these metals damages the ecosystem surrounding the mine and increases the carbon footprint. Finally, many mining companies abandon the mine when it is no longer profitable, without carrying out any environmental rehabilitation process.

---

Mining," *Yale Environment 360,* July 2, 2019. https://e360.yale.edu/features/china-wrestles-with-the-toxic-aftermath-of-rare-earth-mining

193 Michel Penke, "Toxic and radioactive."

The most critical points of extracting and refining rare earth metals for the environment are the radioactivity of thorium, the production of a huge amount of carcinogenic toxins from sulfates, ammonia, hydrochloric acid, and waste leaching into the water. We can certainly state that rare earth mining and processing is a dirty business.[194]

Perhaps all these factors help to explain why we are moving away from the goal of carbon neutrality (emitting into the atmosphere only the amount of greenhouse gases that we absorb in other ways) in order to halt climate change.

## THE TRUE PRICE OF THE CLIMATE CRUSADE

In the Middle Ages, the Crusades became a lucrative business for some. Thus, the Catholic Church legitimized and justified the spoils of the crusaders, which sometimes consisted of conquered lands, peoples, and their resources. Today's crusaders, in the name of the fight against climate change, are none other than the mining companies that set off for Africa or other developing countries in search of mineral deposits to exploit, under conditions of regulatory laxity, profiting from an activity that is much more controlled in the West. In the past, Templars committed atrocities overlooked by their engagement in what was otherwise justified as a holy crusade. Today, what can justify the damages resulting from the fight against climate change and the maintenance of our technified and ultra-communicated society?

The church-monarchy partnership of the earlier era has morphed into today's political-environmentalist partnership. At the COP summits, the most developed countries offer salvation to the developing countries—when they carry out the energy transition. But for this they must first help us to exploit their mines and allow China or the West to produce the wind turbines and solar panels that will take us away from the hell of global warming. But who is going to pay for the energy transition in these underdeveloped countries? Clearly they do not have the economic capacity to carry it out and many have other more pressing domestic problems than flying the flag of the crusade against climate change. However, some do have the minerals, such

194 Jonathan Kaiman, "Rare earth mining in China: The grim social and environmental costs," *The Guardian,* March 20, 2014. https://www.theguardian.com/sustainable-business/rare-earth-mining-china-social-environmental-costs

as rare earths, which make this fight possible. Leaders of the rich world present themselves as green evangelists, even though it is their countries that have brought about the current climate change situation. Companies and corporations that exploit the resources of developing nations rarely help them out of the resource curse in which they find themselves. They bring with them new revenues that are not well distributed among the population and they do not bring development. They have not done so in many cases in exploiting oil resources and most likely will not do so in exploiting countries' mineral resources. Rich nations have benefited from the use of fossil fuels to develop and are still abusing them. Ironically or hypocritically, the world's major development organizations under their tutelage, nowadays, generally refuse to finance the exploitation of fossil fuels that some poor countries could use to lift themselves out of poverty.

In Africa, the exploitation of renewable energy resources is viewed not as a matter of choice but as a remedy for its poverty. We are talking about a lot of wood, straw, and dung, so much that it accounts for half of the energy produced on the continent. Telling poor countries to live and develop on the basis of intermittent energies such as solar and wind, which are not even consolidated in the West and weaker than other clean sources such as nuclear energy, is more than a swindle, it is an outrage. Renewable energies are like teenagers: intermittent, highly variable, and unpredictable. They are not comparable to mature energies such as nuclear in terms of independence and capacity or to gas and fossil energies in terms of availability.

Rare earths, silicon, cobalt, and lithium play an important role in achieving the milestones set in the green agenda against climate change, established by the Paris Agreement in 2015 and previously by the Kyoto Protocol. However, as we can see, the damage from both mining and refining of green metals are acquiring tragic environmental dimensions. We are faced with the paradox of the unsustainability of an energy transformation advertised as sustainable, due to a new type of pollution produced and a limited amount of mineral resources.

The OECD also points out the problems generated in the extraction of critical minerals, their processing, manufacturing, and waste management. According to this organization, the environmental consequences could be so severe that low-carbon technologies would simply change the nature of the environmental problem. It would simply shift the source of the problem from one part of the resource-intensive energy sector of the economy to another part, but the ecological and social hazard would remain. We would be exchanging part of the $CO_2$ pollution and global warming for heavy metal pollution, habitat destruction or resource depletion.[195]

In the same way we would be transferring pollution from one country to another. The hidden price of our crusade is the externalization of pollution and environmental damage and shadow costs paid by the planet. If the crusade continues without a course correction, green bubbles will initially be created before 2050–2060, consisting of countries with very little pollution. Due to bio-diffusion these bubbles would not withstand the onslaught of the 32 billion tons of $CO_2$ dumped globally each year into the atmosphere. The USA, Canada, Europe, Oceania, Japan and South Korea and finally China will only comparatively become "green nations or continents." No more than a quarter of the world's population would see life as green. The rest would have to wait. Some would even see new and numerous mines appear on their territories, leaving them with the pollution from extracting the minerals, others would suffer the pollution from the metal processing plants, but without seeing the benefits of using them to generate wind or solar energy on their territories.

However, the world is not doomed to follow this trajectory. The degree of ecological impact of the extraction processes of critical materials does not depend so much on the types of minerals extracted as on the extraction techniques and processes applied in the countries where they are extracted. For example, diverting the course of a river to access water, dumping tailings in lakes or acid leaching directly into the ground are techniques and processes used almost exclusively in developing countries and differ from those used in Western countries where the energy to power smelting furnaces or processing and refining centers may come from state-of-the-art nuclear power plants or hydroelectric dams. Legislation in more developed countries generally does not allow for significant environmental damage. Regulations, taxes, media pressure and public opinion make companies think twice before starting a project on Western soil.[196] Now we need to stop them going

195 OECD, *Global Material Resource Outlook to 2060: Economic Drivers and Environmental Consequences* (2019).

196 Preston S. Chiaro, "Environmental Strategies in the Mining Industry: One

to the Global South or to oblige them to act there by their Western standards.

## NOT HERE, AND DON'T TELL ME WHERE

The "Not in My Backyard" (NIMBY) effect plays an important role in the climate crusade. Countries do not want the environmental consequences associated with renewable energy production in their own country, i.e., close to home. Therefore, large mining companies tend to open projects in third countries, located in poorer regions where they obtain minerals at a much lower price, with less costly but more environmentally aggressive procedures. Labor is also cheaper and working conditions are more favorable (to the companies—never to workers). Western countries must extend their legislation and environmental protection to developing countries. Otherwise, just as the crusaders took temporary religious vows and were granted leniency for their sins, some Western mining companies flying the flag of the fight against climate change will run wild in developing countries. Their sins will be ignored by governments whose economies benefit from these activities. Current Western legislation on mining in third countries is mostly more a guide to good conduct than a supervised enforcement regulation with economic or criminal repercussions. It is only in cases of clear criminality that some of these companies are forced to sit in the dock.

Such is the case of Glencore, a multinational company at the center of the global raw materials markets and the energy transition. This Swiss company has in recent years faced multi-million-dollar fines for its cobalt mining activities in the Congo.[197] Far from the authority of Kinshasa, Congolese mining is rife with corruption, illegal processes, bribery and child labor exploitation under the control of paramilitary authorities or local non-state armed groups. After duly paying its fines, the company continues to mine the precious metal. On the other hand, the question arises as to what would happen if it decided or was

---

Company's Experience," in Deanna J. Richards (ed.), *The Industrial Green Game: Implications for Environmental Design and Management* (Washington, DC: National Academy Press, 1997), 165–181. https://www.nap.edu/read/4982/chapter/15

197 Global Witness, "Seismic change needed at Glencore following a decade of corruption," July 18, 2022. https://www.globalwitness.org/en/press-releases/seismic-change-needed-glencore-following-decade-corruption/

forced to suspend its activities. China would simply take over, filling the gap left by Glencore. Chinese state-owned companies escape the jurisdiction of Western governments and are impervious to pressure from Western environmental and human rights groups.

The Democratic Republic of Congo supplies about 70% of the world's cobalt, but 80% of its industrial cobalt mines are owned or financed by Chinese companies.[198] In other words, China extracts almost all the Congolese cobalt for its refineries, thus dominating this step in the supply chain. As a result, most of the cobalt, needed in its processed silver metal form for the cathodes of lithium-ion batteries in electric vehicles, computers, cell phones and many of our high-tech electronics comes from Chinese refineries. If its only Western rival in the Congo, Glencore, were to cease its activities, Western dependence on Chinese-Congolese cobalt could be almost total. For more than a decade, Chinese companies have strategically bought up U.S. and European mines in the DRC, leading them to control 15 of the country's 19 cobalt mines.

This scale of presence in the DRC is in line with the "Made in China 2025" policy to transform China into a manufacturing superpower in 10 areas, with an emphasis on electric vehicles. If we consider the data provided by the EU Joint Research Centre report[199] analyzing the imbalance between cobalt supply and demand on the road to transition to electric mobility, the future picture is very worrying. The average demand based on four different scenarios compared to the average supply implies a cobalt deficit from 2025 onwards. This deficit will increase annually and could reach 490,000 metric tons by 2030. World cobalt needs, in any of the scenarios, are such that they double the amount required by 2030. If our "metal-dependent" society does not also want to be completely "China-dependent," Glencore can be both part of the problem and a necessary part of the solution. The same is true of other Western mining companies. These companies, which are needed to secure metals supply chains, can only compete

198 Cade Ahlijian, "Congo's Cobalt Controversy," *Global Edge,* April 20, 2022. https://globaledge.msu.edu/blog/post/57136/congos-cobalt-controversy

199 Patricia Alves Dias, Darina Blagoeva, Claudiu Pavel, Nikolaos Arvanitidis, *Cobalt: demand-supply balances in the transition to electric mobility* (EU Joint Research Centre, 2018), 13–14 and 54–56. https://publications.jrc.ec.europa.eu/repository/bitstream/JRC112285/jrc112285_cobalt.pdf

with Chinese companies if they employ similar rules or if they have the help and backing of their governments.

Not only in Congo but also in many other poor countries, miners suffer from extremely poor working conditions and minimal wages. This leads to revolts such as the one in 2012 in South Africa, which resulted in the death of 34 miners at the hands of security forces, known as the Marikana Massacre. [200] Thus, the final price of rare earths and other rare metals obtained in developing countries does not include these working conditions let alone project any improvement in them, or factors such as carbon emissions from fossil fuels used in mining and transportation, environmental pollution, etc. From an economic point of view, the outsourcing of mining to developing countries involves the externalization of all these costs that are ultimately absorbed by the local population, and ecosystems.

If this trend is not reversed, developing countries will foot the bill for this "sustainable transformation," but only Western countries will receive the net benefits of curbing climate change if the objectives are achieved jointly and globally. Addressing sustainability in a regional framework alone leads to externalizing pollution. Responsible mining and processing, within an appropriate legal framework, would make the energy transformation inclusive and respectful of developing countries. This would follow ESG (Environmental, Social and Governance) procedures, which promote environmental, social and governance protection criteria in such countries. Otherwise, we will exchange toxic oil spills in the Niger Delta and similar situations for desert ecosystems with barren water and soil contaminated by metals.

Environmental protection innovations that the American company Mountain Pass Materials has incorporated into its processes and facilities,[201] or at Neo Performance Materials' rare earth processing facility in Estonia, [202] demonstrate that responsible rare earth mining and processing is feasible. These innovations include the ability to recycle water, regenerate the chemical reagents required for rare

---

200 Abu-Bakarr Jalloh, "Interview: 'A lack of political will,'" *DW,* August 15, 2017. https://www.dw.com/en/marikana-massacre-anger-sadness-and-total-disbelief/a-40102521

201 Mountain Pass Materials, "Sustainability, why are we different?," accessed December 1, 2021. https://mpmaterials.com/sustainability/

202 NEO Performance Materials, "Sustainability," accessed December 1, 2021. https://www.neomaterials.com/sustainability/

earth production, generate power from a highly efficient natural gas cogeneration plant, and dispose of mine waste through an innovative tailings-in-pulp system.

The correct environmental objective should be to export these extraction and processing techniques to developing countries, instead of outsourcing harmful practices whose costs are paid by developing countries.

## THE UNSUSTAINABILITY OF "SUSTAINABILITY": AN ENVIRONMENTAL EPIPHANY

It will be increasingly difficult for citizens of Western nations to ignore the environmental damage from the extraction of critical materials and the production of renewable wind and photovoltaic energy. In political systems with elections every four years, announcing a carbon-free world by 2050 may be a successful political speech but it sidesteps reality. If the predictions of metal shortages come true, Western populations may have an epiphany and become aware of our externalization of mining pollution schemes, and more generally, of political procrastination applied to the problems of energy transition and its consequences.[203] At the same time, developing countries will have absorbed more and more investment from the rare earth mining sector, as their laxer legislation, low labor costs and corrupt ruling classes will allow it.[204]

The Western population and political class will have to choose between continuing to damage the environment in third countries and continuing with the energy transition as currently being undertaken or delaying it in order to seek better solutions while trying to undo the damage already done. What will almost certainly not happen is for Western countries to allow unsustainable, polluting, or insufficiently regulated mining or processing to take place in their own territories. Existing national environmental laws and regulations, together with political pressure from local environmental groups, will prevent this. Our current politicians are heirs to a problem generated by their

---

203 United Nations for Climate Change, *Paris Agreement* (United Nations, 2015). https://unfccc.int/sites/default/files/english_paris_agreement.pdf

204 Mazumbaru S., "Fighting corruption in mining approvals," *DW,* December 5, 2017. https://www.dw.com/en/fighting-corruption-in-mining-poses-tough-challenges/a-41645234

predecessors, leaders who encouraged the development of this crusade against climate change without the required scientific planning and inter-ministerial and cross-industry coordination. But those leaders are no longer sitting in office and today's politicians do not win votes by announcing projected collapses. This short-term vision ignores the limits of our resources.

The awakening of public opprobrium against rare earth pollution can also come from within developing countries themselves—or is perhaps more likely to do so, as these countries suffer their immediate impacts. A case in point is Malaysia, where social unrest and demonstrations led to the closure in 1992 of what was one of the world's few rare earth processing plants outside China, owned by the Japanese company Mitsubishi Corporation. After the closure the company was forced to pay over $100 million to rehabilitate its former site.[205] The Australian company, Lynas Corporation, took over and built a much more environmentally friendly rare earth processing plant in Malaysia. But since 2012, it's faced public protests which led to the further improvement of its procedures.[206] Environmental awareness spread rapidly, and protesters made connections with Japanese and European anti-nuclear activists, who supported their demands. [207]

There are many examples of an emerging social consciousness, leading to people reacting and demonstrating against companies in charge of the extraction or processing or even the final use of rare earths, raising their voices against the outsourcing of our pollution to developing countries and the violation of human rights. The process of sustainable development on a global scale needs to be re-evaluated, as sustainability often ends at the borders of developed countries. Only with the certainty of global inclusiveness will the sustainable process truly have a deep social commitment.

---

205 Siva Sithraputhran, "Citizen backlash keeps Malaysia rare earth plant on hold," *Reuters,* May 8, 2012. https://www.reuters.com/article/us-malaysia-lynas-idUSBRE84808X20120509

206 Michael Montgomery, "Thorium: Rare Earth Liability or Asset?" *Investing News Network,* March 14, 2011. https://investingnews.com/daily/resource-investing/critical-metals-investing/rare-earth-investing/thorium-rare-earth-liability-or-asset/

207 Saleem H. Ali, "Social and Environmental Impact of the Rare Earth Industries," *Resources* 2014, 3(1), 123–134; https://doi.org/10.3390/resources3010123 February 13, 2014. https://www.mdpi.com/2079-9276/3/1/123/htm

The public's social conscience has recently been shaken by a very significant case related to cobalt, which has so many similarities with rare earths. In 2019, a class-action legal complaint was filed by International Rights Advocates against U.S. companies Apple, Google, Microsoft, Tesla, and Dell for the use of cobalt in their products.[208] The cobalt, the organization claimed, comes from the Democratic Republic of Congo, and its extraction is promoting child labor in Africa. International Rights Advocates singled out Glencore, Umicore and Huayou Cobalt as the companies responsible for supplying cobalt to the defendants.[209]

It may seem surprising that Apple, Alphabet (Google) and Microsoft, and until recently Tesla, are listed as leaders in the American stock market Standard & Poor's ESG index,[210] which precisely ranks large companies according to their degree of compliance with ESG standards. This index, which was recently created to channel public and private investments that advocate sustainable development, may not be fulfilling its function. The problem is that globalization has stretched supply chains so far that these mega-corporations do not exercise full visibility over their sourcing. With turnovers larger than the Gross Domestic Product of some countries, and more workers on the payroll than some states, these corporations have the same problem as some countries—they lack clear traceability and awareness of the origin of the materials that make up their products. According to the *Harvard Business Review*, which analyzed all conflict minerals reports

---

208 Although the appeal was dismissed, it sets a precedent and opens a door to similar future prosecutions. The judge stated, "It may be true that if Apple, for example, stopped making products that use cobalt, it would have bought less of the metal from Umicore, which might have bought less from Glencore, which might have bought less from CMKK, which might thus have instructed Ismail to stop buying cobalt from the artisanal child miners, which might have led some of the plaintiffs not to have been mining when their injuries occurred," the judge said. "But this long chain of contingencies, in all its undulation, creates mere speculation, not traceable harm." Danielle Toth, "Judge Dismisses Child Labour Class Action Against Apple, Google Alphabet, Microsoft, Dell and Tesla," *Top Class Actions,* November 3, 2021. https://topclassactions.com/lawsuit-settlements/employment-labor/judge-dismisses-child-labor-class-action-against-apple-google-alphabet-microsoft-dell-and-tesla/

209 Michelle Toh M., "Apple, Google, Microsoft, Dell and Tesla are sued for alleged child labor in Congo," *CNN Business,* December 18, 2019. https://edition.cnn.com/2019/12/17/tech/apple-microsoft-tesla-dell-congo-cobalt-mining/index.html

210 S&P Dow Jones Indices, "S&P 500 ESG Leaders Index," October 2022. https://www.spglobal.com/spdji/en/indices/esg/sp-500-esg-leaders-index/#overview

filed with the U.S. Securities and Exchange Commission (SEC), most multinational companies still do not know where their raw materials come from. Only 1% of companies were able to state with certainty that their products were conflict-free.[211]

The questioning of the fairness of rare earth extraction and processing follows the same pattern. The public is awakening to the full extent of the problem, and its influence is now beginning to reach multinational companies. The same organizations that, in defense of the environment, are getting permits for the extraction of rare earths in Europe, or for the construction of new processing plants in Japan, are asking themselves where our rare earths come from.[212] Their investigations lead them to Burundi, a neighboring country under the influence of the Congo, to Myanmar with a recent coup d'état, to Tanzania or Madagascar, with low levels of governance but high levels of corruption and insecurity.

## PLUNDERING THE PERIODIC TABLE

In this century, humans have begun to plunder the entire periodic table, turning a blind eye to the risks. In 1900, 79% of all materials used annually by humans were biomass, compared to 32% in 2005 and 22% currently projected for 2050. In contrast, the consumption/extraction of mineral elements is increasing at a rate of about 3% per year and will continue to do so until 2050.[213] The situation is reminiscent of the extinction of large mammals caused by their systematic hunting by homo sapiens throughout prehistoric times. If we continue in this way, by 2050 we will have exhausted all our reserves of some elements such as gold and antimony, or others such as molybdenum and zinc within a hundred years.

---

211 EPS News. "Tech Companies Sued Over Minerals-Sourcing Practices," *Passive Components Blog,* December 26, 2019. https://passive-components.eu/tech-companies-sued-over-minerals-sourcing-practices/

212 The environmental platform "Sialatierraviva" lobbied for a political decision to reject the Matamulas rare earth mining project in Ciudad Real, Spain. On its website, the platform itself raises awareness of the dangers of rare earth mining and processing sites in developing countries. http://www.sialatierraviva.org/2016/03/firma-por-un-campo-de-montiel-vivo-sin.html

213 University of Barcelona, "Humans plunder the periodic table while turning blind eye to the risks of doing so, say researchers," *Phys.org,* January 17, 2023. https://phys.org/news/2023-01-humans-plunder-periodic-table-eye.html

Trends in nature are exponential, not linear. Only our short life span, lifestyles disconnected with nature and the influence of outdated capitalist principles have induced us to a lack of perspective that can make us think that the trend is linear, but the exploitation of metal resources actually follows a clear exponential trend. Shortages of a multitude of metals will occur much sooner. But how dare we talk about sustainability when we have already sentenced some of our critical elements to death? The rate of human consumption of materials continues to grow annually, but the recycling rate, relative to that consumption, continues to decrease year after year. On the other hand, the plundering of resources is enhanced by the unreality of our financial economic orientation. Central banks produce unlimited money with which to pay for some very limited resources. The price of these resources is not related to their long-term scarcity; neither is their finiteness or the degradation of the planet factored in. We can produce endless paper, but we cannot replenish the metals. Who calculates the loss of the planet's capital? Nature does not understand our beloved banknotes. The planet understands predators of its resources and biodiversity. In this sense, we are parasites that reduce its biodiversity (geological and animal) to maintain our well-being. The ecological economy must be accounted for by our governments. Perhaps slowing down economic growth is the only way to guarantee our grandchildren a future with some access to resources that we are stealing from them.[214]

The paradox of the "unsustainability of sustainability" shows us that without responsible mining, processing, and recycling, the energy transition will be increasingly questioned by citizens. It is quite feasible that sooner or later they will realize that there is a global energy unsustainability that includes energy crimes such as burning 5.1 trillion cubic meters of gas as surplus from oil wells, enough to supply France, Germany, and Belgium annually. The world will be aware that we throw away the thorium that goes with rare earths, when instead we could use it as nuclear fuel. They will learn that excess energy produced by renewables that cannot be absorbed by the grid is simply thrown away.

---

214 Antonio Valero and Alicia Valero, *Thanatia. Los límites minerales del planeta* (Icaria Editorial, 2021).

Many inhabitants of our planet can begin to demand that politicians act in the interests of real sustainability. Among other measures, they will demand responsible mining in developing countries.[215] In this process of change, some mining companies currently operating there could face legal charges and be forced to stop their activities. On the other hand, applying environmental, social and governance (ESG) measures[216] could sharply reduce their profit margins and affect their business model, forcing them into bankruptcy. Therefore, raising social awareness and demanding coherent actions from the political class and large international companies, on the road to a comprehensive solution, could well secondarily increase a deficit of rare earths and rare metals in general. Involuntarily, in an undesirable way, it would lead us to suffer shortages that would delay the crusade against climate change or supply cuts that would jeopardize our security.

It's not going to be easy to get out of the quagmire we've gotten ourselves into without spending a little time in purgatory. If not us, then our children, or more likely our grandchildren, who will be unable to avoid the reality that limitless growth meant endless destruction of ecosystems and the plundering of resources. When Keynes theorized about our capitalist system, he did not sufficiently take into account the physical limits of the planet. Reality shows us that the existing quantity of critical metals is one of them. The wheel of money may go on turning forever, but not the wheel of resources. As in the case of COVID, an early reaction could save many lives. In this case our Western politicians must internalize the exponential nature of the

---

215 Perhaps the clearest example of such responsible behavior, inside its borders, is China, which in recent years has reduced its own mineral production, thereby reducing pollution, implemented modern ESG standards, remediated damage and tackled illegal mining. Cecilia Jamasmie, "China gets tougher on illegal mining and export of rare earths," *Mining.com,* February 2, 2016. https://www.mining.com/china-gets-tougher-on-illegal-mining-exporting-of-rare-earths/

216 Environmental, social and governance (ESG) criteria are a set of standards for a company's operations that socially conscious investors use to select potential investments. Environmental criteria take into account the company's performance as a steward of nature. Social criteria examine how it manages relationships with employees, suppliers, customers and the communities in which it operates. Governance deals with the company's management, executive compensation, audits, internal controls and shareholder rights. The Investopedia Team, "Environmental, Social, and Governance (ESG) Criteria," *Investopedia,* updated March 22, 2023. https://www.investopedia.com/terms/e/environmental-social-and-governance-esg-criteria.asp

demand for rare metals, the consequences of their exploitation and save us from ourselves as soon as possible.

# 6. THE MINERAL YUAN

## ENERGY TRANSITION WEAKENS THE DOLLAR

The finiteness of metal resources seems to go unnoticed. Most Western countries underestimate the role that these materials can play in the struggle for hegemony. This increasingly intense competition for resources doesn't just play out in the arenas of technology, armaments, or proxy wars. The struggle includes a fierce fight by many countries of the global east and south to escape the dollar's monetary hegemony and the best weapon to achieve it may be rare earths and other "green metals." The current global domination of the U.S. dollar could be swept away by a geopolitical tsunami caused by the energy transition and the struggle to lead it. When the waters recede, we may well see far fewer green dollars and far more red yuan. We may even see a hard currency, or Chinese renminbi (yuan), backed by metals again—as they have almost always been throughout history.

Hong Kong is the strategic enclave where this battle is taking place. Its financial market allows us to observe how investment flows are changing or being redirected. An American investment banking analyst in Hong Kong, who prefers not to reveal his name, tells me that "Capital investment in green energy, such as in the world of renewables and electric vehicles, is growing by leaps and bounds compared to hydrocarbons. We see them in general as safer investments, which are receiving higher flows, higher returns, and lower relative volatility."

As he describes it, "Hong Kong, through its Stock-Connect, is an important gateway for portfolio investment in China, and connecting with its Shanghai and Shenzhen stock exchanges. That is, private investors and foreign investment funds, such as the American BlackRock and Bridgewater Associates can buy shares of Chinese companies."

BlackRock's presence in this city, which serves as its center of operations in the Asia-Pacific region, is not surprising. CEO Larry

Flink wrote in a letter to his shareholders in 2022, "I believe that the decarbonization of the global economy is going to create the greatest investment opportunity of our lifetime."[217] Blackrock's asset manager takes a preferential seat, positioning the company next to the gateway to the Asian giant, knowing that it will be Chinese companies that will take a large share of this market.

It is not by chance that in the past the traditional path to the G8 included the domination of a large share of automotive manufacturing. Nowadays, with the emergence of the expanded 11-country BRICS, the G7 has become less significant in terms of GDP and it is easy to realize that if we combine future electric vehicles investments with wind and solar energy, the capital that China can absorb is enormous. The Asian giant is carving out a niche for itself in the world economy. Without splashy public announcements, it is building via its critical strategic metals monopoly the vehicles that will lead it to the throne of the G20—though Xi was apparently not interested in attending the last meeting. As its ingenuities acquire more strategic and commercial importance and a greater volume of business—and given the West's ongoing sanctions with regard to Ukraine, and the response to same by some countries of the Global South—the chances of a drastic change in the financial system are not just increasing but have become for them an explicit goal and have already begun trading with each other in their national currencies. The result could be the fall of the U.S. dollar as the benchmark currency for international trade and as the main reserve of many central banks. History shows us how the foundations that were laid for the dollar's global enthronement have deteriorated. A dynamic like that of its birth could now bring about the enthronement of a new hegemonic currency, whether the Chinese yuan, various workarounds, or a new currency as may be created by the BRICS countries. As we shift from oil dependence to metal dependence, the yuan would rise on the back of the Middle Kingdom's global hegemony over many critical minerals. Another alternative would be a currency driven by the Beijing government, but with a shared foundation with some of the richest countries in these resources, the BRICS (Brazil, Russia, India, China and South Africa).

---

217 "Larry Fink's 2022 Letter to CEOs: The Power of Capitalism," BlackRock. https://www.blackrock.com/corporate/investor-relations/larry-fink-ceo-letter

As Mark Twain once told us: "History does not repeat itself, but it rhymes." With the idea that there is nothing completely new under the sun, we may find the keys to a possible decline and to the future rise of the yuan by reviewing the beginnings of the rise of the dollar to become the hegemonic currency.

## THE PETRODOLLAR

Between 1940 and 1970, the "American dream" became a reality in the United States. The quality of life grew, stimulated not only by the oil monopoly but also by its unequalled advantageous position provided by the Breton Woods agreements. Signed in 1944 in the eponymous locale in New Hampshire, England, they fixed the dollar as the reference currency for the Allied countries and the respective exchange values with their currencies. Throughout the history of mankind, few nations have had the privilege of having the world's reference currency. The British Empire's sterling had been the de facto benchmark prior to Bretton Woods, and with its signing, Britain handed the precious key to the custodian chest of the world's currency over to the U.S. The main stipulation was convertibility; each U.S. dollar was to have gold backing, initially fixed at $35 per ounce.

U.S. foreign policy was marked by the pressing need to maintain a stable and secure supply of the hydrocarbons that represented the oxygen of its economy. Fundamentally, the crude oil that between 1940 and 1970 was under the control of its five largest oil companies, associated with two other Anglo-Saxon companies in the monopoly known as "The Seven Sisters." But despite its advantageous position, between 1968 and 1971, the U.S. government changed the gold-dollar parity quite frequently. The aim was to finance the costs of the Vietnam War and to cushion the huge economic disruptions caused by the oil crisis. But it was not without consequences. Japan and the European powers were rising again, and as they accumulated dollars as reserves, they began to wonder warily about their convertibility into gold. Nixon needed to break the dollar-gold parity to be able to continue printing dollars without pressure from his European allies. The world watched in astonishment as, on black and white television, the American president announced the unilateral breaking of the international commitments undertaken by his nation at Bretton Woods.

The dollar-gold parity was abandoned, and the value of the dollar was deregulated, becoming a free-floating currency or fiat (lat. "let it be done") currency. Some economists argue that dissolving the gold backing requirement increased the monetary supply and while it may have improved the U.S. ability to pay its bills, it caused the world to lose confidence in dollar of uncertain value.

The situation worsened and became truly compromised when the U.S. oil monopoly, with its perfectly integrated vertical supply and value chain, collapsed. A gigantic wave of nationalization of oil resources simultaneously shook the "Seven Sisters," who lost their oil wells in those Middle Eastern countries with the highest oil production and reserves, such as Saudi Arabia, Iran, Iraq, and Kuwait. The supply chain was broken up, leaving the Seven Sisters with only the parts corresponding to transportation, refining, and marketing. As the situation seemed to stabilize, the major oil producers associated with OPEC then imposed an oil embargo on the nations that supported Israel in the Yom Kippur War. It looked as if the dollar, America's greatest aircraft carrier, might be shipwrecked.

But then, with strategic astuteness, President Nixon played one of the greatest geopolitical cards in modern history. Nixon realized that a dollar without parity and without the backing of any other metal or commodity was not viable. Combining the two problems, oil and currency, he came up with a unique and masterful solution on the advice of his Secretary of State, Henry Kissinger. A new strategic alliance with Saudi Arabia, the largest crude oil producer, assured him that oil would only be sold in U.S. dollars. The Saudi monarchy, which until then had only accepted payments for oil in gold, would now accept them exclusively in dollars. In exchange, the U.S. offered it protection, especially against Israel, and sold it weapons. Oil for weapons, Petrodollars for security. A few years after the agreement was signed, most OPEC countries, led by Saudi Arabia, followed suit and embraced the same pact.

Nixon had managed to secure the possibility of continuing with a monetary expansion that would support his policy and those of his successors for more than 50 years, a period where the U.S. enjoyed world monetary hegemony. The dollar became the petrodollar, thanks to all the oil exchanges that then were forced to take place in the world in dollars. The titanic repercussions of this agreement gave unequalled power to the dollar, since all the countries of the world also had to stockpile dollar reserves to be able to pay for their oil transactions. Accordingly, the world increased its dollar reserves to secure its energy. The world's thirst for dollars grew at the same pace as the thirst for oil, driven by an unstoppable automobile industry. The world was flooded with petrodollars.

But with the gold-dollar equivalence gone, it left the U.S. partially dependent on OPEC countries continuing to accept the dollar as a currency of payment. It is true that part of the ubiquity of the dollar was enhanced by the lack of strong capital controls, unlike the nowadays highly restrictive China policies on the Yuan. But America became over reliant on a monarchy that was anything but democratic, and indeed, was itself subject to change. China is now seeking to buy oil in its own currency.[218] With the new Saudi government and then the UAE now agreeing to sell its oil in yuan, that monopoly has been broken.

While the U.S. government took good care to provide its population with an unbeatable supply of oil at unbeatable prices, its culture and lifestyle became addicted to it. Since then, petrodollars and imported barrels of oil have weighed heavily in American foreign policy, as the conflicts in which the U.S. has been involved in Middle East show. American foreign policy relies heavily on oil to this day. This is evidenced by the fact that the U.S. has never officially condemned the massacres that Saudi Arabia has perpetrated in Yemen, to cite just one recent example.

## FROM PETRODOLLAR TO MINERALYUAN

The situation has changed. The U.S. is now the largest producer of oil and gas, and considering fracking, is already energy self-sufficient. Further, while the U.S. is reducing its purchases of crude oil from Saudi Arabia, the geopolitical weight of oil is diminishing with every wind turbine or solar panel that is installed and with every electric vehicle that replaces a combustion vehicle. The image of black gold is deteriorating, attacked by environmental activists and the profitability

218 Huileng Tang," China says it's moving to buy oil and gas in the yuan — a move that could threaten the dollar's global dominance in the long run," *Markets Insider,* December 11, 2022. https://markets.businessinsider.com/news/currencies/dollar-vs-yuan-china-buy-gulf-oil-energy-rmb-currency-2022-12?op=1

of its exploitation damaged by state ecological taxes. At the same time, the entire flow of capital and investment that used to be captured by fossil fuels is increasingly diverted to the raw materials necessary for the global green energy transition. On the road to decarbonizing the world economy, oil is progressively playing a lesser role as the world's star commodity. The countries called upon to absorb these capital flows will become green giants or "metallo-states" and the countries that cling inexorably to crude oil, the "petro-states," will become fallen angels.

In its best years, the U.S. dominated the auto market and, despite not owning it, controlled the crude oil market. If China succeeds in its green metal agenda, as vehicles electrify it will also gain control of the automobile market and dominate its new fuel—lithium and other critical and strategic minerals. Likewise, with no other major competitors, it will dominate the chosen energy of the future, wind and solar. China has found the same path that brought the U.S. to power. The U.S. used OPEC to secure energy and fuel with crude oil. China uses the Belt and Road Initiative to reach every mine it can in Africa, South America and around the world. The U.S. refines oil on its territory and China refines minerals on its territory. Many of the minerals and their associated metals needed for this energy transition and electric vehicles are already in the hands of China, which also controls their processing stage by transforming them into metals.

Just referring to the green metals, let us recall that China has the hegemony, among others, of refining lithium, cobalt, zinc, silicon, and an exorbitant level of monopoly of the essential rare earths. We could say that China leads an invisible OPEC of green metals. Perhaps this metaphor will soon become a reality, with nations seeking formalized agreements and creating new monopolistic organizations related to these elements, led by the Beijing government. For example, could a new lithium OPEC including Chile, Argentina and Bolivia be possible, perhaps leaving Australia out of the association because of its western alignment? Such an organization would not only hold more than half of the world's current lithium reserves but would also dominate its processing thanks to Chinese factories. In contrast to the Chinese aggressiveness that has already begun to extract lithium from Congo, Zimbabwe, and Argentina and to establish preferential purchase agreements with other countries such as Chile, the U.S. and the EU are smothering some of their best projects. The race for lithium dominance has begun, but the Jadar project in Serbia and the Thacker Pass project in Nevada have not received governmental authorization. Most Western countries are thus abandoning themselves to the designs of the Asian giant.

Given the revolutionary applications of rare earths, the renewable energy transition is deeply dependent on these elements. Curiously, rare earth elements were already at the origin of man's use of energy. Lanthanum, cerium, and thorium were used for oil and gas lighting to improve performance, prior to transitioning to electric lighting. Today, the green revolution aims to save the world from global warming with batteries, electric vehicles, wind turbines, solar panels, energy-saving light bulbs, heat/cold air pumps, etc. With these new applications, the portfolio of essential elements expands to include neodymium, europium, terbium, dysprosium and yttrium.

These elements have become so vital that they are used to obtain almost all energy sources, manage them, and optimize their use. For example, today's oil refining requires the elements lutetium, lanthanum, and cerium, which are used as refining catalysts. Without them, the price of fuel for our vehicles would increase 10% to 30%. Even nuclear energy production is dependent on rare earths because they are used in reactor control rods and as a nuclear or neutron "poison consumer." This means that they can absorb neutrons produced in the reaction in the nuclear reactor, allowing their regulation and control in combination with other materials. None of the conventional first- and second-generation nuclear power plants are free from dependence on rare earths either. Five rare earth elements are fundamental in the control of nuclear energy production—samarium, gadolinium, holmium, dysprosium, and terbium. Even so, the quantities needed per Gigawatt-hour produced are not comparable to the nearly half a ton of rare earths produced via an off-shore wind turbine. Erbium's prominence in the nuclear world has extended to the point where it has been used in combination with uranium as nuclear fuel for some Russian power plants, thus increasing their safety.[219]

As China takes over not only the manufacture of these metals but also the renewable energy goods requiring these metals, the volume

219 Ricardo Prego Reboredo, "Rare earths, a key piece in the energy puzzle," in *Energy and Geostrategy* (Spanish Institute for Strategic Studies, 2021), 295–361.

of the market traded in yuan and transactions with this currency is growing. The yuan-mineral is pushing the petrodollar out of the throne room. China no longer bases its economy only on exporting plastics and cheap products, needless to say. China is conquering the final and fundamental links, those with the largest share of the world market, giving added value to its products.

## PETROYUAN + MINERALYUAN

Chinese President Xi Jinping is learning from history, not only using the strategy of Nixon and other historical leaders of backing their currencies with a key commodity but perfecting that strategy. Is the world prepared for a new Nixon-like shock? In the West, we live in a bubble of relative economic security that we consider stable. But, if China were to only accept payment in yuan for critical materials, in the form of minerals, processed elements and their finished products, governments and their central banks would be forced to kowtow, given the immense demand for these products and their strategic importance. As they did in the 1970s to secure oil access, nations would buy yuan-mineral currencies as reserves to ensure access to such precious metals for their production chains.

While the steamroller of the petrodollar's destruction was already in motion, the conflict in Ukraine has accelerated it. Now it is not just the *anticipation* of the petrodollar's decline; major players such as India, China and Russia are already conducting the oil trades between them in rupees, rubles, or yuan. The largest Western mining company, BHP, of Anglo-Australian origin, now accepts yuan for iron ore sales to China, to the benefit of the yuan-mineral. Argentina, which has applied to join BRICS, is also building yuan reserves as it increases its lithium sales to China.

In a move whose medium-term repercussions were perhaps not sufficiently calculated by the White House, the U.S. froze Russia's dollar reserves in response to the Russian invasion of Ukraine. The U.S. thus inadvertently added fuel to the fire for the petrodollar burnout, as some non-allied nations, many of them autocracies, took note of the potential danger to their own dollar reserves. The world has taken note that the U.S. has taken strong action against the reserves of a third country for a conflict occurring outside its borders and that of its NATO allies. With justified distrust, other third countries are considering exchanging dollar reserves for other reserves outside the Western circuit such as traditional gold or yuan. Even Israel, a loyal U.S. ally, is buying yuan for the first time as a reserve currency to the detriment of the dollar, whose weight in its reserves is decreasing. Holding reserves in yuan facilitates and favors the flow of economic transactions between the countries that hold them and China. Similarly, Iran and Venezuela are increasingly comfortable with the idea of selling their oil in yuan and building state reserves with this currency. The fall of the world's reference currency could be simplified with this equation: Petrodollar Fall = Petroyuan Boom + Mineralyuan Boom (renewables and electric vehicles).

There is a concern to be raised regarding the U.S.'s erstwhile enduring relationship with Saudi Arabia, the implicit leader of OPEC and the country that opened the door to its monetary monarchy. The relationship between the two countries and in particular between their two current leaders, President Biden and Saudi Crown Prince Mohammed bin Salman (MbS), has deteriorated, now resembling a failed marriage more than a strong alliance. Meanwhile, Saudi Arabia is pursuing a unilateral oil production policy independent of the wishes of its American partners. The U.S., for its part, is tempted to cut off arms sales to the Saudi kingdom and to suspend all arms cooperation. The U.S. has not only drastically reduced its purchase of Saudi oil, but as the main exporter of crude oil and its refined products, it has become a competitor operating outside OPEC. The common interests for this marriage that catapulted the petrodollar to monetary hegemony no longer exist. The new conjuncture is the germ of infidelities and even of Saudi Arabia's search for a new partner before a total breakup takes place. China is the chosen one and not without reason.

The Asian giant has been reluctant for many years to import its oil by paying in petrodollars and has tried to source its supplies mainly from countries outside the OPEC circuit. Sudan, Angola, Niger, Nigeria, and Equatorial Guinea are African countries that are part of China's energy security policy, which, while seeking diversification, is fleeing from the petrodollar. Its military presence in these countries shows the clear determination of the Communist Party of China to defend its energy interests and the interests of its companies located there. Saudi Arabia has been one of the main victims of this anti-petrodollar stance. Despite the exponential growth of Chinese crude imports, the Saudi monarchy has watched helplessly as it progressively ceased to be the main supplier of crude to the Asian giant. It is not only that since 2016 its total crude oil imports exceeded those of the U.S., but also that, to Saudi frustration, American requests for its crude oil decreased from 60% to less than 20% in a few years. The U.S. went from importing 1,500 Saudi barrels a day in 2005 to just 500 in 2020.

In March 2022, Crown Prince Mohammed bin Salman announced his intention to accept China's purchase of crude oil in yuan. The petrodollar was trembling, and President Joe Biden announced his visit to Saudi Arabia, supposedly to ask it to increase its crude oil production in the face of the lack of Russian oil. He also intended to keep prices under control so as not to favor the Russian economy, sustained by sales of its oil and gas. But perhaps Biden's visit reflected a hidden and pressing concern about the new Chinese-Saudi Arabian axis.

The rapprochement between Mohammed bin Salman and Xi Jinping seems unstoppable. While MbS endured President Biden's harsh pre-campaign criticism, the Chinese government has reached out to him in times of greatest difficulty. Thus, following the announcements by Aramco, the state-owned company with a monopoly on Saudi crude oil, of a new expansion in the form of an IPO, China has publicly shown its support and interest in the purchase. Although not yet materialized, its simple interest has already empowered Prince MbS to reciprocate China's goodwill. Gratitude, understanding, and common interest are all present in the launch of the massive joint venture between Aramco and the Chinese government in the Shandong region. This mega-project involves a colossal Saudi investment in the creation of an integrated refining and distribution business model in the Asian giant.[220] The crude oil purchased by China to feed this refinery will be bought in yuan, marking a milestone in the decline of the petrodollar.

The Beijing government has gone one step further and made available a worldwide financial instrument which allows any country to buy oil in yuan with excellent guarantees. The tool is crude oil barrel

---

220 Simon Watkins, "China and Saudi Arabia strengthen alliance with new megaproject," *OilPrice.com,* June 29, 2022. https://oilprice.com/Energy/Energy-General/China-And-Saudi-Arabia-Strengthen-Alliance-With-New-Megaproject.html

futures; these have been on sale since March 2018 on the Shanghai International Energy Exchange[221] and are backed by an unusual convertibility into gold. The launch has been so successful that the selling rate of these futures has risen sharply since their inception and is beginning to rival western-designated oil sales futures (Brent and WTI) sold on their stock exchanges.

Xi Jinping is aware of the enormous relevance and implications of turning his currency into an international reference currency. The possibility of actually replacing the petrodollar would entail the deployment all the resources of the Chinese strategy and not only incorporate Nixon's masterstroke maneuvering but intends to improve upon it. The Chinese government has long advocated a multipolar order; it does not seem to want to reach the throne unaccompanied. After the creation of the New Development Bank in 2015, the last meeting of the BRICS partnership announced the intention to launch a new joint currency to serve as a global reserve alternative to the dollar.

Although it is true that the International Monetary Fund's Special Drawing Right (SDR), in which many of the international reserves are constituted, also includes currencies other than the dollar, such as the yen, the euro and more recently the yuan or renminbi, given the speed and lack of visibility with which the Russian reserves were frozen, the BRICS aspire to create their own basket of alternative currencies. This basket would include reais, rubles, rupees, renminbi and rands. As can be seen, the renminbi is already in a winning position as it is in both the Western and BRICS baskets. It is also true that in the sunrise of this new multipolar currency order, until now even if the SDR yuan percentage has increased, it's been at the expense of the Yen and the EUR. The USD has remained consistently around 40–42 percent of the SDR.

## ANOTHER FIAT CURRENCY DETHRONED?

China has inevitably noticed that the U.S. ability to freeze Russian accounts containing U.S. dollars will likely lead many countries to be wary of holding significant U.S. dollar reserves, or remining beholden to the SWIFT system. The new Chinese currency could therefore be

---

221 Shanghai Futures Exchange, "INE Crude Oil Futures Launching Ceremony," March 26, 2018. https://www.shfe.com.cn/content/2018-yyQH-en/index.html

backed by a basket of commodities and gold. The Beijing government seems to be thinking long term, aware that fiat money would give temporary power to its government but that backing the currency with a physical asset, such as gold, would give it stability and protect citizens from inflation and bad fiscal policies.

The future cannot belong to short-termism. This lesson is well engraved in the Chinese DNA, since China was the first nation in the world, about 700 years ago, to officially use fiat money. Marco Polo described in astonishment[222] the existence of a paper currency that had replaced one of our nowadays green metals par excellence, copper. This paper currency only had value thanks to the reputation of the dynasty of Kublai Khan Yuan and the power of his army, but it promoted commercial exchanges without having to transport heavy strings of copper coins. However, the end of fiat currencies has historically always been the same, as those who rule succumb to the temptation to print money; their outcomes were already implicit in their origins. The Yuan dynasty printed ever-increasing quantities of its paper currency, which led to galloping inflation and contributed to the collapse of their dynasty in 1368 AD. Although the successor dynasty, the Ming dynasty (1368–1644 A.D.) also began printing paper money without backing, it suspended the program in 1450 A.D. and chose silver as its currency.[223]

Given that all currencies without the backing of some material with an intrinsic value have failed and disappeared throughout history, fiat currencies with the U.S. dollar as their flagship, could well have their years numbered. The world may well return to hard-backed currencies. As the energy transition and the fight against climate change are driven by metals, this physical backing could come in the form of our aforementioned green gold. Copper, silver, and gold certainly could form part of the "basket of metals," together with other green

---

222 Marco Polo and Rustichello of Pisa, "Book Second, Part I, Chapter XXIV: How the Great Kaan Causeth the Bark of Trees, Made into Something Like Paper, to Pass for Money over All His Country," in Colonel Sir Henry Yule (trans. and ed.), *The book of Ser Marco Polo, the Venetian: concerning the kingdoms and marvels of the East*, Vol. 1 (London: John Murray, 1903). This book is in the public domain and can be read online at Project Gutenberg. https://www.gutenberg.org/files/10636/10636-h/10636-h.htm

223 Kallie Szczepanski, "The Invention of Paper Money," *ThoughtCo.*, updated October 17, 2019. https://www.thoughtco.com/the-invention-of-paper-money-195167

metals that could be exchanged for the new Chinese or BRICS currencies. It is no coincidence that these countries have been increasing their gold reserves in the last decade, while many Western countries have been decreasing them. The exception is South Africa, but it has some of the largest gold mines in the world.

Many of these green metals have fallen under the monopoly of the Communist Party of China, which has sufficient authority in this market to dictate the accepted currency to be used in order to trade, buy and sell these critical materials or their derivatives. Thus, the renminbi would progressively acquire an international role similar to that of the Chinese Gross Domestic Product at world level, simultaneously eroding world confidence in the dollar.

Ray Dalio, the CEO of Bridgewaters Associates, warns in his book "New World Order" of this danger and calls for the solidarity of the American people and good work to get out of the problem. This visionary and experienced investor narrates how the high rate of American indebtedness and an excess of public spending without equivalent state revenues could lead to a situation close to financial bankruptcy. In his view, the U.S. bankruptcy would be caused by the loss of credibility of its currency in favor of another. Once this loss of currency credibility occurred, the U.S. would not be able to finance itself through foreign debt and its federal reserve would print banknotes and buy them itself to solve it. Another way out, "option B," is a massive tax increase that neither Democrats nor Republicans seem willing to undertake. Massive money printing, as happened with COVID, would lead to inflation and the loss of purchasing power of a middle class that would become even more polarized.

This maddening spiral, this public debt trap, is frighteningly reminiscent in its modus operandi of a typical pyramid or Ponzi scheme. If third countries stopped buying the U.S. dollar, the house of cards would fall. But replacing the world's currency requires building open markets with a lot of fluidity and volume. The numerous financial structures created by the U.S. ensure the continuity of its currency as the hegemonic currency. This inertia is difficult to break, and China has so far shown itself to be hermetic and has controlled its capital flows. It is difficult to say whether, if it manages to conquer the automobile market and with the increase in renewables, it will take the already announced step of completely opening up its society to consumption.

Perhaps we will see a new order in which even if the dollar were to fall, it would not be replaced by the yuan in a similar monetary market. De-globalization can create new types of markets or distort existing ones. "Doctor Catastrophe," Nouriel Roubini, known for predicting crashes such as that of cryptocurrencies or the 2008 crisis, believes that we are heading towards a bipolar monetary order. According to this economist, the dollar will give way to the yuan. Geopolitics will prevail and as a result of the struggle between both factions, part of the dollar's functions as the global "unit of account," "means of payment" and "store of value" will deteriorate and lose weight in favor of the Chinese currency.[224]

It seems that an important part of the dilemma we are facing is whether the oxygen of the world economy is a dollar, with its financial structures in line with its hegemony, or whether it is trade and production, which seems to be absorbed by China. The U.S. has a level of global state reserves of 60% and its public debt is 40% of the world's annual sales. The debate is on: will all countries and their inhabitants continue to accept ever more abundant paper with which fewer and fewer real goods or products can be bought? Will the American Empire maintain its credibility, or will an alternative prevail? What is clear is that while we debate, China continues to consolidate its control of materials that dim the stardom of oil, materials which allow it to take over supply chains and gobble up new market shares.

The International Renewable Energy Agency (IRENA) sets the total budget for the global energy transition to 2050 at 131 trillion dollars. This is the amount of money needed to establish an energy system that prioritizes technological pathways compatible with the 1.5°C maximum global warming compared to pre-industrial levels. Given that we have 28 years to make this transition, the annual investment corresponds to $4.7 trillion per year. This amount is more than double the global volume associated with the oil and gas extraction and production market, according to a market study conducted by IBISWorld,[225] a leading business intelligence company. The annual

---

224 Nouriel Roubini, "A bipolar currency regime will replace the dollar's exorbitant privilege," *Financial Times,* February 5, 2023. https://www.ft.com/content/e03d277a-e697-4220-a0ca-1f8a3dbecb75

225 IBISWorld, "Global Oil & Gas Exploration & Production Market Size 2005–2025."

investment required to implement the energy transition nearly equals the total global revenues generated by the total oil and gas industries, estimated at $5 trillion[226] in 2021.

Just as the demand for oil exploded from 1960 onwards, thanks to internal combustion engines for cars, ships and airplanes, sixty years later it is the consumption of rare earths and critical metals that rises with the adoption of green technology. The balance continues to shift towards the metallic world if we take into account that rare earths and other green metals are also indispensable for the manufacture of countless products beyond the purely energy-related ones, and their uses, unlike those of oil, continue to expand. Proof of this is the difference in the number of new patents registered. Between 2016 and 2019 the registration of new patents related to rare earths increased exponentially.[227] While in this period patents related to low-carbon technologies grew on average by 3.3% per year, the registration of patents related to fossil fuel technologies began a significant decline.[228]

A currency backed by such rare earths as lithium, copper, cobalt, and uranium as well as by the BRICS partnership could be a key element in this transition. This association brings together 43% of the world's population and 30% of the earth's territory blessed with an abundance of natural resources which, despite having an average GDP less than half that of Western countries, has an average debt of about half that of its Western counterparts. And, for instance, when adjusted for local prices: based on purchasing power parity, China's share of world GDP is 18.9 percent, according to the International Monetary Fund, surpassing the United States at 15.4 percent.[229] It is

226 Rebecca McClay, "How the Oil and Gas Industry Works," *Inevestopedia,* September 24, 2022. https://www.investopedia.com/investing/oil-gas-industry-overview/

227 Thorium Energy Alliance, "China Rare Earth Patents vs U.S. Patent 2019" (graph). https://thoriumenergyalliance.com/resource/china-rare-earth-patents-vs-us-patent-2019/

228 European Patent Office and International Energy Agency, *Patents and the energy transition: Global trends in clean energy technology innovation* (April 2021), 10. https://documents.epo.org/projects/babylon/eponet.nsf/0/3A283646135744B9C12586BF00489B38/$FILE/patents_and_the_energy_transition_study_en.pdf

229 Ana Swanson, "The Contentious U.S.-China Relationship, by the Numbers," *The New York Times,* July 7, 2023. https://www.nytimes.com/2023/07/07/business/economy/us-china-relationship-facts.html

not surprising that Saudi Arabia, Algeria and Iran, all OPEC members, have announced their willingness to join the BRICS alliance. The rise of this club of countries is demonstrated by the 22 new official membership applications, dwarfing the timid enlargement of NATO with only two new members (Sweden and Finland). The Global South is moving ever closer to the BRICS[230] bloc, which in its last summit in August 2023 made public its acceptance of Argentina, Egypt, Ethiopia, Iran, Saudi Arabia. and UAE as members.

Nor is it surprising that the name of the bank that could be chosen as the future recipient of the BRICS currency is the New Development Bank. This bank established by the BRICS countries in 2015,[231] aims to finance infrastructure and sustainable development projects in the BRICS and other emerging economies, fighting the dollar, and using local currencies as much as possible. The NDB has issued bonds in local currencies such as Chinese yuan, Indian rupee, Brazilian real, and South African rand, and has also extended loans in these currencies to its borrowers. In words of its president Dilma Rousseff: "Local currencies are not alternatives to the dollar," she said. "They're alternatives to a system."

The NDB is not for now a recipient of the BRICS currency, but rather a promoter of de-dollarization and financial cooperation among the BRICS and beyond. Its name is a nod to the developing countries. With the idea of laying the foundations for healthy economies together, it could represent a counterpoint to the expansionary monetary policies promoted by the International Monetary Fund and the World Bank, as well as the U.S. Federal Reserve and other Western central banks—pursuing development, taking into account the material limits opposed to the search for the "El Dorado" of infinite growth[232]. In addition,

---

230 Antony Sguazzin and S'thembile Cele, "BRICS Expansion Plan Draws Interest From More Than 40 Nations," *Bloomberg News,* July 20, 2023. https://www.bloomberg.com/news/articles/2023-07-20/brics-expansion-plan-draws-interest-from-more-than-40-nations

231 Filip De Mott, "China-based BRICS bank aims to de-dollarize debt by expanding local currency lending," *Markets Insider,* August 22, 2023. https://markets.businessinsider.com/news/bonds/china-brics-bank-dedollarization-dollar-dominance-debt-local-currency-lending-2023-8

232 New Development Bank, "Financing for a sustainable future," consulted on August 1, 2023. https://www.ndb.int/

they created a liquidity mechanism called the Contingent Reserve Arrangement to support members struggling with payments[233].

If the dollar falls, it will show us once again the historically proven unviability of fiat money. Without banking credibility, due to massive money supply increases by the Federal Reserve, the accumulation of debt (123.4% of GDP in December 2022), and a lack of hard currency backing, the dollar had only the prestige of American democratic institutions and its army as a pillar to maintain its hegemonic currency. With the current electoral malaise and with 43% of Americans saying a civil war is at least somewhat likely in the next 10 years,[234] one might think that the dollar is only sustained by the American war machine and the global financial inertia of the structures created. The winds of change are blowing. If they are not harnessed by the U.S., they may quickly turn into a hurricane that will sweep away the hegemony of the dollar. The U.S. has allowed itself to make strategic mistakes and lose wars in recent years. Now with a real competitor it needs to sharpen its strategic boldness.

## CHINA IS NOT READY … YET

If China has not yet given its currency the final push to the throne, it is because China is not yet fully prepared. It is waiting for the right moment. For the time being, the variations in the value of its currency respond to its government's interventions. Although the yuan is theoretically a floating fiat currency, it is state-directed to benefit its exports. If it were to appreciate in value, China's products would become more expensive and lose many customers. Anchoring the yuan to the physical and real value of commodities would deprive the Communist Party of China of this fiduciary maneuverability. China has kept its currency under pressure, devalued because it was an exporter of raw materials and commodities. This means that the yuan is worth less compared to other currencies, such as the U.S. dollar or the euro.

---

233 Astrid Prange, "A new world order? BRICS nations offer alternative to West," *DW,* April 10, 2023. https://www.dw.com/en/a-new-world-order-brics-nations-offer-alternative-to-west/a-65124269

234 Clara Hernanz Lizarraga, "43% of Americans Say a Civil War Is At Least Somewhat Likely in Next 10 Years," *Bloomberg News,* August 30, 2022. https://www.bloomberg.com/news/articles/2022-08-30/is-a-us-civil-war-coming-43-of-americans-say-at-least-somewhat-likely-by-2032#xj4y7vzkg

The main reason has been to boost its exports. A weaker yuan makes Chinese goods cheaper and more competitive in the global market, which can increase the demand for them. This helped China's economic growth, which is largely dependent on exports.[235] But today its higher value-added products would hold up better to price variation. In other words, it is possible that solar panels, cell phones, 5G network and telephony components, electric cars and all products made with rare earths or critical materials in Chinese hands would withstand well the new international value of the yuan. Plastics, textiles and similar products would not. This path has been trodden by other nations in the past.

It would currently hurt China very much if its own U.S. bond reserves were to depreciate as a result of the falling dollar. But here, the existence of signs or indications of an attempt to erode the dollar in favor of the yuan are obvious. The Chinese interbank government bond market (CIBM), created in 1997, is already the second largest after the U.S. market. And there is no doubt that, whether it obtains fiat leadership or not, the Beijing government is putting in place the structure that will support its new currency if it becomes queen. China has already developed its own alternative to the international bank transfer system (SWIFT), called the Cross Border Interbank Payment System (CIPS). Also, after creating its central bank digital currency or digital yuan, it is leading the development of its cross-compatibility in cooperation with the Bank for International Settlements (BIS). The Beijing government does not want to jump without a network, so, like so many other things, it is manufacturing one.

---

235 Neil Irwin, "Why Did China Devalue Its Currency? Two Big Reasons," *The New York Times,* August 11, 2015. https://www.nytimes.com/2015/08/12/upshot/why-did-china-devalue-its-currency-two-big-reasons.html

# 7. RARE EARTHS AND WORLD HEGEMONY

## THIS IS HOW U.S. HEGEMONY ENDS: NOT WITH A BANG BUT A WHIMPER [236]

Western civilization is repeating one of the characteristic milestones of history, the discovery and use of new metals. In the prehistoric era, the discovery of copper, bronze, or iron metallurgy brought about important changes for mankind that shifted the hegemony from some diasporas in the Mediterranean basin to others. The shortage of bronze between 1800 and 1700 BC led various pirate civilizations in the Mediterranean to attack fortified cities to loot the bronze and turn it into weapons. Anatolia, using what is now known as "substitution technology," succeeded in making higher quality weapons from a much more abundant metal, but through a more complicated metallurgical process. The metal was iron. Its use spread and the Iron Age began around 3000 B.C..[237] At the peak of Roman Empire, 300 B.C., Rome was mining copper as far north as Anglesey, in modern-day Wales; as far east as Mysia, in modern Turkey; and as far west as the Rio Tinto in Spain and could produce up to 15,000 tons of refined copper a year. Romans not only used iron but also copper and bronze in armor, helmets, swords, and spears. But their hegemony was also based on other technological advancements supported by its metallurgical knowledge. Their extensive water systems and engineering ability made frequent use of copper and bronze in plumbing-related fittings, including tubing, valves, and pumps. Coinage also developed thanks to Roman Empire metallurgy.[238]

---

236 T. S. Elliot, *The Hollow Men* (1925).

237 Juan Manuel Chomón Pérez y Andreas Ganser, "Rare earths and the struggle for world hegemony," Inicio IEEE, December 21, 2021. https://www.ieee.es/contenido/noticias/2021/12/DIEEEO141_2021_JUACHO_Tierras.html

238 Terence Bell, "The Ancient History of Copper," *ThoughtCo.*, updated

Today, rare earths could well lead to limiting the technological growth of the United States and favoring that of China, with a major impact on the struggle for superiority and thus on international security. Let's look at electrical capacitors as an example. Almost 90% of the capacitors in the world have a multilayer of dysprosium, a kind of metal ring in the middle of its body. They are the smallest in size and their special characteristics have made them ubiquitous, equipping countless electronic devices in use today. They are so small that they cannot be installed manually; only specially designed industrial robots can insert them onto electronic boards. There are other capacitors without dysprosium, but they are larger and serve different purposes. Some rely on tantalum, also a critical metal, while still larger ones are made of aluminum, for example. These capacitors mainly leave Neo's factories in China for Samsung Electronics in South Korea and Murata in Japan, and from there they are inserted on to their semiconductor boards to equip telephones, screens, computers, robots, converters, and cars. In the event of a dispute, China could temporarily paralyze the world's electronics. U.S. dependence on Chinese rare earths is almost absolute, with an added high dependence on other metals processed by Chinese firms, such as arsenic, gallium, natural graphite and tantalum, as shown by the U.S. Geological Survey Agency in 2021.

This competition between the United States and the Asian giant implicitly involves a struggle between two socio-political and economic models for ascendancy and reaches its peak in the field of rare earths, revealing the vulnerabilities in what is the world's oldest standing democracy and leader of globalist liberal capitalism. The most visible battle is ongoing trade disputes, but the struggle goes beyond the economic realm. The competition involves a race for technological superiority,[239] military superiority, diplomatic influence and control of supply routes. In this competition, the Beijing government is steadily resorting to rare earths to win.

Historically, technology has played a decisive role in the quest for international power[240] but today it is a double-edged sword. While

---

January 25, 2020, https://thoughtco.com/copper-history-pt-i-2340112

239 The Chinese government recognizes leadership aspirations in the official publication, *Made in China 2025.*

240 Oriol Farrés, "La creciente rivalidad estratégica China-EEUU y sus ramificaciones regionales" ("The growing China-US strategic rivalry and its regional

its use and enjoyment represent a growing value to the economy and improves our quality of life, technological advantage serves as a facilitator and promoter of economic power, driving a multitude of industrial sectors (aerospace, telecommunications, armaments, medicine, energy, etc.). Arguably, much of the West's global hegemony was achieved through technological superiority, not least in weaponry. The negative side is its destructive potential. Consequently, technology is increasingly analyzed from a security perspective. Both the West and China have come to the realization that without control of supply routes, it is not feasible to protect supply chains that have been decentralized, expanded, and diversified as globalization has progressed. And, without a continuous supply of critical metals, there is no technology, and they will falter.

Some of the technologies currently being developed could be disruptive in their own right, revolutionizing our lives both positively and negatively, such as artificial intelligence (AI), quantum computing, biotechnology, nanotechnology, new wireless communications networks (e.g., 5G), metadata and big data exploitation, digitization of the economy, and satellite technology. These technologies may also alter the international hierarchy. They all find chemical and physical support in the use of critical materials such as rare earths. It is no coincidence that their uses and applications have developed in parallel over the last 40 years.

What is most striking about the disruptive technologies currently under development is the confluence and combination of several of them in new applications. But there is growing concern that their promising use may turn into new risks to public and national security. These technologies are mostly dual-use, in the sense that they can be used both to serve military or nefarious purposes with enormous destructive capability, as well as civilian purposes promoting social and economic development.[241] Increasing geopolitical tensions bring their negative potential under the scrutiny of security actors, raising

---

ramifications"), *Anuario Internacional CIDOB* (June 2019). https://www.cidob.org/articulos/anuario_internacional_cidob/2019

241 Camino Kavanagh, *New Tech, New Threats, and New Governance Challenges: An Opportunity to Craft Smarter Responses?* (Carnegie Endowment for International Peace, August 29, 2019), 2. https://carnegieendowment.org/2019/08/28/new-tech-new-threats-and-new-governance-challenges-opportunity-to-craft-smarter-responses-pub-79736

concerns such as cybernetic attacks or a non-related collapse; artificial intelligence turning against humanity to save the planet; lethal robots answering to no ethical code; long-lived and supremacist superior humans; hyper-connected economic, food and energy grids collapsing at the same time; maximum social control by authoritarian governments, etc. Technological purgatory can be imagined in different ever more catastrophic versions, but most to the point is the fact that it seems unquestionable that due to its potential we are at a turning point where obtaining a technological edge and maintaining it can tip the balance of world power.

China has already made public its plan to achieve independence in 10 key technologies by 2025, and when it comes to the supply of materials which form the physical basis of these technologies, its dominance is unmatched.[242] China is moving steadily towards strategic autonomy.[243] Conversely, with China having a monopoly on rare earths, the maintenance of the technologically based U.S. hegemony depends on what happens with China. In 2021, a press release from the Energy Department's Office of Fossil Energy reported that the U.S. still imported 80% of its rare earth elements directly from China, with the remaining portion coming indirectly from China through other countries.

Some advocates of globalization argue that interconnectedness and economic co-dependence prevent conflicts. China might not be interested in conflict if its own electronics industry, which also depends on intermediate products from Western countries, were to be crippled through lack of supply. The Beijing government could be faced with high unemployment rates, destabilizing demonstrations and riots. This argument forgets that many past and present wars and conflicts such as the war in Ukraine do not take into account their loss of capital or the domestic well-being of their nations or behave as wholly rational actors. The frustration of the people and the irrational emotional

---

242 Jack Lifton, "Only through a Secure Supply of EV Metals (Rare Earths) can a Hegemony Be," *Investor News,* May 26, 2021. https://investorintel.com/critical-minerals-rare-earths/only-through-a-secure-supply-of-ev-metals-rare-earths-can-a-hegemony-be/

243 James Kennedy, "China Solidifies Dominance in Rare Earth Processing (UPDATED)," *National Defense,* March 21, 2019. https://www.nationaldefensemagazine.org/articles/2019/3/21/viewpoint-china-solidifies-dominance-in-rare-earth-processing

desires of leaders is sometimes directed outward in the form of violence. Germany learned this lesson first-hand regarding Nordstream 2 and found itself hamstrung in its efforts to sanction Russia for its invasion of Ukraine, while scrambling to find stop-gap efforts to meet its enormous natural gas demands.

But the Chinese Communist Party's path to technological superiority need not involve the use of violence. An abrupt cut-off of supplies could only be justified in very extreme circumstances and is likely unnecessary. The difference may lie in the planned development of a long-term industrial strategy that includes seemingly trivial fiscal measures which nonetheless serve as a springboard for technological development, such as the selective application of Value Added Tax (VAT) within the Great Wall. Success may lie in laying the right foundations for technological supremacy, and if the United States does not clean up its own, its hegemony will end not with a bang but with a whimper.

## CHINESE COPYING AND IMPROVEMENT

China learns from its American rival and co-opts successful recipes, adapting them to its culture and industries. It copies technologies that were considered obsolete in North America and revolutionizes them, such as the LFP (Lithium-iron-phosphate) batteries[244] of American origin, but long since abandoned by the U.S. These batteries have now been improved by Chinese companies such as BYD and are leading the battery market in China. Thanks to their modifications, they provide better performance and safety than NCM (Nickel Cobalt Manganese) batteries and make it possible to dispense with cobalt and nickel. Overtaken by the Chinese leadership in the sector, Western vehicle manufacturers can only follow. At the national level, the Beijing government is executing its own variation of American post-war industrial strategy, improving it through strategic control of many critical materials and the aspiration for independence in certain sectors.

---

244 "LFP Batteries are Winning the EV Race – But Where's the (Ex-China) Supply," *Investing Whisperer*, consulted on January 1, 2023. https://investingwhisperer.com/lfp-batteries-are-winning-the-ev-race-but-wheres-the-ex-china-supply/

With the fall of the Berlin Wall, the West rested on its laurels and cashed in on the peace dividend. With the fall of the USSR, the West's exultant assertion of unipolarity and embrace of Fukuyama's claim that it marked *"the end of history"* made it forget about China's potential. Complacency has lulled us to sleep, and we remain torpid even as we hear drums in the distance. The Chinese government's novel and secretive applications of rare earths may not have served merely as a catch-up with the United States technologically, but rather as a technological leap which puts it ten years ahead of its competitor. The next few years will uncover how true this is. China has been preoccupied with laying the physical and chemical foundations that have enabled it to carry out a technological revolution in pursuit of world leadership, albeit in the context of a multipolar world. Beijing financed its rare earths and metals industry and absorbed the West's related technological know-how and is now in a privileged position to achieve hegemony, were that to be its aim.[245]

The clear-sighted vision of the Chinese government's "National Technology Research and Development Plan" of 1986, which also included the conquest of rare earths, has survived to the present day and who better than the current leader, Xi Jinping, a chemical engineer, to grasp the importance of these super-elements, enhance their development and maintain their control? In contrast, it is unsurprising that there are no chemical engineers specialized in rare earths outside China, as Teresa Lorens from IGME told me, or that "China produces many more geologists than the whole of Europe" according to geologist Isabel Pino. Today, the effects of a limitation on China's rare earths exports could facilitate its ability to achieve hegemony during a key moment. By the time a possible dispute at the World Trade Organization (WTO) is resolved, China may already have taken the necessary step to position itself clearly ahead of its main rival, and sufficiently leverage its technology, especially emerging and disruptive technologies, to solidify its position.

For the time being, to maintain the cruising speed that allows it to overtake the USA in the race for world leadership, in 2019 China imposed a de-facto decades-long export ban of its critical minerals and concentrates such as rare earths, with strategically applied export

245 James Kennedy, "China Solidifies Dominance in Rare Earth Processing."

tariffs. Companies producing metal powders or rare earth metals must pay tariffs (13%) if their buyer is outside the Great Wall. The opposite is true for finished products containing rare earths. The companies that export them do not have to pay VAT, which is known as a non-tariff barrier, on the transaction. The VAT does not violate World Trade Organization rules. China manages to move up the supply chain to the production of the final product by withholding raw materials and primary products beforehand.

## THE ALARM SOUNDS: SENKAKU

When China banned rare earth exports to Japan as a diplomatic weapon in 2010, it was not yet a worthy contender for world hegemony. This ban was in retaliation for seizing the crew of a seagoing vessel that was fishing in Japanese national waters off the Senkaku Islands. The seagoing vessel took hostile action against the Japanese coast guard when it was warned to leave the area. A two-month near-total blockade of rare earth shipments was followed by three years of heavy export quotas. If the initial embargo had lasted longer than two months, the Japanese companies' reserves would have disappeared, and they would have had to stop production. China's own industry would also have suffered the consequences of not receiving Japanese electronic products. That year, the price of rare earths increased tenfold.

But Japan learned its lesson well. Its current rare earth strat
is now more than 15 years old. Under the name "Genso Senry
it seeks to secure the supply chain, while investing in innovat
recycling by supporting Japanese domestic companies. It
Tokyo government that was the first to understand and in
ize the fair relationship between oil and metals. The re
criticality of rare earths and oil to its energy security i
state agency Japan Oil Gas and Metal Corporation
coordinates all energy actions, providing financial in
of them and ensuring compliance with national pr
ronmental targets. These targets include achievi
by 2050 and exploiting new rare earth deposit

246 JOGMEC provides loan and debt guarantee
support, information gathering and provision, and geo
development of metallic resources. JOGMEC websit
https://www.jogmec.go.jp/english/index.html

Japanese strategy has made it possible to reduce Japan's dependence of these metals on the Chinese market,[247] not only in the renewable energy sector but also in the defense sector.

Once again, the similarities with the oil world are striking. The Chinese government's reaction to the Senkaku conflict was reminiscent of that of the Saudi monarchy in response to the Yom Kippur conflict in 1973. Then, OPEC imposed an oil embargo on Western countries that had supported Israel in its war against Egypt and Syria. The price of a barrel of oil increased threefold in one year. Just as the world reacted and turned to nuclear energy to seek a certain independence from oil, in the case of the embargo on rare earths, from 2010, Japan also tried to find solutions to the Chinese embargo. It allied itself with Australia through saving its company, Lynas, from bankruptcy in order to obtain its metals, and it simultaneously boosted substitution. Shortly before, in 2009, the Australian government had blocked the attempted purchase of Lynas by the state-owned China Nonferrous Metal Mining Company.[248]

Other Western countries, the USA and the EU joined Japan in a complaint to the World Trade Organization (WTO) concerning the Chinese restrictions in the form of quotas.[249] After a long legal dispute, the WTO ruled the embargo as illegal. This event triggered a reaction not only from Japan but also from the U.S.-led Western world to this problem, which until then had gone unnoticed. Faced with the imminent threat of closure of the Lynas processing plant in Malaysia,[250] Japan once again came to the rescue and its government granted a loan of 133 million dollars.[251] The loan, channeled through the new JARE

---

247 Julian Ryall, "Japan moves to secure rare earths to reduce dependence on China," *South China Morning Post,* August 17, 2020. https://www.scmp.com/week-asia/politics/article/3097672/japan-moves-secure-rare-earths-reduce-dependence-china

248 Keith Bradsher, "China's Plans for Mines Are Blocked," *The New York imes,* September 25, 2009. https://www.nytimes.com/2009/09/25/business/bal/25mine.html

249 Shannon Tiezzi, "Japan Seeks Chinese Compensation Over 2010 t Collision Incident," *The Diplomat,* February 14, 2014. https://thediplomat. /2014/02/japan-seeks-chinese-compensation-over-2010-boat-collision-incident/

250 Melanie Burton and Roushni Nair, "Lynas faces part closure of Malaysian arths plant by July," *Reuters,* February 13, 2023. https://www.nasdaq.com/ /lynas-faces-part-closure-of-malaysian-rare-earths-plant-by-july

1 "Australian rare earths miner Lynas receives $133m from JARE," *Mining*

(Japan Australia Rare Earths) organization, will be used to speed up the construction of the new Lynas rare earths processing plant, not in Malaysia but on Australian soil. But the hiatus between the completion of the Australian plant and the closure of the Malaysian plant will leave the world almost entirely in the hands of Chinese rare earths. For the time being Lynas Malaysia Sdn Bhd's operations will not be allowed to carry out "cracking and leaching" (C&L), two of its fundamental processes in the country after December 31, 2023.[252]

## THE U.S. REACTS

Under President Donald Trump, Congress approved, as part of the emergency COVID measures package, $800 million to fund research dedicated to rare earths and critical materials to counter Chinese dominance. The new law also required the U.S. Geological Survey to begin calculating the amount of metals needed to meet the country's needs. Since then, several governmental entities[253] have been trying to tackle the supply chain problem of rare earths and other critical materials. It is a difficult assignment, considering the problem affects several industrial sectors and their associated government ministries: defense, energy, agriculture, environment, and the economy.

U.S. President Biden, also aware of the magnitude of the problem, took further steps in 2021 to tackle it. A 100-day review of supply chains in the key areas of medicine, raw materials and agriculture concluded that "decades of underinvestment, coupled with public policy choices that favor quarterly results and short-term fixes, have left

---

*Technology,* March 8, 2023. https://www.mining-technology.com/news/lynas-133m-from-japan/

252 Sinar, "Lynas not closing down, just no 'cracking and leaching' after Dec 31," *SinarDaily,* May 9, 2023. https://www.sinardaily.my/article/195579/malaysia/national/lynas-not-closing-down-just-no-cracking-and-leaching-after-dec-31

253 The principals are the Department of the Interior (DOI), the White House Office of Science and Technology Policy, the Department of Agriculture (USDA), the Environmental Protection Agency (EPA), and the Department of Energy, the U.S. Development Finance Corporation, and the Department of Defense (DOD). White House, U.S. Government, "FACT SHEET: Biden-Harris Administration Announces Task Force on Supply Chain Disruptions to Address Short-Term Supply Chain Discontinuities." https://www.whitehouse.gov/briefing-room/statements-releases/2021/06/08/fact-sheet-biden-harris-administration-announces-supply-chain-disruptions-task-force-to-address-short-term-supply-chain-discontinuities/

the system fragile."[254] Critical materials, especially rare earths, held a pivotal role in these supply chains.

Aware of the relevance of this misunderstood issue and the danger to its weapons systems, the Department of Defense (DOD) now deploys incentives, grants, loans, loan guarantees and purchase agreements in relation to strategic and critical materials and their research and development (R&D). Its biggest bet is on a joint agreement between the Australian company Lynas and the DOD to develop the capability to process heavy rare earth elements with a new manufacturing facility in Texas, known as Blue Line. The intervention of the DOD[255] is vital in trying to secure the supply chain; otherwise, American civilian companies, such as M.P. Materials, exploit the minerals from their mines focused only on the pursuit of immediate economic benefits, without capitalizing on the strategic relevance of obtaining each of the 17 metals processed from the rare earths.

Like the DoD, the Department of Energy also provided access to more than $3 billion in loan guarantees to support technologies that improve energy efficiency, such as technologies for mining, extraction, processing, recovery, or recycling of critical materials.

Surprisingly, in February 2021, on the anniversary of Executive Order 14017 ordering the aforementioned review of supply chains, a new but brief government report stated that if the measures taken were successful, the current dependence on one product, Chinese permanent magnets, would be reduced. The report cited this one product, of which China produces 87% of the world's total, but did not allude to a whole string of products made with Chinese rare earths that directly or indirectly affect its safety. Whether this omission was intentional or a dangerous oversight is unclear.

To support its sister departments, the U.S. Department of the Interior is also taking action. In 2022, with the support of the White House Office of Science and Technology Policy, it created a working group composed of agencies such as the Department of Agriculture

254 Rhys Thomas, "Biden creates task force on supply chain disruptions," *Supply Chain,* June 9, 2021. https://supplychaindigital.com/supply-chain-risk-management/biden-establishes-supply-chain-disruptions-task-force

255 U.S. Department of Defense, "DOD Announces Rare Earth Element Award to Strengthen Domestic Industrial Base," February 1, 2021. https://www.defense.gov/News/Releases/Release/Article/2488672/dod-announces-rare-earth-element-award-to-strengthen-domestic-industrial-base/

and the Environmental Protection Agency to identify locations where critical minerals can be produced and processed in the United States.

Another option, not yet widely exploited at the national government level, would be to promote entrepreneurship to create supply chains outside China, such as that of the American company Energy Fuels, which supplies the Canadian company, Neo Performance Materials, with a rare earth concentrate from the mineral monazite, stripped of its radioactive uranium and thorium traces. The race against the clock has begun but North American analysis centers such as Adamas Intelligence,[256] among other experts[257] in the sector, see difficulty in meeting future needs for rare earth metals mined and processed on American soil before the first shortages occur. As this moment approaches, more alarm bells will start ringing from different sectors and the government will have to adopt a more interventionist policy.

The outcome of this struggle for control of rare earths may well be determined by the "tempo" or speed of reaction of the U.S. and its allied states, and by China's exploitation of this clear geostrategic advantage for as long as it manages to maintain it. In the interim, and in the absence of specific regulation at the global level addressing rare earths' strategic importance, international diplomacy may end up taking on regulatory and mediation roles in the face of rare earths-related conflicts. Western alliances may serve to prevent China from using the strategic export reduction card, or to resolve tensions and problems if it does resort to it.

In the search for containment measures, the White House is promoting and relaunching the dormant alliance of Indo-Pacific democracies. This coalition, the QUAD (Quadrilateral Security Dialogue Nations), consisting of the United States of America, Japan, Australia and India, aims to counteract this situation by cooperating in the financing of new production technologies and development projects

---

256 Adamas Intelligence, *Rare Earth Magnet Outlook to 2035* (Q2 2022). https://www.adamasintel.com/rare-earth-magnet-market-outlook-to-2035/

257 "MP Materials . . . could have a chance of being in the light rare earth separation business by 2024. Even so, to achieve this MP would have to hire outside agents." Jack Lifton, "Lifton on Biden and the security of supply of rare earths," *Investor News,* January 24, 2021. https://investorintel.com/markets/technology-metals/technology-metals-intel/lifton-on-biden-and-the-security-of-the-supply-of-rare-earths/

and by developing new international regulations.[258] Nevertheless India, as a BRICS member, is playing a delicate balancing act, engaged in expanding trade with Russia and on the diplomatic level, refusing to invite Ukraine to the forthcoming G20 meeting. In March 2021, the respective QUAD presidents participated in a meeting in which participants publicly recognized China's dominance over rare earths. A major problem they identified was that any deficit of a third country in its supply chain was automatically absorbed and filled by China, which always ended up refining the metals. This occurred regardless of where the minerals were mined.[259]

Both Australia, a member of QUAD, and Canada are both mining powers that are playing a key role in the establishment of these strategic alliances that are helping to reduce China's monopoly. The Canadian stock exchange accounts for 43% of the world's public mining companies, as listed on the Toronto Stock Exchange (TSX and TSXV). In the case of Australia, in addition to its mining wealth and large companies, there is also explicit state support. Through its Australian Export Finance Agency,[260] the Australian government encourages the establishment of companies dedicated to the extraction and production of critical and strategic materials through various financial solutions. Australian companies such as Australian Strategic Metals and Lynas are developing international supply chains outside China, such in the United States, South Korea, Japan and Malaysia. Thanks to these companies, particularly Lynas, dependence on China[261] has been slightly reduced in recent years. Another impetus for this model is the Asian giant's creation of vertically integrated international companies,

---

258 Nikkei Staff Writers, "Indo-Pacific international relations: Quad strengthens cooperation on rare earths to counter China," *Nikkei Asia Review,* March 11, 2021. https://asia.nikkei.com/Politics/International-relations/Indo-Pacific/Quad-tightens-rare-earth-cooperation-to-counter-China

259 Panos Mourdoukoutas, "America, Australia, And Japan Try To Limit China's Rare Earth Dominance -- It Won't Be Easy," *Forbes,* August 6, 2019. https://www.forbes.com/sites/panosmourdoukoutas/2019/08/06/america-australia-and-japan-try-to-limit-chinas-rare-earth-dominance-it-wont-be-easy/

260 Priscila Barrera, "Rare Earths Outlook 2021: REE Magnet Supply to Remain Tight," *Investing News Network,* January 20, 2021. https://investingnews.com/rare-earth-outlook-2021/

261 U.S. Geological Survey, "Mineral Commodity Summaries 2020" (Washington, DC: U.S. Department of the Interior, 2020).

which contain all steps in the supply chain and receive immense state backing.

## A FIGHT WITH THE SAME RULES?

Yet, since the only way to compete and not lose is to use the most beneficial standards for the producing companies, i.e., Chinese standards, the U.S. has finally resorted to direct and intervene in its domestic market instead of relying on a free-market capitalism that is insouciant with regard to security concerns. This intervention in the domestic economy is reflected in its Inflation Reduction Act,[262] which narrowly passed in the House and Senate in August 2022. Nonetheless, support is strong, as seen by its $437 billion endowment. Among its provisions are incentives for the green energy sector and an expansion of the President's budget for the Defense Production Act of 1950. Already only manufacturers of electric vehicles or renewable energy that source components and materials produced in America will be eligible for subsidies and tax breaks. This could provide the catalyst needed to support the development of the rare earth supply chain.

Until now, the CEOs of Western companies have played with their hands tied behind their backs, always with an eye on share prices and quarterly results, in order to satisfy their shareholders. By moving to China, their companies enjoyed environmental, tax and wage advantages and a guaranteed supply at a good price. This new law may finally mark the beginning of an attempt to rebuild the American industrial base as part of a national security strategy. Such measures will prevent the migratory hemorrhage of domestic companies seeking out the competitive advantages offered by the Beijing government. For the U.S., in the long term, the surrender of its technology, the loss of jobs and the loss of control of supply chains are much more costly than the short-term benefit in terms of shareholder return.

Even so, Chinese state-owned companies continue to compete in a different league. They have unlimited capital, abundant available talent fresh out of their universities or trained in the West, and assured material resources. China provides the ultimate support for its industrial strategy through these companies, which are building a highway

262 U.S. Congress, *H.R.5376 - Inflation Reduction Act of 2022,* August 16, 2022, https://www.congress.gov/bill/117th-congress/house-bill/5376

to hegemony. Even the U.S. Inflation Reduction Act, long awaited by many American businessmen and patriots, may have undesirable side effects. Semi-isolationist self-sufficiency may be detrimental to the industry of other allied countries. South Korea,[263] France and Germany threatened to denounce the new law to the World Trade Organization and take other action in response if an agreement is not reached. Understandably, after the conflict in Ukraine, Europe is not at the forefront of global innovation; its economy is based primarily on production of finished goods such as automobiles, aircraft, renewable energies, chemicals, pharmaceuticals, etc. If we add to the exodus of European companies to the Chinese mecca a further migration to the USA, and add to the low prices of American energy, which have an impact on the final price of goods, the subsidies announced by the new law, the new panorama turns the USA into a prospective El Dorado for European companies. Automobile and renewable energy producers are unintentionally invited to flee Europe. EU exports to the U.S. could be also hampered.

Paradoxically, the United States, the driving force behind the World Trade Organization, is undermining the foundations of this organization in favor of the security of its supply chains and its industrial base, prioritizing its strategic autonomy. At the same time, on the moral borderline of sarcasm, but with arguable legal grounds, the Chinese Ministry of Commerce[264] also lashed out against the provisions of the U.S. anti-inflation bill. According to the Beijing government, this law may violate WTO rules, referring to its advantageous status of special membership as a "most favored nation." The Chinese government announced its intention to take action against the act. And it will not be the first time that this happens. It is within the realm of possibility that the U.S., in the face of a hypothetical complaint before the WTO by China, the European Union or South Korea, will have to withdraw some measures of its Inflation Reduction Act (IRA). But, for the time being, in 2023 the EU has set out its Green Deal Industrial

263 Ji-Hoon Lee, Jae-Yeon Ko and So-Hyeon Kim, "Korea may file complaint with WTO against US' Inflation Reduction Act," *The Korea Economic Daily,* August 22, 2022. https://www.kedglobal.com/electric-vehicles/newsView/ked202208220024

264 Global Times, "China's Commerce Ministry says US anti-inflation bill's EV provisions may violate WTO rules," September 22, 2022. https://www.globaltimes.cn/page/202209/1275909.shtml

Plan, aiming to change the economics of industrial decarbonization and it also relies upon the Recovery and Resilience Facility's dedicated climate subsidies to offset the IRA's effects on the EU economy/[265] It replicates partially the measures of the IRA. The green subsidy race has already started and probably South Korea and other countries will do the same. Japan and U.S. also announced an agreement to secure free trade on critical materials used to make electric vehicle batteries. This represents a backdoor to gain access to the Inflation Reduction Act's generous tax breaks.

Globalization could be blowing up and the explosion could take much of world trade and some of its pillar organizations such as the WTO with it. It is yet another instance of the U.S. taking actions in an effort to protect its hegemony.

Nonetheless, the U.S. has shown in other human security crises an astonishing capacity to react. Despite the difficulties in obtaining a vaccine against COVID, the strong interventionist stance adopted by the U.S. government in Operation Warp Speed[266] showed the power of its institutions. In both cases, rare earth and coronavirus, a similar need for intervention associated with a threat to human and national security is identified. But the threat of rare earth deficiency is much more obscure and therefore does not generate the same forceful reaction. Government intervention in the form of creating public companies, direct support for existing ones and the development of state programs are proven recipes for ensuring the security of its citizens.

But there are even more aggressive measures which might be applied, such as those used by China: A citizen of Beijing or Shanghai who wants to buy an internal combustion car must sign up on a public list and participate in a lottery system. After waiting a few years and with a dash of luck, he or she may win the lottery and be granted a license and registration plates. This program, called the Vehicle Ownership Restriction, started in 2011 and grants many more licenses to electric vehicles; the times to obtain them are shorter as well. On

---

265 Christian Scheinert, "EU's response to the US Inflation Reduction Act (IRA)" (briefing), European Parliament, Policy Department for Economic, Scientific and Quality of Life Policies, June 2023. https://www.europarl.europa.eu/RegData/etudes/IDAN/2023/740087/IPOL_IDA(2023)740087_EN.pdf

266 U.S. Congressional Research Service, "Operation Warp Speed Contracts for COVID-19 Vaccines and Ancillary Vaccination Materials," March 1, 2021. https://crsreports.congress.gov/product/pdf/IN/IN11560

the other side of the Pacific, American citizens exercise their freedom to buy the car they want. But even with the new federal EV tax credit rules of the Inflation Reduction Act's and its focus on clean energy, very few EVs currently qualify for the full $7,500 tax credit. However, protectionism is clearly reflected, as among the electric vehicles that don't qualify are about nine models, mostly from foreign manufacturers, including Hyundai, Volkswagen, BMW, Rivian, Nissan, and Volvo. Obviously, both systems entail support for domestic development of their electric car industry but the Chinese support is drastically higher.

At the other extreme, U.S. passivity and leaving the problem in the hands of the self-regulation of a theoretically efficient capitalist system could progressively grant more hegemonic weight to China. The Middle Kingdom could leverage its strength thanks to its mastery of the periodic table, the enabler of its technology. Technological overtaking could be accompanied by a triumphalist narrative disseminated through information campaigns, which would show China as a world leader in several technological areas. If China were to massively promote a vision of a China with green cities, with clean energy and clean air, without crime and with the latest technological developments, this would serve to bury its "deviations" in terms of human rights, restrictions on individual freedom, and shed light on its actual improving environmental situation. Thanks to its rapid electrification China will soon stop being the biggest polluter on earth in spite of its second world largest population.[267]

## THE THUCYDIDES TRAP

As China tries to overtake the West without a blinker and in the right lane, we will have indicators that will reveal a reality that may be alien to many Westerners locked within narrative bubbles. Here are some of them:

- 42% of the world's e-commerce is carried out by China, which has 700 million inhabitants with Internet access, more than the U.S. and Europe combined.
- One out of every three "unicorns" in the world (companies worth more than 1 billion U.S. dollars) belongs to China.

267 German Lopez, "China´s two climate directions," *The New York Times*, August 14, 2023. https://www.nytimes.com/2023/08/14/briefing/china-climate.html

- The largest video game company on the planet is China's Tencent, and it is not even its core business.
- The number of Chinese quantum computing patents and the most powerful quantum computers are alternating, according to sources and dates in the past year, between China and the U.S.
- As for satellites specifically related to defense, in 2022, China put into orbit 45, the U.S. 30 and Russia 15.
- China has hypersonic missiles in service and the U.S. is only now beginning to field its Long-Range Hypersonic Weapon platforms.[268]
- On January 2, 2019, China published pictures of the dark side of the moon and plans on using the satellite responsible for transmitting these photos as a communications node for a moon base it plans to build in 2027.
- In July 2023 a private Chinese company launched into orbit the world's first methane-liquid oxygen rocket, sending what could become the next generation of launch vehicles into space.
- In several areas of Artificial Intelligence use, China has already surpassed the United States. For example, in voice recognition technologies, where Chinese companies are ahead of U.S. companies in all languages, including English. China's iFlytek has 700 million users, twice as many as Apple's Siri.

Undoubtedly, the struggle of opposite narratives and information campaigns to show China or the U.S. as winner in the fight for technological dominance has already begun. The evolution of these or similar indicators will tell us the reality of the competition's outcome. But so long as the struggle for technological dominance continues to be based physically and chemically on rare metals, it is not out of the question that we will witness conflicts such as those that took place to

268 Richard Parlato, "1st Multi-Domain Task Force deploys the Army's first Long-Range Hypersonic Weapon System," *U.S. Army,* March 30, 2023. https://www.army.mil/article/265349/1st_multi_domain_task_force_deploys_the_armys_first_long_range_hypersonic_weapon_system

obtain bronze in prehistoric times, as above mentioned, before reaching any "substitution technology." Part of the U.S. strategy to fight China's monopoly on rare earths is to copy this solution and boost the technology for substituting these metals.

This is what its Department of Energy intends to do with the R.E.A.C.T. initiative[269] (Rare Earth Alternatives in Critical Technologies). But it will do little good if it substitutes one material for another still dominated by China, or if it focuses only on wind turbines and electric vehicles. Nor would a substitution that produces a poorer or more expensive product be of any use. In the end, consumers will not be willing to pay more or lose advantages for the sake of a security issue that doesn't affect their daily lives. Beyond substitution, the prescription for the U.S. to overcome this chronic weakness is not much different from what the EU needs: exploitation of its domestic deposits; creation of processing, refining and metallurgy centers; increasing reserves of rare earth metals and their critical objects by both companies and governments; efficient recycling; and secure international supply chains.

A possible outcome of a failed U.S. strategy, which would lead it to fight to obtain these metals irrespective of an embargo by the Beijing government, could bring us closer to the trap announced by the philosopher Thucydides: the eponymous Thucydides' Trap. According to the ancient Greek philosopher, the shift in the balance of power always leads the declining power to challenge the rising power, to retain dominance. In addition to the still simmering territorial tensions between China and Japan over the island of Senkaku, there are now, maybe U.S. fueled, renewed Chinese aspirations for speedier reunification with Taiwan. And, as the U.S.-China trade war competition takes on pre-conflict overtones, the tension is also focused on the island, which is home to Taiwan Semiconductor Manufacturing Company (TSMC). Drawing parallels with the past Senkaku altercation, it would not be surprising if history repeated itself, this time with an incident between the Chinese and U.S. navies near the island of Taiwan, leading to a ban on the export of rare earths to the U.S. and Taiwan itself and a de facto block on high-performance microchip manufacturing.

---

269 ARPA-E, "REACH: Rare Earth Alternatives in Critical Technologies." https://arpa-e.energy.gov/technologies/programs/react

Both China and the U.S. are taking precautions. The Asian giant, as established in its "Made in China 2025" plan, seeks self-sufficiency in the field of manufacturing precious microchips. On the other side of the Pacific, the U.S. is trying to recover what was once one of its flagship technological empires by subsidizing its company Intel and trying to relocate the manufacture of these semiconductors within its borders. But China has the rare earths and other critical materials needed to manufacture the ubiquitous and all-powerful microchips and the U.S. does not. Its manufacturing depends on light rare earths (lanthanum, cerium, praseodymium, neodymium, promethium and samarium) that have a "very high risk" of going into supply disruption in the next few years. They also depend on other critical rare metals as gallium and germanium.

Therefore, and not by chance, on August 1, 2023, the Asian giant was taking a new step in the metals war. The U.S. was attempting to corner its technology. Its companies were suffering the ravages of the Western ban on the sale of chips and the machinery needed to produce them. Trying to slow the Chinese advance, the United States with its CHIPS Act, Europe and Japan are limiting the export of chips and equipment needed for their production to China. Disruptive technologies such as artificial intelligence, which could tip the balance of power, depend on chips such as those designed by U.S. giant Nvidia. But all semiconductors are just an entelechy without a physical backbone to support them.

China was applying the ancient Talion law, tit for tat, an eye for an eye, a tooth for a tooth. China has imposed export controls on eight gallium and six germanium products. According to former Vice Minister of Commerce Wei Jianguo, these controls "are just the beginning." Beijing had also previously announced restrictions on exports of rare earths, which could come as early as November. The Western world forgets that if chips are the brain of electronics, these critical metals are its neurons. While the West has its head in the software clouds, the Communist Party of China (CPC) also strives to reach them but has its feet on the ground. The foundations of its industries are based on its land, its products are made from the minerals it extracts and, above all, from the metals it refines. China cited national security reasons that allow it to restrict its exports without breaching World Trade Organization regulations. In this case, the control mechanism is based on the obligation of exporting companies to obtain a specific license.

These materials are essential for the production of chips, but also for the manufacture of modern weapons systems, fiber optics, 5G and 6G stations, and the solar panels that equip our satellites, among others. They are enablers, not by chance, of technologies in which China wants to be a world leader. So now, the Chinese Ministry of Commerce has turned off the tap of the world's supply of germanium and gallium. Last year, China produced about 98% of low-grade primary gallium, the main raw material in the gallium supply chain, according to the U.S. Geological Survey (USGS), and about 60% of the global germanium market, according to the European industry association Critical Raw Materials Alliance (CRMA).[270]

China has learned to use its strategic weapon of the rare metals monopoly to its advantage without harming itself. An abrupt and prolonged cut in rare earths such as the one that started in 2010 could not be sustained for long as its industry would also suffer. Speaking in silver or speaking in critical metals, the Chinese rare earths embargo of 2010 was like shooting flies with cannons. China has since studied how and when to use the restrictions on its critical metals. Germanium for example is critical for the manufacture of the solar panels that equip satellites, for the production of fiber optics, and for the production of various modern weapons systems. These are technologies in which China wants to be a world leader. The restriction of its exports has certainly been well analyzed before being implemented. China no longer uses its rare metal restrictions only reactively but also for strategic purposes.

In the West's attempt to leave China behind technologically, chips have become the first objects in contention, but could the weapons systems of our armies be next? As we shall now see, the supply chains of critical minerals are as decisive for the economic world order as they are for the security world order.

270 Andy Home, "China flexes critical metals muscles with export curbs," *Reuters,* July 10, 2023. https://www.reuters.com/markets/commodities/china-flexes-critical-metals-muscles-with-export-curbs-2023-07-10/

# 8. WESTERN ARMIES WITH FEET OF CLAY

A new arms race has begun; the development of lethal weaponry equipped with artificial intelligence is reshaping the battlefield. But our Western armies are running in this new competition with feet of clay. The physical basis of this technology are the metals which it simply does not possess. A storm could soften their feet, causing them to fall—a cut in the supply of these metals would limit Western weapons' efficiency or render them inoperable. Many countries have not defined a list of critical metals for war. They are unaware of the importance of vanadium for the hardness of their steels, of tungsten so that their warheads do not melt, of germanium to obtain infrared vision, of niobium for super-resistant alloys, of the lightness of titanium as resistant as steel. . . . They look away and rely on outsourcing.[271]

Many conflicts show how air power, well integrated into a joint strategy, is the key to victory. A study[272] conducted by researchers at the University of Florida provides quantitative evidence of the conclusive positive relationship between air superiority and battlefield outcomes between 1932 and 2003. The results of this research show how air superiority better predicts victory in a war than other well-known factors such as regime type, civil-military relations, and a general measure of military power.

The more advanced an army is, the more rare earths it needs. As the air domain is the most technologically advanced and my specialty is military piloting, let me show you the importance of rare earths in this context.

---

271 *The Economist,* "Gallium, germanium and indium: the curious strategic metals that China will stop exporting and worry the West," July 15, 2023. https://www.infobae.com/economist/2023/07/15/galio-germanio-e-indio-los-curiosos-metales-estrategicos-que-china-dejara-de-exportar-y-preocupan-a-occidente/

272 Richard Saunders and Mark Souva, "Air superiority and battlefield victory," *Research & Politics,* November 20, 2020. https://doi.org/10.1177/2053168020972816

## THE ROLE OF RARE EARTHS IN THE UKRAINE WAR

In aviation, the best software on the market is useless if it is not accompanied by the best materials that enable it to carry out its algorithmic commands. Rare earth metals enable the development of more efficient, agile, and intelligent military capabilities and combat systems.[273] These elements are essential for, among others, night vision devices, communications equipment, navigation systems, batteries, stealth technology, drones, target designation lasers and communications satellites. An example of their importance can be seen in their use in the Ukrainian war. The man-portable missiles (MANPADs and ATGMs) that have proven so relevant could not maneuver if their actuating fins were not equipped with rare earths. These missiles have not only denied free use of airspace below 10,000 feet to Russian aviation but have been capable of destroying expensive tanks while being able to be used by a single soldier with minimal training. Given the overwhelming existence of MANPADs operated by Ukrainian personnel, Russian aviation has been forced to fly either high or at night. The dreaded MANPADs operated by the Ukrainian military were joined by even more powerful air defense weapon systems on loan from the West as the conflict progressed. One example is the NASAMs air defense systems whose radars provide 360-degree coverage, identifying and tracking as many fighter planes as drones or helicopters up to 120 kilometers away. Their radars, like almost all current radars, including those for civilian use, depend at a minimum on rare earths such as europium and lutetium.

Air superiority is usually achieved by the more powerful nation in the initial stages of a conflict. This was not the case in Ukraine. Russia was unable to deny the enemy the use of airspace, to freely support its own ground troops, or to conduct intelligence or logistical airlift within the area of operations. Their maneuverability and firepower were reduced. Forced to fly in this complex scenario, Russian aviation required an increasing number of precision-guided bombs to be effective and reduce casualties. The other option was to use

---

273 Juan Manuel Chomón and Andreas Ganser, "How Relevant are Rare Earths to Europe's Security and Defence?," *European Security and Defence,* October 7, 2021. https://euro-sd.com/2021/10/articles/exclusive/23989/how-relevant-are-rare-earths-to-europes-security-and-defence/

dumb, gravity bombs, flying so low that the pilot cannot see even the pilot's own shadow or so high that accuracy becomes unachievable. And so this is what they did. Russian air raids were often forced to resort to these tactics because smart bombs were in short supply, either exhausted or reserved because of their extreme expense and dependence on both technological elements from the West and critical materials such as rare earth neodymium, praseodymium, dysprosium, samarium and terbium. Russian aviation has suffered the ravages of the technification of air power and the elongation of its supply chains. Many of the technologically advanced components aboard its fighters such as the Sukoy-30 or Sukoy-35 come from foreign companies. The supplies of those located in Western countries were cut off, limiting the sustainability of the Russian air fleet and reducing its operability. The U.S. government declared that Russia's global military procurement network was in its sights and took action to destroy it. However, neither the U.S. nor the allied bloc of liberal democracies in general have credible power to attack supply chains at their initial stages. Attacking the raw material, as was done in World War II, might be easier than going after the myriad companies that sell the technological components that equip modern weapons systems.

In Ukraine, with neither side achieving air superiority, drones entered the scene. Turkish models of the Saheb 135 or its Russian version Geran 2 are launched in swarms to destroy Ukrainian electricity grids and their fuel depots, leaving General Winter to act against the population, as it has done in other wars. The Western side sent to Ukraine one of the most powerful drones on the market, the Predator whose optronic systems for surveillance of critical and high-risk facilities such as ports, airports, industries, thermal and nuclear power plants need rare earths. Despite being completely different drone models, none of these drones could fly without the rare earths that equip them.

In the case of fighters, as they are more complex weapon systems, even more metallic elements are required. A state-of-the-art fighter is a flying periodic table. For example, titanium, used for the first time in 1960 in the U.S. Air Force's dazzling SR-71 Blackbird, provides high structural strength despite its light weight. Rhenium, a metal that is exceedingly rare in the earth's crust, thanks to its melting temperature of 3180 degrees Celsius, has been used since the 1980s in alloy with nickel, to enable gas turbine blades to withstand the high temperatures at the turbine's engine outlet.

The latest applications of rare earth metals have been used on board the F-22 Raptor since 2005. This U.S. fighter uses the rare earths yttrium, terbium and erbium in its optical, sensing and fiber optic systems. The weight of rare earths in new weapons systems, both in terms of importance and physicality, is only increasing. The spearhead of American aviation, equipping several allied Western militaries, is the F-35 Lightning II fighter, which entered service in 2015. Although a 2013 Congressional Research Service report indicates that the aircraft contains 920 pounds (400 kilograms) of rare earth metals that equip various systems,[274] when interviewing a senior executive from one of its critical supplier companies, he indicated that,

> I really don't think our American colleagues have the slightest idea of how many rare earths are in their aircraft or their origin. When the product reaches them, it is already inserted in very small quantities in the final product, ten or twelve steps down the supply chain, far from the mine. No one traces its origin back to the mine. If we mix the hermeticism and secrecy of the defense industries with the opacity of the rare earths market, the curtain is so thick that no one seems to be able to look through it.

What suppliers and experts openly admit is that without access to the rare earths monopolized by China, as is the case with many other metals, the U.S. F-35 would not be able to fly. Although this military leviathan still has laws that oblige its armies to source only metals produced on U.S. soil, in the case of rare earths it has been necessary to bend the rules. In 2022, a bipartisan bill was drafted in the U.S. Senate that could prohibit defense contractors from procuring rare earth metals from China by the end of 2026 and force the Pentagon to create a strategic stockpile of these elements by 2025. But is this possible?

While the Pentagon and defense contractors were complacently enjoying the golden decades, several of these companies supplying

274 Russell Parman, "An elemental issue," *U.S. Army,* September 26, 2019. https://www.army.mil/article/227715/an_elemental_issue.

weaponry to the U.S. government, with government authorization, have sold it weaponry containing Chinese rare earths. Subcontracting was identified as the source of the violation, but the issue is so pervasive that the U.S. government had to issue a legal exemption to avoid having to disable weapons systems such as the F-35.[275] The U.S. government, aware that parts of its F-35s are carrying rare earths from China, is forced to give an extraordinary authorization for them to continue flying while efforts to solve the problem are pursued. But several years have passed since the first warnings with no viable solution in sight. If the same type of investigation were to be carried out for the aforementioned lasers, radars, missiles, night vision systems, etc., it would likely unearth some uncomfortable truths. Visualizing the problem is a simple affair, as no rare earths are refined outside of China. It would therefore be easy for the Middle Kingdom to establish an embargo that would degrade the operability of Western armies, if not rendering them altogether useless. It would all depend on the rate of replenishment required for each Western weapon system of elements containing heavy rare earths or even light rare earths if they stopped arriving from China.

The bloc of liberal democracies should be learning lessons either from the past or from the effects of their own embargoes and sanctions and review the supply chains of their militaries. He who does not know history is condemned to repeat it, and past examples also tell us that our Western weapons systems are in the hands of China. Following the invasions of Iraq and Afghanistan, demand for the metal germanium, used by the U.S. military, skyrocketed. Consumption of this material for thermal vision systems, night vision goggles and guided weaponry rose from 5,000 tons in 2003 to 30,000 tons four years later.[276] Today almost 60% of germanium metallurgical production takes place in China. Similar figures of Chinese monopoly of various metals, in their mineral or processed form, such as the elements cobalt, lithium, manganese, tungsten, wolfram, antimony, bismuth, graphite, fluorspar and germanium, cannot be ignored in the development of military capabilities.

---

275 John Shiffman and Andrea Shalal-Esa, "Exclusive: U.S. waived laws to keep F-35 on track with China-made parts," *Reuters,* January 3, 2014. https://www.reuters.com/article/us-lockheed-f35-idUSBREA020VA20140103

276 David S. Abraham, *The Elements of Power,* 164.

In the case of the U.S., the relevance of rare earths and their Chinese dependence was already identified in 2010 by the National Defense Stockpile Center, but by 2019, almost ten years later, the situation had not changed substantially. This time it was the U.S. Congressional Research Service that recognized this dependence. It pointed out that some of its main weapon systems such as the F-35, produced in the U.S. but also exported to its allies, contain rare earths.

The rare earths used for the creation of permanent magnets (samarium, neodymium, praseodymium and dysprosium) in the defense world are today irreplaceable[277] due to their high performance. They are essential for several reasons. They make it possible to develop miniaturized electric motors of great power, resistant to high temperatures and capable of supporting remarkably high weights without any energy expenditure. Rare earths were not chosen for their abundance in the earth, but for their unrivaled performance.

Examples of missiles that are part of the American weapons spearhead are the American Patriot, Sidewinder and Tomahawk missiles, in which these metals are essential. The powerful Patriot, a surface-to-air missile with a range of 160 km and a speed of Mach 5, uses neodymium and samarium in electric motors. Its radio-frequency guidance systems require gadolinium, yttrium and samarium to magnetically control the flow of electronic signals that allow them to navigate. The SideWinder short-range, heat-seeking air-to-air missile has rare-earth magnets in its fins to control the flight path. Smart bombs, precision guided munitions, Tomahawk cruise-type, anti-ship (ASM) and surface-to-air (SAM), as well as bunker busters require dysprosium, neodymium, praseodymium, samarium and terbium.

One of the best radars in service today, the North American Aegis Spy-1, which is expected to remain in service for 35 years, has cobalt and samarium magnet components that will have to be replaced during the radar's lifetime. Future generations of some defense system components, such as radar transmitter and receiver modules, will

277 Karl A. Gschneidner, Jr., "Neodymium: Supply, Demand, Substitution, and Recycling" (Ames Laboratory, U.S. Department of Energy and Department of Materials Science and Engineering, Iowa State University), presented at *Critical Materials Flow in an Age of Constraint,* U.S. DOE's Office of Intelligence, Woodrow Wilson International Center for Scholars, Washington, D.C., May 25, 2011. https://www.wilsoncenter.org/sites/default/files/media/documents/event/gschneidner_neodynium_supply_demand_substitution_and_recycling.pdf

continue to rely on rare earth materials.[278] The U.S. in 2009, following the identified delay in the production of some weapons systems due to the lack of rare earths lanthanum, cerium, europium and gadolinium, acted accordingly by increasing its war reserves of some of these metals. Disturbingly, these reserves in other nations such as Europe are non-existent. But what is really worrying for the West is that if it ever had to use them in weapons production, it would not know how to do so. China does not just own the metal powders but its entire supply chain, including the human expertise. Thus, CEOs such as Raytheon's stated in June 2023 that it is impossible to undo dependence on China; for the time being, one can only aspire to reduce the risks.[279]

## THE METALLIC REVOLUTION

In August 2022 I was visiting the Heritage Foundation in Washington, D.C., one of the world's most prestigious security think tanks. From its location you can walk to both the Capitol and the U.S. Supreme Court, and it's not uncommon for select members to be called for consultation by any one of the numerous public institutions within a two-kilometer radius of their offices. As one of the main analysts told me during the visit, if many Western countries were to enter a conflict similar to the one in Ukraine, their stockpiles of smart weapons would not last more than a month. This calculation includes the typical guided bombs units (GBUs), a fundamental part of practically all Western fighters' armament loadouts, as well as the missiles comprising their artillery systems. Unsurprisingly, both also require rare earths.

Western news outlets regarding the war in Ukraine often claim Russia faces ammunition shortages, but the conflict is likewise devouring the artillery, air defense, and ammunition reserves of Western countries. After the fall of the Berlin Wall, NATO progressively focused increasingly on the fight against terrorism, which replaced the preparation for "classical" large-scale combat operations (LSCO). Consequently, their arsenals and defense budgets decreased, and their

278 "Rare-Earth Elements (REE)," GlobalSecurity.org, consulted on November 22, 2022. https://www.globalsecurity.org/military/world/china/rare-earth.htm

279 Sylvia Pfeifer, "We can de-risk but not decouple' from China, says Raytheon chief," *Financial Times*, June 19, 2023. https://www.ft.com/content/d0b94966-d6fa-4042-a918-37e71eb7282e

forces tailored themselves to irregular warfare. After talking to various experts, opinions vary, but roughly speaking, if China were to turn off the tap of its precious metals abruptly and completely, it would take at least a year for the military industry in many Western countries to react. That is, to manufacture the intermediate products that normally come from the Asian giant and to secure supplies from outside China. Those were just estimates, but what is a reality is that some critical materials, such as heavy rare earths, can only be purchased through China. As a result, Western combat capabilities would be compromised. As we do not replenish material, our anti-aircraft defenses will become less and less operational, the precious theatre air picture of and ability to engage targets in all weather and with reduced collateral damage will be degraded. The achievement of vital air superiority would be put in question.

The Chinese government is as aware of the potential of its rare earth weapon as its People's Liberation Army is of the current superiority of its missile program. In 2018, during an awards ceremony for China's military industry, reserve General Luo Yuan of the People's Liberation Army, made headlines with his commentary on how China could take on its biggest rival, the U.S.[280] He said:

> Historical experience tells us that America's main fear is its dead. Now we have DF-21D missiles and DF-26 missiles which are carrier killers. If we sink one of their carriers we will cause 5000 casualties, if we sink two 10000 casualties—don't you think America will be afraid? [281]

Both the latest version of the Dong-Feng 21 (DF-21D) and Dong-Feng 26 (DF-26) are anti-ship ballistic missiles (ASBM)

---

280 The Heritage Foundation, "2022 Index of U.S. Military Strength."

281 "Major General Luo's Speech at the 2018 Military Industry Awards Ceremony and Innovation Summit," Shenzhen (trans. by Sarah Kirchberger), December 20, 2018 (accessed July 23, 2021). https://www.kunlunce.com/ssjj/guojipinglun/2018-12-25/130147.html

See also J. D. Simkins, "'We'll See How Frightened America Is' – Chinese Admiral Says Sinking US Carriers Key to Dominating South China Sea," *Navy Times,* January 4, 2019 (accessed July 21, 2021). https://www.navytimes.com/news/your-navy/2019/01/04/well-see-how-frightened-america-is-chinese-admiral-says-sinking-us-carriers-key-to-dominating-south-china-sea/

capable of carrying both conventional warheads and several nuclear warheads. While the DF-21 has also become an anti-satellite and space-capable anti-missile weapon, the DF-26 has a range of more than 5,000 km and can accurately strike targets on the island of Guam from the Chinese coast. This island serves as an American stronghold located in the Pacific, 2475 km from Taiwan and approximately 3000 km from the Chinese coast. It is home to two U.S. strategic bases, one naval and one air base, which has led to the DF-26 missile being dubbed the "Guam Express" or "Guam Killer." Given the secrecy and hermeticism that surrounds all types of new weaponry, even more so if it belongs to China, it is not possible to know for certain if these missiles' components incorporate the same rare earths that are necessary for similar, albeit archaic, Western models. What is certain is that the materials incorporated in the new Chinese missiles have allowed them to modify their trajectory at speeds of Mach 10. In other words, they fly at 10 times the speed of sound, without cracking or igniting, while ensuring the reception of signals from satellites or radars. This disruptive technology requires advances in materials engineering to support and accompany software developments. Some of the uses of the numerous Chinese rare earth patents registered in recent years, the number of which dwarfs those of the rest of the world, could well be behind China's technological edge and its new weapons, such as these missiles or the even newer YJ-21 or DF-ZF.

To the astonishment of the U.S. military, the Chinese Navy successfully tested the maritime version of the DF-21, the YJ-21 hypersonic anti-ship missile, in March 2022 from an on-board vertical launcher. This makes the large Chinese Type 055 destroyers the most dangerous ships on the planet, capable of neutralizing any of the American aircraft carriers, as there is currently no defense against maneuverable hypersonic missiles.[282] What is the point of having state-of-the-art fighter planes with exorbitant prices if a hypersonic missile can destroy the platforms from which it takes off, be they airports or aircraft carriers? A prolonged war also needs a war economy to

---

282 FP Explainers, "Is the era of carrier groups over? China's DF-21D and DF-26B missiles may have ensured just that," *Firstpost,* August 2, 2022. https://www.firstpost.com/explainers/explained-is-the-era-of-carrier-groups-over-chinas-df-21d-and-df-26b-missiles-may-have-ensured-just-that-10999531.html

support it. How much does a U.S. aircraft carrier cost and how much does a hypersonic missile cost?

Another new type of weapon system, even more worrying and whose technology has no equivalent in the U.S. Army, is the DF-ZF, a hypersonic glide vehicle. Thanks to the carrier rocket that carries it into orbit, this vehicle, which includes protective countermeasures, can attack targets in flight. If necessary, it can fly over the South Pole without being detected by U.S. radar. After an orbital cruise phase outside the atmosphere, it re-enters the atmosphere at Mach 10 and before reaching the target it performs a relatively flat, gliding trajectory. Russia also has similar missiles such as the Avangard (capable of reaching an astonishing Mach 27, if the claims are true) or the Kinzhal, used in the Ukrainian war in the spring of 2022.

The most advanced and effective Western air defense systems such as the Israeli Iron Dome, are fully automated and dependent on artificial intelligence systems. They incorporate in addition to their ground-to-air interceptor missiles the latest development in the sector—the Iron Thunderbolt, a laser weapon that also intercepts rockets and missiles. However, until directed energy laser weapons are sufficiently developed, Chinese hypersonic missiles will be able to penetrate the defenses of the Israeli Iron Dome or the most advanced American carrier group. Although companies such as Lockheed Martin have already developed laser weapons such as ALADIN, Chinese hypersonic missiles seem indestructible for the time being. Moreover, none of these Chinese missiles will be intercepted by the laser weapons that equip frigates, destroyers or aircraft carriers, without the use of the rare earth metallic elements yttrium and terbium, which, being heavy rare earths, come exclusively from China.[283] Chinese rare earths fly under the radar of many Western armies. It is an "elemental" problem.

The U.S. is lagging behind in this new race to reach its goal of autonomous and intelligent lethal weaponry. Its hypersonic missiles are only now being fielded and are not fully operational. The U.S. was at a disadvantage because until 2018 it was bound by the Intermediate-Range Nuclear Forces Treaty signed with Russia in 1986, which prevented it from developing this type of weapon. On the other hand, according to Dr. Peter Leitner, Pentagon advisor on matters related

283 Russell Parman, "An elemental issue."

to the trade of strategic materials, when the Chinese government acquired the American company Magnequench, it did so to advance its development of long-range cruise missiles.[284] As is the case in many joint ventures, China will have already copied all the technology that Magnequench had and possibly developed it further for use in new, purpose-built factories. But the company that now owns Magnequench is Neo Performance Materials, and its majority shareholders have been Westerners (formerly Americans and now Australians) for more than 10 years. The U.S. also has several hypersonic missile programs under development, although they remain nascent. One of the most advanced projects is under development by the American government agency DARPA (Defense Advanced Research Project Agency), which was initially optimistically expected to equip the U.S. Air Force by the end of 2023. It is the Hypersonic Air Breathing Weapon missile manufactured by Raytheon Technologies.

Despite the difficulty in knowing the exact metallic composition of the new Chinese missiles, what is known is that the systems that send signals to guide the trajectory of the missiles are essentially either radars or satellites. These radars require, at a minimum, europium and lutetium, and the satellite networks require various rare earth elements for the coating of optical lenses and glasses, their sophisticated communication and navigation systems, thermal control systems, fiber optics, solar panels, microelectronic components, batteries, etc. Both deploy dual-use technology, which can be used for both civil and military purposes. The main constellation of Chinese military navigation satellites is Bei Dou, but there are other constellations that act as sensors and communication networks such as Gaofen, Yaogan, Jilin, Tian-lian and Hainan. The latter can identify and track ships longer than 30 meters regardless of the prevailing weather between the 30 North and 30 South parallels. The biggest technological revolution is represented by the Jilin-1 network, which will have 138 operational nanosatellites by 2030 and can search any part of the world in 10 minutes. It has the capacity to identify and track aircraft, but its main advantage is that in case they are disabled or destroyed they can be readily replaced and at a lower cost.

---

284 Richard Mills, "Rare earths in the crosshairs of new high-tech arms race," *Mining.com,* October 29, 2018. https://www.mining.com/web/rare-earths-cross-hairs-new-high-tech-arms-race/

While the U.S. defense industrial base has been consolidating into a handful of private government-subsidized macro-companies, behind the Wall, public centers such as the Chinese Academy of Military Sciences or the China Aerospace Science and Technology Corporation have infinite resources. The Beijing government is committed to everything that sounds strategic, and new weapons technology is inherently strategic. Accordingly, these programs have ample access to credit, access to personnel from the best Chinese universities or Chinese scientists trained in the best Western universities, availability of the best materials and unrestricted support from other institutions.

The disruptive capability of China's new satellites and missiles and the technological transformation of the People's Liberation Army show how critical it is to master the materials engineering that drives technology, in this case weapons technology. No less important, though, is the availability of rare earths and critical materials required to subsequently produce independently. It is a metallic revolution and a generalized mastery of the periodic table: a conceptual and physical possession. Without the physical possession of metal, the staggering growth of the Chinese navy in the last decade, which already surpasses the American navy in number of ships, would have been impossible. In the end, these are tons and tons of floating metal.

The two jewels in the American crown in terms of security are its Ballistic Missile Defense System, which is its shield, and its Prompt Global Strike, its sword. Both are an attempt by the U.S. to achieve absolute security. But that security is already only a mirage. The sword, the aircraft carrier groups, can be broken by the aforementioned DF-21, DF-26, YJ-21 and DF-ZF missiles. As for the American shield, it has been put in check by the threatening development of new weapon systems. Chief among these is the intercontinental cruise missile, the DF-41, which equips new Chinese ballistic silos, each capable of 250 missiles, located in the provinces of Gansu and Xinjiang and Inner Mongolia. It is joined by the JL-3 intercontinental missile, which will soon equip Chinese nuclear-powered submarines. Both missiles, in addition to reaching Mach 25, are maneuverable and therefore hardly detectable by satellites. With a range of between 12,000 and 15,000 km, they could reach New York in 30 minutes, and are unable to be stopped by the American anti-missile protection system.

It may well seem that the U.S. and indeed all Western militaries, despite having maintained the technological edge in military software and its applications, have fallen behind in the mastery of the periodic table and in particular have lost the technological edge in the use of metals that it does not possess in usable quantities. Today, the U.S. stockpile of critical metals for national defense is but a fraction of what it once was; its stockpile of materials is valued at less than $1 billion. Adjusted for inflation, it is less than 1/40th of its value in 1952. When the cold war ended many of these metals were sold.[285]

Western armies move with feet of clay, weakened by a lack of materials, such as rare earths, whose supply is not assured, and by a comparative backlog in materials engineering capacity that does not allow them to develop some of the capabilities already in the hands of their major competitor.

## BACK TO THE TERRIBLE TWENTIES SUPPLY/ SUPPLY CHAIN PROBLEMS

In the EU, the situation is no better than in the USA. While its Common Security and Defense Policy is still in its adolescence, a joint industrial policy[286] has fostered economies of scale. Europe presently has defense giants such as OCCAR, EADS (Airbus), Rheinmetall AG, Leonardo, Thales, Safran, Indra, etc. It has also resorted to the decentralization of its contracts. Defense companies collected their "peace dividend" and favored the "just in time" business culture[287] by reducing stockpile inventories. Strategic independence, once fundamental in Europe, was declining and military procurement was giving way to the quarterly results of companies, so eagerly awaited by investors.

---

285 Clark M., "The National Defense Stockpile Is Small but Important-And Should Be Bigger," Dec. 2022, https://www.heritage.org/defense/commentary/the-national-defense-stockpile-small-important-and-should-be-bigger#:~:text=The%20National%20Defense%20Stockpile%20is%20a%20little%2Dknown%20and%-20less,to%20continue%20playing%20this%20role.

286 This is evidenced by Directive 2009/81/EC on defense procurement and Directive 2009/43/EC on transfers of products related to the European defense market. In addition, the European Defense Agency subsequently published the Code of Conduct on Procurement and the Code of Best Practice in the Supply Chain, as well as the Code of Conduct on Offsets.

287 Government of Canada, "The Trouble with JIT in Military Operations: a Review," Jan. 2022," https://www.canada.ca/en/army/services/line-sight/articles/2022/01/the-trouble-with-jit-in-military-operations-a-review.html.

Business competitiveness was winning out over the security of the location of supply chains for national defense.

The EU's European Defense Agency published a Code of Conduct on Procurement, Offsets and Good Practices in the Supply Chain. Unfortunately, these are only guidelines for European nations, which do not entail any obligation to comply. Moreover, where states have procurement rules, companies can use Article 346 of the Treaty on the Functioning of the European Union (TFEU),[288] to exempt themselves from compliance. Let's cut to the chase: the security of European supply chains is generally in the hands of subcontractors. In most cases, there is no national legislation obliging them to assume legal responsibility in this respect.

However, control of the supply required to produce and keep weapon systems operational has proven vital in the past. Europe has already forgotten the tungsten lesson of World War II. Germany needed the metallic element wolfram (also called tungsten) during this period of war to harden its shells, artillery guns and tank armor. Wolfram mines existed in England, but curiously they belonged to Germany. Although the British were slow to react, these mines were eventually expropriated. The Allied bloc also pressured a neutral Spain into denying sales of the strategic metal to Germany, in order to weaken its capabilities. Finally, it was the U.S. purchase of Spanish wolfram from Germany itself that, together with the Allied maritime blockade, prevented German access to the precious metal. But that was not the end of the story. The war spurred Nazi ingenuity. The regime resorted to extracting wolfram present in tailings from zinc mining. These tailings, previously despised as a by-product, contained the precious tungsten. Thus, the Nazi war machine, faced with a lack of supply, had found a way to satisfy its hunger for the metal.[289]

The U.S. began after World War II to comprehensively study the accessibility of critical materials needed in wartime,[290] but by the

288 Vincenzo Randazzo, "Article 346 and the qualified application of EU law to defence," European Union Institute for Security Studies, *Brief Issue* 22, July 2014, https://www.iss.europa.eu/sites/default/files/EUISSFiles/Brief_22_Article_346.pdf

289 Leonard Caruana and Hugh Rockoff, "A Wolfram in Sheep's Clothing: Economic Warfare in Spain, 1940–1944," *The Journal of Economic History* 63(1) (March 2003), 100–126. http://www.jstor.org/stable/3132496

290 United States Congress, Senate Committee on Interior and Insular Affairs, *Stockpile and Accessibility of Strategic and Critical Materials to the United States in*

1970s had forgotten this WWII lesson. The tungsten of that time is the rare earth of today, and the same world hegemon that has made globalization possible is now forced to create a Supply Chain Disruptions Task Force[291] to reassess the security of its supply chains. The results of the study show their fragility and deterioration, in which rare earths play a highly relevant role. The situation of the EU rare earth supply chain, in which there are no binding laws either at interstate or national level, also leaves its military and by extension its security policy in a situation of great vulnerability in the face of the predicted shortage of rare earths.[292] In the case of its flagship product, permanent magnets, China produces 95% of those used in the EU.[293]

A hypothetical future projection of China's past threats or diplomatic uses of rare earths suggests that it could sanction defense companies that could directly or indirectly jeopardize its security. These could include, for example, companies selling arms to any country with which China is in conflict, which could be sanctioned with limitations, interruptions or bans on their supply of rare earths—with the threshold of sensitivity that would trigger a rare earth blockade of a given company to be set by the Chinese government. Thus, recently, in the journal *China's Modern Defense Technology*, Chinese researchers denounced the enormous military potential of SpaceX's StarLink and called for the development of capabilities to monitor this constellation of satellites in low Earth orbit, and to deactivate or destroy the network. Among other concerns, the scientists pointed out the ability of this satellite network to detect their hypersonic missiles, exponentially

---

*Time of War,* 1953. https://www.worldcat.org/title/853188335

291 The White House, "Fact Sheet: Biden-Harris Administration Announces Supply Chain Disruptions Task Force to Address Short-Term Supply Chain Discontinuities," June 8, 2021. https://www.whitehouse.gov/briefing-room/statements-releases/2021/06/08/fact-sheet-biden-harris-administration-announces-supply-chain-disruptions-task-force-to-address-short-term-supply-chain-discontinuities/

292 KU Leuven University, echoing earlier publications by the International Energy Association, quantifies between 7 and 26 times the increase in current rare earth consumption needed by 2050 to reach the EU's climate targets. "Study quantifies metal supplies needed to reach EU's climate neutrality goal," *EurekAlert!,* April 25, 2022. https://www.eurekalert.org/news-releases/949848

293 European Raw Materials Alliance (ERMA), "Ensuring access to the raw materials for the European Green Deal: A European Call for Action," September 30, 2021. https://erma.eu/european-call-for-action/

increase the data transmission of U.S. aircraft such as the F-35 and its drones. They also argued in July and October 2021 that this network had already put their satellites in danger of collision, a fact that was denounced by the Chinese government before the UN. The ban on the export and use of rare earths could be a perfect tactic to disable the StarLink satellite network, which has a history of military use, including as a means of military communication by the Ukrainian military.

The technology and associated capability to destroy satellites via missiles is only available to a handful of major powers (USA, China, India, and Russia) and its use is highly controversial. After destroying a satellite, the space debris generated puts a large number of other satellites at risk, as not all the debris re-enters the atmosphere. A ban on the export of rare earths to StarLink would lead in the medium term to the disabling of this or other satellite networks. It would be an action within the so-called gray zone, since it does not imply the use of force and as such would avoid an escalation towards a conventional military confrontation.

Some European vulnerabilities, in this case only theoretical, could include the French company Dassault Aviation[294] and the European company Airbus,[295] which have sold both Rafale fighter and transport aircraft (A400M and C295) to India and Indonesia, respectively. In some cases, these agreements involve not only the sale but also a certain transfer of technology, since in the final stages of the sales programs the aircraft are produced in the buyer country.

These theoretical examples are not at all far-fetched if we look at the growing geopolitical tensions in the Indo-Pacific region. China has been engaged in a border dispute with India for years. It also actively claims, through its fishing militia, part of Indonesia's Exclusive Economic Zone in the Natuna Sea, and in late 2019 an incident escalated into military action.[296] Just as China threatened sanctions by

---

294 "Dassault welcomes India's purchase of 36 Rafale" and "Indonesia buys Rafale" (accessed April 25, 2022). https://www.dassault-aviation.com/

295 "India formalizes purchase of 56 Airbus C295 aircraft" and " Indonesian Defense Ministry orders two Airbus A400Ms," 2021 (accessed April 25, 2022). https://www.airbus.com/

296 Evan A. Laksmana, "Indonesia's response to China's incursions in North Natuna Sea unsatisfactory: Indonesian," *ThinkChina,* December 10, 2021. https://www.thinkchina.sg/indonesias-response-chinas-incursions-north-natuna-sea-unsatisfactory-indonesian-academic

cutting off the supply of rare earths to U.S. companies on national security grounds, it could also target sanctions against Dassault and thus France for selling armaments to countries that threaten its security or national interests. Obviously, this example could be extended to other European weapon system manufacturers, such as the frigate manufacturers that have a growing presence in the Indo-Pacific and are expected to increase.[297]

Many modern frigates incorporate a total of more than 1.5 tons of rare earths, but the case of the French Rafale fighter is particularly significant as this aircraft can carry nuclear weapons. If this aircraft were to be rendered inoperable for lack of rare earth-based components something as crucial to France as its nuclear deterrent capability would be decimated. But the EU and its defense companies such as Dassault, manufacturer of the Rafale, are no exception.

Just as this scenario in the Indo-Pacific Region is feasible, another plausible scenario is to imagine that China would support Russia via armaments in the Ukraine conflict. If Western countries were then to initiate sanctions against China,[298] these could be met with retaliatory measures such as a limitation on exports of Chinese rare earths.

As geopolitical tensions increase, the EU, Japan and Australia appear to be becoming more aligned with U.S. foreign and security policy, and the so far limited sanctions exchanges with China, mainly over claims of mistreatment of the Uyghur minority, could spread to other areas, such as rare earths and the defense sector. The dependence of the Western defense sector on Chinese rare earths along the supply chain is a bitter barrier to our strategic autonomy, technological sovereignty and may limit our ability to react and sustainability of operations.

So far, the European Union's measures to try to secure the supply of rare earths have always been of a civil-industrial nature.

---

297 This is provided for in the "EU Strategy for Cooperation in the Indo-Pacific," published in April 2021. It states the EU's intention to ". . . cooperate with the navies of its partners, and develop their capabilities where appropriate, to establish global surveillance in the interests of maritime security and freedom of navigation, in accordance with international law . . . ."

298 Jennifer Rankinin and Vincent Ni, "EU leaders urged to be tough on China if it backs Russia in Ukraine," *The Guardian,* March 31, 2022. https://www.theguardian.com/world/2022/mar/31/eu-leaders-urged-to-be-tough-on-china-if-it-supports-russia-war-in-ukraine

No one is guaranteeing the supply of rare earths to major European arms manufacturers. No Western defense company is going to operate at a loss voluntarily to secure either our independence from China or the required war reserves for our armies. However, the EU could emulate its American big brother and act according to its Common Security and Defense Policy. The Defense Fund or programs such as the Permanent Structured Cooperation should promote the self-supply of critical materials for defense.

The necessary minerals are to be found on European soil. Opening new European mines such as those identified by the EURARE body in Europe[299] is an option, but perhaps the time has come to review history and imitate the Germans, when at the end of World War II, they resorted to bargain-hunting in their mines to recover wolfram. Many European mines contain rare earths as by-products which can likewise be extracted.

As indicated above, the USA has already gotten down to work, funding a pilot project in 2022 with 140 million euros through the Bipartisan Infrastructure Law (BIL) to pursue the recovery of rare earth elements from coal ash and other mining by-products. This initiative will also create jobs in the Appalachia region of the United States, where the coal industry was threatened with closure. The closure has been cancelled, with other mining by-products possibly also to be used. The old, abandoned iron mines near New York City contain fluorapatite ore in their remnants that is richer in heavy rare earths than even coal ash.

This same U.S. infrastructure law also allocates three billion euros to the recycling of rare metals. Governmental support is the only way for such projects to proceed. For the rare earth recycling process to be profitable it must be done on a large scale, with a high degree of automation, provide a final product equivalent to the original and be a less polluting process than usual production. Rare earth recycling is already a reality and has been applied by Western companies such as Neo Performance Materials, Fraunhofer, Germany's Siemens Energy and Geomega. The largest source of materials for recycling comes from wind turbines used to generate power, especially offshore wind

---

299 EURare, "Location of REE occurrences and deposits in Europe" (accessed April 25, 2021). http://www.eurare.org/countries/reemap.html

turbines. Each of these turbines contains more than 500 kg of neodymium, making recycling easier and more cost-effective.[300]

In China, supported by large state programs, 20% of rare earths are recycled.[301] Exceeding this figure, according to many experts, seems difficult. But to secure supply, if there is insufficient supply of minerals, the West will have no choice but to increase the recycling of rare earths and to resort to substitution as far as possible. On the other hand, despite the positive aspects of these initiatives, they require years to become operational. This period constitutes a window of opportunity for China which, aware of the West's weaknesses, could use them to challenge the West and achieve its objectives. Taiwan, the Senkaku Islands and the exclusive economic zone in the China Sea, the Spratly Islands (claimed from the Philippines) may be at stake, but also the North Pole, the exploitation of the ocean floor or the moon, in this critical period characterized by Western strategic insolvency. Not without reason, this decade has already been dubbed by many defense analysts as "the terrible twenties " due to supply and supply chain problems.[302]

300 Shayan Khakmardan and Raoul Schmitt, *Recycling Processes for the Recovery of Rare-Earth Magnets of Wind Turbines,* April 2020, https://www.researchgate.net/publication/347033394_Recycling_Processes_for_the_Recovery_of_Rare-Earth_Magnets_of_Wind_Turbines

301 "China's Ganzhou to launch RE waste recycling projects," *Argusmedia,* April 12, 2021. https://www.argusmedia.com/en/news/2204285-chinas-ganzhou-to-launch-re-waste-recycling-projects

302 Mackenzie Eaglen with Hallie Coyne, *The 2020s Tri-Service Modernization Crunch* (Washington: American Enterprise Institute for Public Policy Research, March 2021), 1. https://www.aei.org/wp-content/uploads/2021/03/The-2020s-Tri-Service-Modernization-Crunch-1.pdf

# 9. THE FIRST BATTLES

## THE NATURAL RESOURCES CURSE

In his ship's logbook, Christopher Columbus mentioned the word gold 139 times and the word God 51 times. The Spanish adventurers set sail in the 16th century for the New World after having sold their properties to finance their voyage. A Franciscan, Benedictine or Jesuit priest would bless them and set sail with them, justifying the holy enterprise of Catholicizing and expropriating the natives by bringing them salvation and eternal life. The Spanish adventurers always carried two things with them, a bible and a weapon. Their hearts harbored both courage and ambition and for most of them the possibility of making a fortune accompanied the work of evangelization.

In the same way, our companies are today setting off in search of the minerals that will bring us clean and eternal energy from the wind and the sun, invoking the holy fight against climate change and the holy name of energy transition. This time the narrative tells us that this energy will mean the end of wars for resources; renewable energies are unlimited and will offer nations independence from each other.

But just as Spanish soldiers decimated indigenous populations in South America with their diseases and skirmishes, mining companies and governments that directly or indirectly operate their mines in Africa and other developing countries also sometimes sow destruction of ecosystems and harm local populations. Just as Spanish soldiers took gold and silver from South America, which then served the Spanish crown to finance its wars in Europe, mining companies are today taking rare earths and critical minerals to carry out the energy transition in Western countries and in China. Then as now, mineral resources are sometimes a source of misfortune, from paradoxical impoverishment to the emergence of conflicts. The resource curse is a situation in which, despite their abundance of non-renewable natural resources, some countries go on to experience stagnant economic growth or even economic contraction, often due to external forces.[303] This curse is currently affecting some countries in Africa, Southeast Asia and South America. In turn, faced with shortages of critical minerals, governments and companies compete to secure the supply of rare earths. This competition has historically sometimes led to struggles and conflicts, as in the case of South American gold and silver in the 16th and 17th century, Southeast Asian spices, or Peruvian guano in the 19th century, which, when used as a fertilizer revolutionized agriculture in Europe. More recent examples include minerals such as coltan from the Congo, from which the silvery tantalum metal so necessary for electronic components is obtained, blood diamonds from Sierra Leone or Kuwaiti oil.

Even in the case of Ukraine's invasion it is difficult to discern to what extent its resources play an important role in the conflict. According to a recent assessment by SecDev, an Ottawa-based research and analysis group, Ukraine has the potential to become a "critical minerals superpower." Not only does it rank fourth globally in terms of total natural resource value, but it is believed to have the largest amount of recoverable rare earth resources in Europe, rivaling those recently announced by Turkiye. Of the list of thirty critical elements defined by the EU, 21 are available on Ukrainian soil. Thus, in July 2021 the EU invited Kiev to join its Critical Raw Materials Alliance and its Industrial Alliance on Batteries. The Vice-President of the European Commission justified this new alliance by arguing that when Russia finishes building the Nord Stream 2 gas pipeline to Germany, Kiev would lose revenue by decreasing gas transit through its territory and the sale of minerals could compensate as a new source of revenue to Ukraine.

The Donbas region is rich in coal that has fueled its steel plants and smelters for nearly a century and the Dnieper-Donetsk region is home to approximately 80% of Ukraine's oil, natural gas and coal production reserves. Furthermore, shortly before the invasion, Shell Oil Co. and Chevron Corp were applying for exploration of gas deposits, as a preliminary to exploitation in the contested Black Sea. In its waters, Ukraine is believed to have the second largest natural

---

303 Ekmen P., "From Riches to Rags: The Paradox of Plenty and its Linkage to Violent Conflict" *Goettingen Journal of International Law* 3 (2011) 1, 473–493.

gas deposits in Europe, estimated at 1.2 trillion cubic meters of proven reserves, and possibly as much as 5.4 trillion cubic meters.

From ancient times to the present day, resource conflicts, both intrastate and international, have been fueled by the scarcity of critical and strategic materials. A strong unsatisfied demand and a pressing thirst for the resource leads to a struggle to obtain it. Today, in the case of rare earths, and some rare metals, the reasoning remains the same. This time it is electrification as a means of transport for the world's growing energy production and the automobile, both based on critical materials, which are in increasing demand. As so often in the past, scarcity fuels competition for their procurement, invoking the emergence of conflicts.

Although inter-state conflicts between major players cannot be ruled out, humanity has not witnessed a conflict between two nuclear powers since World War II.[304] Given the Ukraine conflict's outbreak is shadowed by the prospect of superpower nuclear confrontation,[305] the most likely option is that an escalation of tension[306] would be channeled in the form of conflict taking place in third countries, possessors of the resource. In other words, in the form of proxy wars.

This concerns more than just the current conflict in Ukraine. Elsewhere, two or more powers could thus confront each other indirectly, outside their borders in other scenarios. They would do so through state actors and/or armed non-state groups, financing, selling armaments and training powers and factions who favor their interests.[307] The same "curse" that fell on oil and gas rich countries like Kuwait, for example, could now be transferred to Burundi, Zambia, Tanzania, Namibia, Brazil, Madagascar, Malawi, or Myanmar for having mines that can exploit rare earths, or uranium in the case of Niger.[308] In fact, heavy rare earths have already been used as con-

---

304 The countries with nuclear arsenals that have come closest in recent years to a traditional armed conflict have been India and Pakistan, but the conflict has never reached those proportions.

305 Andrew Mumford, "Proxy Warfare and the Future of Conflict," *RUSI Journal* 158, no. 2 (April 2013): 40–46. https://www.tandfonline.com/doi/full/10.1080/03071847.2013.787733

306 Dominic Tierney. "The Future of Sino-U.S. Proxy War," *Texas National Security Review* 4, no. 2 (Spring 2021). https://tnsr.org/wp-content/uploads/2021/03/TNSR-Vol-4-Issue-2-Tierney.pdf

307 Andrew Mumford, "Proxy Warfare."

308 Samuel Obedgiu, "Niger: Will Rare-Earth minerals increase Africa's

flict-enhancing minerals. Myanmar and Burundi are showing early pre-conflict stages that may be related to rare earths.

Given the large, unsecured investments required to open new rare earth mines, the environmental constraints and the average time required of more than ten years, the growing demand for rare earths encourages the more intensive exploitation of existing mines. The same applies to the processing and transformation centers already in operation both inside and outside China, which are being expanded. In other words, existing supply chains will become the main arteries of market supply. Even if new ones are progressively developed or new mining projects such as those in Australia, Brazil, Burundi, Canada, Malawi, Russia, Tanzania, and Uganda are completed, they are not scheduled for completion until 2027[309] and it is not clear whether their production will be sufficient.

In the meantime, we will witness the competition between various players who populate the rare earth "arena" sands, vying to obtain precious resources: miners, automobile manufacturers, arms industries, advanced technology producers or clean energy developers. Inextricably linked to these are their governments, trying to negotiate for them a favorable position in the world economy by an assortment of means. The implications of these companies' activities as they relate to the security of their citizens are not lost on many. Many of these nations therefore make maximum use of their economies as an instrument of power, to such an extent that their use may correspond to the very early, pre-conflict phases. The best example is China's Belt and Road Initiative, renamed as the Global Development Initiative. Behind this seemingly win-win initiative,[310] China is trying to obtain international priority in the supply of minerals or raw materials[311] by controlling many critical infrastructures in other countries. Behind a

---

geo-political bargain power in the world," *Idrakpost,* August 18, 2023. https://www.idrakpost.com/en/d/203/niger-will-rare-earth-minerals-increase-africa%E2%80%99s-geo-political-bargain-power-in-the-world

309 Richard Roy Blake, *The Rare Earth Crisis,* 155.

310 United Nations, "Global Development Initiative's Work Addresses Common Challenges, Helps Achieve Sustainable Development Goals, Secretary-General Tells Ministerial Meeting," September 20, 2022. https://press.un.org/en/2022/sgsm21470.doc.htm

311 Laura-Anca Parepa, "The Belt and Road Initiative as continuity in Chinese foreign policy," Journal of Contemporary East Asia Studies 9, no. 2 (November 2020): 175–201. https://www.tandfonline.com/doi/full/10.1080/24761028.2020.1848370

harmless trade there is always the Chinese flag and its national geopolitical interests included in the framework of its security strategy.[312]

The Beijing government doesn't mind losing money as they venture into Africa, unlike Western companies. Chinese companies have been investing in the production and extraction of African rare earths. Some examples are the Baluba mine in Zambia or the Gakara mine in Burundi. Over the past decade and a half, China has been very active in obtaining exclusive mining rights in African countries. Many of these have been accompanied by large-scale infrastructure projects carried out by the Beijing government. Deals have been struck, for example, in the Democratic Republic of Congo and Kenya, where China has agreed to provide $666 million for a data center and a highway.[313] The Chinese muscle behind the development of this new Silk Road is some of the 97 Chinese state-owned macro-enterprises, managed by the Beijing government, in particular by its State-owned Assets Supervision and Administration Commission. One of those directly involved in the extraction and processing of rare earths is, for example, the company Shenghe Resources, very active outside China's borders and with footprints in Singapore, Vietnam, the USA and Greenland.

President Biden and the G7 leaders have hit back with the creation of the Build Back Better World (B3W) initiative, which aims to be an alternative to China's Belt and Road Initiative, promoting sustainable growth and curbing, of course, climate change. It seeks to boost green economic recovery and the creation of resilient supply chains for critical materials is a priority. However, America needs the support of its European partners, given its projection on the African continent, especially towards its extractive sector. As the Atlantic Council (NATO's main decision-making body) points out, African countries are becoming decisive terrain, key to securing critical supply chains.[314]

---

312 Asia Society Policy Institute, "Weaponizing the Belt and Road Initiative," September 8, 2020. https://asiasociety.org/policy-institute/weaponizing-belt-and-road-initiative

313 "How Rare-Earth Mining Has Devastated China's Environment," *Earth.org,* July 14, 2020. https://earth.org/rare-earth-mining-has-devastated-chinas-environment/

314 Marianne Schneider-Petsinger and Patrick Schroeder, "To build back better, the US must reach out across the Atlantic," *The Hill,* July 1, 2021. https://www.msn.com/en-us/news/politics/

Emerging nations with production of rare earths and other critical materials are caught between China's monopoly and the supply needs of Western countries. Some large companies in the latter are already showing signs of not being willing to wait for their governments to react. Companies such as Volkswagen are (unsuccessfully) trying to take over the best lithium mining projects in South America, such as the one belonging to Neo Lithium in Argentina acquired by China in May 2022.[315] Tesla resorts to buying some critical minerals from companies facing legal charges and actually convicted for sourcing minerals illegally like Glencore or fleeing from other resources like rare earths by recently announcing the manufacture of its new motors dispensing with them.

Bolivian lithium is a case in point in this struggle for strategic mineral resources: According to some media Elon Musk was directly accused by Evo Morales in 2020 of backing the coup to gain access to Bolivian lithium. Subsequently when a Bolivian election replaced the coup government, China´s state enterprises were the new government's preferred choice.

Germany was the first to arrive but not the first to be served. The Bolivian state company Yacimientos de Litio Bolivianos (YLB) YLB and Germany's ACI Systems agreed in October 2019 to set up a joint venture to exploit lithium from Bolivia, with the main product to be lithium-ion batteries but the agreement was cancelled. Finally, in 2023, Bolivia's Luis Arce government signed a $1 billion agreement with three Chinese state firms CATL, BRUNP, and CMOC (CBC) and the Bolivian YLB to explore lithium deposits in the South American nation.[316] In some other states the sellers of these critical minerals are armed non-state actors (ANSAs) who, taking advantage of low governance, seize resources and leverage them to finance themselves.

While I was attending the General Staff course at the German Bundeswehr Leadership Academy, I had the good fortune to meet numerous student officers from African countries. One student, a Malian army commander who prefers to remain anonymous, told

315 Zijin Mining, "Zijin Mining Completes Acquisition of Neo Lithium," February 5, 2022. https://www.zijinmining.com/news/news-detail-119227.htm

316 Joseph Bouchard, "In Bolivia, China Signs Deal For World's Largest Lithium Reserves," *The Diplomat,* February 10, 2023, https://thediplomat.com/2023/02/in-bolivia-china-signs-deal-for-worlds-largest-lithium-reserves/

me how illegal mining works in his country and how these ANSAs operate. He related that, "In the area of Gao and Kigali, in the north of the country, the Tuareg tribes dominate the mining rights. Their labor force is often migrants passing through on their way to Europe or sometimes local workers." With an air of desperation, he stated that, "The area is out of control, the Tuareg insurgent groups ally themselves with terrorist groups that change their names and in turn integrate with new ones that appear in the area." He mentions the names of some of them, "Islamic State of Grand Sahara (ISGS), Jama'at Nusrat al-Islam wal-Muslimin (JNIM), which changed its name to become Al Qaeda in the Maghreb, " and then adds that "they divide the territory." According to this officer, their main sources of financing are lithium, uranium, gold and bauxite, which is then sold not only to the Chinese, but also to Americans. It first passes through the hands of several traders and then through South African or Canadian front companies that make the traffic legal. With a smile full of resignation he concludes, "I am sure that in your countries, nobody knows where the lithium in your car battery or the uranium in the nuclear power plants comes from, nor who extracted it and how they extracted it."

These pro-independence and terrorist groups will now have to deal with the feared Wagner group, which, representing the interests of Russia, has replaced the French army in Mali and in some other Sahel countries as Sudan and the Central African Republic for instance. The Bamako government, after a couple of failed coup attempts, has decided to replace the traditional guarantor of its security with this infamous PMC (private military company). Russia gets direct access to Mali's resources, as they are not all controlled by illegal mining. In this case, France has taken a step back and avoided entering a veiled conflict with Russia over resources.

Proxy wars, delegating the fight to ANSA groups, have today become a substitute for classic military operations. They are used to achieving objectives without suffering many of the disadvantages of conventional wars, such as the high number of casualties, the high exposure to public opinion, the escalation of conflicts between nuclear powers or even the high costs.[317] Sometimes the indirect action in these proxy conflicts consists of supplying weapons, personnel or economic

317 Dominic Tierney. "The Future of Sino-U.S. Proxy War."

funding to both government forces and ANSAs. The objectives of these proxy wars may include political regime change in a state. The new government will know how to return the favor in the form of commercial advantages or ideological alignment, allowing supporting nations favored access to resources[318] such as rare earths.

Despite its ostensible historical policy of non-interventionism, China is actively involved in protecting its external interests. Beijing is not left out of this current trend and has resorted in recent years to the use of up to twenty different international PMCs in countries such as Iraq, Sudan, or Pakistan.[319] If necessary, it also uses its own troops, as in 2007 when China deployed 4,500 soldiers in Nigeria to protect its oil assets.[320] At the same time, China has developed a more interventionist policy in some regions, such as sub-Saharan Africa.[321] Not only has it greatly increased its investments in this region, but it has also increased its diplomatic and military presence.[322]

Indeed, competition for precious resources such as rare earths are likely to turn into proxy wars and the best breeding grounds for same are countries with low levels of governance. The attempt to secure the supply of rare earths needed to meet future demand may pit China against the U.S. Similar to China, the U.S. government has also shown interest in participating in established mining companies on an African continent, which is in the midst of a mining frenzy for rare earths and other critical materials.[323] The Wagner Group's growing presence in Africa could be followed by other PMCs and its activity could become an endemic evil on this continent. As my Malian colleague pointed

---

318 Tony Allan, "Avoiding war over natural resources," International Committee of the Red Cross, January 11, 1998. https://www.icrc.org/en/doc/resources/documents/misc/57jpl4.htm

319 Frank Hoffman and Andrew Orner, "The Return of Great-Power Proxy Wars," *War on the Rocks*, September 2, 2021. https://warontherocks.com/2021/09/the-return-of-great-power-proxy-wars/

320 JoAnne Wagner, "'Going Out': Is China's Skilful Use of Soft Power in Sub-Saharan Africa a Threat to US Interests?," *Joint Forces Quarterly* 64, no. 1 (2012): 101.

321 Mark O. Yeisley, "Bipolarity, Proxy Wars, and the Rise of China," *Strategic Studies Quarterly* 5, no. 4 (Winter 2011): 75–91.

322 Sam LaGrone, "AFRICOM: Chinese Naval Base in Africa Set to Support Aircraft Carriers," *USNI News*, April 20, 2021. https://news.usni.org/2021/04/20/africom-chinese-naval-base-in-africa-set-to-support-aircraft-carriers

323 Farhana Bashir, "Rare Earth Deposits in Africa," *Eventackle Intelligence*, April 20, 2021. https://intelligence.eventackle.com/rare-earth-deposits-in-africa/

out to me, "My opinion is that with mercenary groups like the Wagner Group, things can get complicated; they may want to keep part of the mines or their rights." He added, "They become a kind of covert shareholder of the mining companies and want their dividends to be part of the minerals extracted." He continued his reflection by saying that "The population continues to not take advantage of our resources and, these military companies may be interested in the continuation of conflicts to justify their presence and ensure their contracts. In the long run they may even take power away from the government." Despite the first-hand knowledge in this officer's words, the truth is that the trend of using these groups continues to grow, including in Mali.[324] Sometimes they may even end up at each other's throats. This was attested to during the Syrian conflict by the confrontation between U.S. Blackwater paramilitaries and Russian paramilitaries of the Wagner Group. The skirmish did not lead to any political or military escalation; it would not be surprising if the pattern were repeated. It is not unimaginable to see clashes between security companies such as the U.S. Blackwater and the Chinese-contracted Frontier Services Group. Both companies would seek to defend their respective interests related to rare earths or other critical materials at any point along the Belt and Road Initiative. Proof of the lack of morality and that these companies and their personnel go "wherever the money takes them" is that the CEO of the new PMC Frontier Services Group is none other than the former CEO of Blackwater, Mr. Erik Prince.

## GREAT GREEN POWERS AND CURSED COUNTRIES IN THE NEW "GAME OF STONES"

Rising natural resource prices for countries with weak governance can become a source of instability leading to conflict. The "resource curse" in its most extreme form has already hit the Democratic Republic of Congo (DRC). A sharp rise in global demand for batteries increased the value of the mineral coltan. The increase in the price of these resources makes them a target for the greed of the various armed groups who use their sale to resupply themselves

324 Jared Thompson, Catrina Doxsee, and Joseph S. Bermudez Jr., "Tracking the Arrival of Russia's Wagner Group in Mali," Center for Strategic & International Studies, February 2, 2022. https://www.csis.org/analysis/tracking-arrival-russias-wagner-group-mali

with weapons and to further intensify their struggle. During the "World War of Africa" (1998–2003), with its epicenter in the Congo, seven countries of the so-called Great Lakes Region were involved, resulting in four million people killed. These figures make it the most devastating conflict in terms of casualties since World War II, with more dead than the Afghanistan, Korean and Vietnam wars combined. The mineral resources that were plundered, especially in the east of the country, played a major role in the conflict, along with the convergence of national and international economic interests, channeled by political elites, military, businessmen, rebel leaders and government administrators.[325]

The situation is in danger of repeating itself. According to estimates by the International Energy Agency, the market for green metals will increase sevenfold between now and 2050. Historically, this increase in demand for materials used for energy purposes is unparalleled, although it is reminiscent of the global race for hydrocarbons. Between 1940 and 1970, the demand for hydrocarbons as a source of energy in rich countries rose from 20% of energy supply to 70%. At the global level, the production of barrels of oil increased by almost 2.5 times, rising in 30 years from four billion barrels per day in 1940 to almost 10 billion barrels per day in 1970.[326] However, in the case of the metals needed for the energy transition, heralded as the fuel of the future, the increase would be almost three times greater. The energy transition entails a raw materials transition that will either empower or doom countries with mines and reserves of this new "green gold."

According to U.S. Geological Survey agency (USGS) data, there are currently only fifteen rare earth producing countries. Despite the existence of other projects, they still do not have open quarries. This center also points out that, among the current green giants with the highest global profits from the exploitation of cobalt, copper, aluminum, lithium, nickel, and silver are China, Australia, Chile, Russia, Brazil, Indonesia, Peru, the Philippines, and Mexico. These countries stand to benefit greatly from an energy transition towards

---

325 Sara Nordbrand and Petter Bolme, *Powering the Mobile World: Cobalt production for batteries in the DR Congo and Zambia* (SwedWatch, November 2007): 26. https://www.germanwatch.org/sites/default/files/press_release/2269.pdf

326 Elliott Gue, "The Supply Side of Oil," *Seeking Alpha,* July 15, 2012, https://seekingalpha.com/article/721841-the-supply-side-of-oil

renewable energies. Controlling materials is the key to controlling industrial sectors such as the automobile industry. But it is not only the economic benefit that will increase the geopolitical relevance of these countries, but also the strategic possession of metals on which humanity is relying to enable the fight against climate change and its own energy security. These metals will give them, as happened with Qatar or Saudi Arabia in the past concerning oil, a leverage point in their negotiations and role at the international level. Rare earths will give countries whose territories encompass such reserves an increasing geopolitical relevance. This relevance will be supported not only by the high value represented by the trade of all the finished products containing them, but above all by their criticality and strategic value.

By 2040, *The Economist* estimates, there will be more than ten autocratic countries in the world deriving more than 20% of their income from raw materials and more than 20 autocracies with more than 10%.[327] According to the World Bank's website,[328] among the fifteen countries with already open rare earth reserves, four of them (Burundi, Madagascar, Myanmar and Tanzania) do not score 50% in terms of governance. As metal prices rise some companies are venturing into territories where they would not normally tread.

These countries could follow the drift of Nigeria, a country politically destabilized for many years by the growing exploitation of a new resource. The black gold rush brought insecurity to a poor country along with its newfound colonial independence. Although in the 1960s it exported a multitude of commodities from cocoa to tin, two decades later, 97% of its exports were oil. But the new source of income was accompanied by political chaos and the total destruction of the Niger Delta ecosystem. It is not surprising that centers such as the Organization for Economic Cooperation and Development in Europe foresee that countries rich in tungsten, tantalum, tin and gold could become victims of resource conflicts. Some of the countries richest in these resources are located in the Great Lakes region.[329] These

327 Paris Kolwezi and San Pedro de Atacama, "The transition to clean energy will mint new commodity superpowers," *The Economist*, March 26, 2022. https://www.economist.com/finance-and-economics/2022/03/26/the-transition-to-clean-energy-will-mint-new-commodity-superpowers

328 The World Bank, Worldwide Governance Indicators (2020) (accessed Nov. 2021). https://databank.worldbank.org/source/worldwide-governance-indicators

329 OECD, *OECD Due Diligence Guidance for Responsible Supply Chains*

lakes bathe the territories of Tanzania, Uganda, Rwanda, Congo, and Burundi, where the richest deposits of rare earths on the face of the earth are supposedly located.

## RARE EARTHS FORETELL BLOODSHED IN AFRICA: THE CASE OF BURUNDI

Burundi, the poorest country in the world and the only one to have left the International Criminal Court, is not exactly a haven of peace. A coup d'état in 1993, the inadequacy of its physical and governmental structures to accommodate international displaced persons from other neighboring countries, widespread poverty and unequal access to land make it more of a ticking time bomb.[330] The wealth contained in this highly unstable country's rare earth mine can easily trigger a resource war. I have not personally been to Burundi, but I have spent almost half a year in the nearby countries of Uganda and Djibouti. In a country where policemen are paid $15 a month, every time an opportunity for money presents itself, legality goes out the window.

Until the discovery of rare earths, Burundi did not have many resources with which to boost its economy, other than some gold it sold to China and the United Arab Emirates. Yet instability had already manifested itself. The 1993 conflict demonstrates the lack of security in Burundi's recent history, leaving approximately 300,000 dead, 800,000 exiled or displaced to neighboring countries, and 700,000 internally displaced persons.[331] History shows that elections are also often fraught with danger in Burundi and can lead to conflict, as happened in 2015.[332]

The thesis that rare earths may eventually trigger internal conflict in Burundi is reinforced by the historical link between minerals and

*of Minerals from Conflict-Affected and High-Risk Areas: Second Edition* (OECD Publishing, 2013). http://dx.doi.org/10.1787/9789264185050-en

330 Jeremy Lind and Kathryn Sturman, *Scarcity and Surfeit: The Ecology of Africa's Conflicts* (Pretoria: Institute of Security Studies, 2002), 179. https://library.au.int/scarcity-and-surfeit-ecology-africas-conflict-3

331 Juana Brachet and Howard Wolpe, *Conflict-Sensitive Development Assistance: The Case of Burundi,* Social Development Papers, Conflict Prevention & Reconstruction, Paper No. 27 (The World Bank, June 2005): 9. https://www.accord.org.za/conflict-trends/conflict-great-lakes-region/

332 Juana Brachet and Howard Wolpe, *Conflict-Sensitive Development Assistance,* 13.

conflict in the Great Lakes region. The background goes back to the struggle over Congolese coltan, from which the metallic element tantalum, classified as a conflict mineral, is extracted. Insofar as newly independent African states did not change their colonial borders which had imposed divisions on ethnic groups, the transnational ethnic factor means that, in the absence of effective border control between states, the ethnic groups involved can readily cross borders when a conflict occurs. Their own ethnic group may provide them with refuge, weapons or even financing from the neighboring country. This support is mainly obtained from the exploitation of mineral resources through mining and illegal trafficking. And, ultimately, it can serve to finance any kind of conflict in the area. The presence of these refugees is itself a source of instability, even for their own ethnic group and for the region of the neighboring country, where competition for resources increases.[333] Proof of this is the Hutu and Tutsi groups, parts of Burundi's social structure which were directly involved in the conflicts in eastern DRC between 1996 and 2003.[334] Both parties to the conflict were able to recruit fighters from their ethnic groups in Rwanda and Burundi, resulting in a regionalization of the conflict.[335]

Some countries try to discourage the search for minerals in these areas through their national legislation that dictates the limits their companies must not cross when operating in or receiving minerals from other countries. Two fundamental problems render many of these laws ineffective: First, as explained in the later chapter entitled New Laws, many of these laws lack clear penal consequences for non-compliance. The second problem is the difficulties in the traceability in the supply chain, from the extraction of many minerals mined in developing countries through intermediate stages until it reaches a company that integrates the metals into an initial or final product. In many developing countries, most mines are not legally registered and are not regularly inspected by the competent state authorities. Subsequently, after the ore has been extracted, refined or not, numerous intermediaries,

333 ACCORD, "Conflict in the Great Lakes Region," May 5, 2016. https://www.accord.org.za/conflict-trends/conflict-great-lakes-region/

334 ACCORD, "Conflict in the Great Lakes Region."

335 Herbert Weiss, *War and Peace in the Democratic Republic of the Congo,* Current African Issues No. 22 (Nordiska Afrikainstitutet, 2000). https://www.files.ethz.ch/isn/105528/22.pdf

sometimes located in different countries, are part of the chain of sale of the ore, which makes it easy for the supplying companies to claim that these minerals come from places through which, in reality, the ore is simply passing through. Let us imagine that the uranium from Niger is sold through several intermediaries until it reaches Senegal. Company X buys it there, assuring afterwards in the documentation that the origin of the mineral is Senegal, as assured by its Senegalese provider.

The most disturbing issue is that if the legislation of some countries is effective in preventing the purchase of minerals from conflict zones, or minerals extracted through the work of enslaved children, their legislation is in fact blocking its national enterprises and leaving the door open for competitors from other countries that are not subject to similar norms. In other words, their legislation eliminates their companies as global competitors and favors those of their opponents. In this globalized world, the power vacuums left by some countries are filled by others.

The consequences of not enforcing laws on a global scale becomes even more evident when the country that bans the purchase of conflict minerals ends up buying finished products containing them without knowing its content or without asking where the raw materials they are made from come from.[336]

The cobalt also mined near Burundi has striking similarities to the rare earths dilemma. In terms of control of metal production, for example, China manufactures more than 80% of the world's cobalt metal,[337] used in batteries and electronics. In order to supply itself, China tries to displace Western companies and buyers in Africa. In the case of cobalt this fact is more easily observable, as 80% of cobalt originates from the Democratic Republic of Congo, where, via the Chinese embassy, the creation of an association of thirty-five companies dedicated to the exploitation of this metal has been promoted.[338]

336 Heidi Vella, "Inside China's move to monopolise cobalt," Mining Technology, June 4, 2018. https://www.mining-technology.com/features/inside-chinas-move-monopolise-cobalt/

337 Chang Che, "China is becoming the world's battery factory," *The China Project,* March 30, 2021. https://supchina.com/2021/03/30/china-is-becoming-the-worlds-battery-factory/

338 Statista, "Major countries in worldwide cobalt mine production" (accessed November 2021). https://www.statista.com/statistics/264928/cobalt-mine-

China captures, thanks to cobalt and other elements, the market for electric batteries. Its giant production companies, such as CATL, which are also subsidized by the Chinese government, are proof of this. Beijing thus captures the supply chain associated with batteries and other technological components that use cobalt.

Since 2018, despite the huge production of its domestic mines, China has become a net importer of rare earths. China scours every corner of the globe greedily trying to get its hands on rare earth minerals,[339] and Burundi, in the Great Lakes region, is home to one of the world's largest deposits of rare earths.

The race to grab rare earths at Rainbow Rare Earths' Gakara project in western Burundi has begun. Malta-based investment company TechMet has funded a rare earths separation facility worth $3 million. The British company, majority owner of the mine, claims it is the world's highest-grade source of rare earths; its concentrates could contain 67% of a cocktail of these elements;[340] 10% of the mine is still owned by the Burundi government, and seven other companies of British, Chinese and Russian origin also have an unspecified share of the project. But work on the mine is currently on hold. The Burundian government does not want to let its rare earths go without making the most of them and has not had the final word. A renegotiation of the concession agreements for the exploitation of the mine is underway.[341]

Although the U.S. government is not on the list of owners, it has already shown interest in participating in the exploitation of the mine and in acquiring its production.[342] The Defense Logistics Agency, which is responsible for securing supplies for the Pentagon, has also

---

production-by-country/

339 Li Liuxi and Denise Jia, "China became a net importer of rare earths in 2018," *Caixin Global,* March 16, 2019. https://www.caixinglobal.com/2019-03-16/china-became-net-importer-of-rare-earths-in-2018-101393333.html

340 JP Casey, "Into Africa: the US' drive for African rare earth minerals," *Mining Technology* September 18, 2019. https://www.mining-technology.com/features/into-africa-the-us-drive-for-african-rare-earth-minerals/

341 Rédaction Africanews with AFP, "Burundi suspends rare earth mining in dispute over wealth," *AfricaNews,* July 23, 2021. https://www.africanews.com/2021/07/23/burundi-suspends-rare-earth-mining-in-row-over-riches/

342 "Burundi: Will US involvement help Rainbow Rare Earths gets its mine reopened?" *Africa Intelligence,* November 9, 2021. https://www.africaintelligence.com/mining-sector_exploration-production/2021/11/09/will-us-stake-help-rainbow-rare-earths-get-its-mine-reopened,109703702-art

been in talks with Burundian company Rainbow Rare Earths Ltd about future supply,[343] as has German company ThyssenKrupp AG.

China-Burundi relations are at their best in history. In 2017, China funded the construction of the presidential palace, the parliament and granted scholarships and training to Burundian citizens.[344] The U.S. then upped the ante, but in its own way. After suspending long-standing sanctions on the Burundian government, it granted it economic aid in the form of critical medical supplies and equipment for Burundian hospitals battling the COVID-19 outbreak.[345] It also initiated a new military training program for its National Defense Forces.

In one of the most conflict-prone scenarios, the major players are already showing their interests. A competition is beginning that could escalate into a conflict with the emergence of any non-state armed group, for example, as a result of the upcoming elections or the frustration of an area of the country neglected by the president. In states such as Burundi, the absence of the rule of law, the lack of institutions, poverty and ethnic tensions also favor regional smuggling, the illegal flow of arms, the criminalization of the economy, drug trafficking and money laundering. It is in this kind of complex general framework that mercenaries finally appear, defending the interests of third parties or rebel groups who sell minerals to finance their activities.[346] Unfortunately, even NGOs, regional news and humanitarian aid can be weaponized by the U.S., China, or other countries in pursuit of their interests.[347] But Africa cannot afford to be torn asunder by a second Cold War, this time driven by the opposing interests of China and the United States who, ideologies aside, are also trying to secure their supply of minerals. There are responsible rare earth mining projects in Africa that can serve as an example and a source of inspiration for

---

343 JP Casey, "Into Africa."

344 Xinhua, "China-Burundi relations at best time in history: president spokesperson," *Xinjhua Net,* January 27, 2018. http://www.xinhuanet.com/english/2018-01/27/c_136928010.htm

345 U.S. Department of State, "U.S. Relations with Burundi," Bilateral Relations Fact Sheet, Bureau of African Affairs, updated May 15, 2023. https://www.state.gov/u-s-relations-with-burundi/

346 Juana Brachet and Howard Wolpe, *Conflict-Sensitive Development Assistance.*

347 Gearóid Ó Colmáin, "Are the US and 'Israel' mounting Proxy Wars in Ethiopia?," *Al Mayadeen,* July 15, 2021. https://english.almayadeen.net/articles/opinion/1494594/are-the-us-and-israel-mounting-proxy-wars-in-ethiopia

other countries on the continent. Not far from the Gakara project in Burundi is the Makuutu project in Uganda, which I visited in March 2023.

## NEW MINING IN AFRICA: THE UGANDAN MAKUUTU PROJECT

At a time when strategic alliances are essential, the West could seek to offer Africa a more appealing alternative. Responsible mining projects like Makuutu can lead the way for others like it and help the West to begin escaping the Chinese yoke. Uganda could provide proof to other African countries that developing a rare earth mining industry that favors its people, respects the environment and supports governance is possible. It is easy to talk about ESG criteria for mining in Africa from a classroom in Hamburg or from a terrace in Madrid. But the dimensions of these criteria change after visiting the suburbs of Kampala and the agricultural area surrounding the ionic rare earth mining project at Makuutu in the Jinja region, 100 km east of the capital. Walking through the Makuutu sub-county, accompanied by the Rwenzori Rare Metals team,[348] I realized what the creation of up to 1600 jobs, 800 direct and 800 subcontracted, really entails. Mining development with an inclusive nature for the local community could serve to curb the mass exodus to the city caused when droughts occur. It would also promote the development of much needed schools and medical centers that are almost non-existent in the area. Admittedly, the displacement of the indigenous population will be necessary in order to extract the minerals, but the alternative of compensating them through individualized negotiations or relocation a relative short distance from their habitual residence has as its counterweight a vital development for an area on the verge of insalubrity (malaria, typhoid, dysentery, yellow fever, etc.), where the average citizen lives below the poverty line. This mining project will serve to alleviate the region's exposure to the environmental stresses that climate change is mercilessly exacerbating.

In Uganda as a whole, and particularly in Makuutu, the concept of subsistence agriculture is an omnipresent reality in almost all its

348 Rwenzori Rare Metals (consulted on March 13, 2023). https://rwenzorimetals.com/

landscapes. It is enough to leave any of the main roads of the country for a few meters to find yourself surrounded by small single-family plots of no more than 300 square meters each, connected by small dirt tracks. A tiny house made of adobe or low-quality brick, with thatched or metal roofs, no sewage system and often no electricity or running water dominates each plot. The fertility of the soils is such that with these small areas a family, usually with more than three children, can subsist. Even so, by not letting the land routinely lie fallow, and without using fertilizers, the productivity of their land decreases year after year. In each one of them a banana tree, some chickens, yucca plants, from the root of which flour is obtained, or sweet potatoes and very little else, is enough for them to be self-sufficient. Land concentration, economies of scale and the generation of surpluses for trade seem to be alien concepts in many regions of Uganda, where the few existing large estates of a certain size are used to produce mainly coffee and sugar cane.

Unfortunately, when the droughts come, the single-family plots are not enough to feed so many mouths. In many cases, the women leave with their children for the capital, Kampala, in search of food. There they try to help out at the small handicraft stalls that line the sidewalks of the roads and streets, in order to provide sustenance for their children. Meanwhile, the children spend the day in the same street, just a few meters away, but with little attention paid to them. Accidents are not infrequent; noisy and hurried "wedding-weddings" (motorcycles) run over some of these children. The development of a minimum industrial capacity in agricultural regions could curb this dramatic way of life. Responsible mining is a solution to the problem and Rwenzori Rare Metals could be proof of this.

On a global scale this kind of project has an undoubted strategic value. Together with the Myanmar mines or the similar Chilean project Aclara, the Uganda project will be one of the few projects that will produce these precious and necessary metallic elements such as terbium and dysprosium outside China. Today there are only six heavy rare earth processing centers in the world, five in China and one in Vietnam, also owned by China. But countries like the U.S. that aspire to have a complete supply chain of heavy rare earths within a few years would do well to imitate the Beijing government and try to secure these invaluable resources as soon as possible.

However, as told by South African Warren Tregurtha, the CEO in charge of the Makuutu project and Rwenzori Rare Metals, although American and Japanese customers have already shown interest in the project, it was the Chinese who made the first move. In 2021, the China Aluminum Company, CHINALCO, signed a Memorandum of Understanding with Australia's Ionic Rare Earths,[349] which currently owns 51% of the Makuutu project, and intends to expand its ownership. Although the agreement is currently dormant, it is quite possible that China is patiently waiting for Rwenzori Rare Metals to obtain the mining permit and start extracting the first minerals. In the absence of more favorable alternatives, the valuable Ugandan heavy rare earths could be in China's hands within a year or two, following the path of many others. These Chinese advances may well be coordinated with the development of the critical infrastructure that would enable it to extract the country's minerals by connecting them to the port of Mombasa in neighboring Kenya, already under Chinese control. The Meter Gauge Railway, a project financed and built by The Chinese state-owned Chinese Railway and Bridge Cooperation (CRBC), serves as the connective tissue. This railway, which has rehabilitated some of the dilapidated former British colonial-era infrastructure, has now completed its connection between Uganda's capital, Kampala, and Malaba in Kenya. The railroad has a freight station at Jinja, in the vicinity of the Makuutu mining project.

However, the fact that another similar rail project has so far been denied to the Beijing government—the Standard Gauge Railway project, which is likely to be awarded to a Turkish company—shows that Chinese expansion has limits in Uganda. It is interesting to recall that in 1972, under the dictatorship of Amin Dada, 90,000 Asio-Ugandan citizens, many of them of Indian origin, were expelled from the country and had their property expropriated, having been accused by the dictator of milking the country like a cow. Even though the mention of Amin Dada evoked visceral comparisons to a brutal butcher in the West, many Ugandans I talked with surprisingly did not view this eviction unfavorably. It is likely that the current government of President Museveni would prefer to have, as in the case of the railways, several alternatives beyond Chinese companies to sell their minerals to.

349 Ionic Rare Earths, "Project: Makuutu Uganda" (consulted on March 24, 202). https://ionicre.com.au/makuutu-uganda/

Proof of the government's support of Makuutu's mining project is the approval of its 900-page environmental impact study, which the company's County Manager, Patiente Singo, proudly showed me. The next step, the mining permit application, had to be renewed due to the enactment of a new national mining law. Warren Tregurtha told me how, when the project was launched in 2016, the local inhabitants did not make it easy for them to pass through their roads. Today, after a massive public relations campaigns involving three radio programs on three different stations, a television program, information brochures, and the inclusion of five community liaison officers from the community on the payroll, things have changed. As we visit the project facilities to tour the progress in the exploration phase, the villagers greet us with a smile, and the county personalities show up and come over to say hello. In this network of sub-counties, counties, districts, and kingdoms with clans and tribes, it is essential to show "recognition" to each of the local authorities. Evidently, the community has much more to gain than to lose with the exploitation of the mine, but it is necessary to respect the political channels and local customs.

It is not easy to explain to a local community and regional leaders with a low cultural level that the processing by leaching of the clays has nothing to do with the polluting chemical processes of the well-known Chinese Bayan Obo mines. The main advantages of these ionic clays, which have been produced by exposing granite rocks to environmental erosion, is that they do not contain radioactive elements such as thorium or uranium. Moreover, its extraction is as simple as collecting sand with a shovel and transporting it to an area where it is piled up in the form of small hills. Since it is not hard rock, it does not need to be fragmented by blasting with explosives, nor does it need to be subsequently ground. Moreover, the use of ammonium sulfate to extract the rare earths, spraying the ionic clays, accumulated in the form of small hills 3 meters high, will generate nitrates as residues that serve as fertilizers for the soil. Once the rare earth elements have been decanted, the concentrated solution containing them will be taken to the processing plant and the remaining piles of soil, already fertilized with nitrates, can be reused to fill the excavated pits.

According to the company's geologist James Opio, in charge of the exploration, "After extracting and sending to the laboratory more than 300 samples extracted throughout the entire surface of the project, it is now sufficiently well mapped and updated." Warren adds that, "The economic viability of this project is based both on the richness of the grade of the clays in some of the rare earth elements and the ease of extracting them." He continues, "To give you an idea, there is no need to fracture the minerals here; these metallic elements are stuck to the clay grains as if they were magnets. Figuratively, it is as if it were enough to use a stronger magnet to separate them. In this case the magnet is ammonium sulfate, a commonly used fertilizer." The solution obtained from leaching will then be concentrated in the plant by reverse osmosis and the rare earth elements will finally be decanted in the form of carbonates. As Warren told me, "There are just over 50 companies in the rare earth world. Many of them are run by geologists who focus on the grade of the elements in the ore. Without an accurate economic view of the whole project, many are doomed to failure. I am an economist and I know that this project is economically viable and that it is economically beneficial to this community."

A clear governmental intervention by countries such as Australia, Japan, USA, or the European Union could serve to promote this type of project for the benefit of rural populations in developing countries, while supplying them with these vital elements. However, inaction will be equivalent to leaving these projects in the hands of the gravitational pull exerted by colossal Chinese companies such as CHINALCO or China Rare Earths Group, which will end up absorbing either their products or the entire project. Behind acronyms such as CHINALCO is a metallurgical giant that has 68 affiliated companies and operates in more than twenty countries. Since 2008, CHINALCO has been on the Fortune Global 500 list, and its branch, Chinalco Rare Earths and Metals Company (Jiangsu), which will become part of the giant China Rare Earths in 2022, already operates several rare earths separation plants in the province of Jiangsu.[350] These companies shoot with the almost unlimited gunpowder of the Beijing government.

350 ASX, "Ionic RE signs MOU with CHINALCO for potential investment, offtake, and mine development," April 7, 2021. https://ionicre.com.au/wp-content/uploads/post/210407i.pdf

# 10. NEW RESOURCE TERRITORIES, NEW LAWS, NEW SOLUTIONS

Humanity continues to evolve, and despite the threats to our cultures, homo sapiens has always had resources at its disposal. Solutions to problems such as rare earths may well simulate outcomes already experienced in the past. This may well lead us to colonize new unpopulated territories, create new alliances, enact new laws, and worship new gods.

## MINING THE OCEAN FLOOR

The colonization of the planet has not yet come to an end, Javier assures me. He is head of the section dedicated to the scientific exploration of the ocean floor at the Spanish Geological and Mining Institute (IGME-CSIC). "The moon is much better mapped than the ocean floors of the planet," says this 48-year-old geologist, who exudes enthusiasm as he describes several of the projects under his direction. "There is a lot of national underwater mapping that is still unfinished, and if we go more than 200 miles from the coasts, practically nothing," he adds. The Tropic seamount discovered by his institute, hidden in the submarine extension of the Canary archipelago in the waters of the Atlantic Ocean, could harbor one of the world's largest mines of cobalt and tellurium. An area of only one square kilometer contains up to 170 tons of rare earths. If we consider that the Tropic seamount has a platform at the top with an area of 120 square kilometers, it is easy to intuit the immense repercussions of its discovery in 2011, and its possible exploitation.

As we discuss the subject, he shows me the building that houses both the offices of the staff working for the Spanish Geological Survey and the Geominero Museum. But the building itself serves as an artifact. Some of the first meetings between European geologists were held there in 1926, presided over by the monarch Alfonso XIII. At that time, not even all the rare earths that today shape our lives had been discovered. Javier regrets how the grandeur of this building has been diluted by neglect. Europe has progressively lost its passion for geology. The geology faculties have emptied since the 1990s, and many European mines have closed. "Fortunately, a resurgence is taking place," he says, "but we still need many experts to run and develop a multitude of programs. Particularly in the world of underwater minerals, it is very difficult to find experts." He is one of the leading scientific authorities in Europe and finds it difficult to find counterparts and collaborators with specific training. "These are essential, because underwater mining could become the major market for some rare metals such as cobalt or rare earths."

When I think about the exploitation of the seabed, two questions come to mind automatically, as if they were springs: Is it economically viable? Is it polluting? His answer to the first question surprises me with its pragmatism. "If there are companies that are dedicated to it, and that have invested large sums in the sector, it is because that is how they see it. Being the spearhead also means that when these exploitation techniques are reproduced on a large scale, these companies will be very well positioned to surf the wave and enjoy it."

One of the best-positioned pioneers is the privately-owned Dutch company Allseas, whose main source of revenue is the manufacture and installation of submarine cables. Subsea mining is much simpler than it might seem. The giant ship manufactured by this company simply sucks up metal nodules deposited at certain points on the seabed, without the need to excavate a single cubic centimeter of rock. The technology of these absorption pipes originates from oil companies; this underwater mining could well be considered the new hydraulic fracturing—"fracking"—of mining. In this case, the cable-driven robot from the vessel slowly advances along the seabed. Its robust traction chains emulate those of a tank. In October 2022, the vehicle travelled 83 km at a depth of three kilometers in the NORI-D area of the Pacific Ocean. It did so under a research permit from the International Seabed Authority (ISA), created in 1994 within the UNCLOS (United Nations Convention on Law of the Sea) and based in Jamaica. While sending the metal nodules through the umbilical cord that connects it to its mother ship, it gently expels the excess sediments through its diffusers, which easily settle back on the sea-floor. Thanks to this remote-controlled underwater "tank," the Allseas' flagship ocean mining vessel Hidden Gem, in cooperation with The Metals Company, recovered 3,500 tons of metal nodules from the sea floor. These nodules contain very high grades of manganese, copper, nickel, cobalt and other rare metals.

Javier points out, "In the North Pacific region, between the USA and Japan, there is a great submarine wealth of metallic nodules and manganese crusts. The energy and processes needed to separate the metals contained in the nodules are much less than those needed to extract them from land mines. In a land mine, you need to move a lot of tons of rock to access ores with a high metal grade. In the case of nodules, it is enough to collect these 'metallic balls' from the seabed. Once extracted, the nodules have a much higher grade than the ores in the mine."

But despite the much-reduced effort involved, the volume and quantity of nodules should not be underestimated. The net amount extracted of a metal such as neodymium or cobalt from settlements such as Tropic can exceed that of many mines. Given the composition of these polymetallic nodules, they may be ideal for supplying new automotive lithium batteries, which typically require around 35 kg of nickel, 20 kg of manganese and 14 kg of cobalt. The nodules have all these metals plus a high concentration of copper. Created by sedimentation, they only grow about a centimeter every million years.

Imagine discovering the first gold or copper mines, or the first oil fields. This is, in a sense, what Allseas is doing. In 1940, to obtain 100 barrels of crude oil from the wells of Saudi Arabia, you needed to expend one barrel's worth of energy. Today, it takes the energy of ten barrels; the energy rate-of-return has dropped from 100 to 10 in just 83 years. While not exhausted yet, spoliation has taken its toll on oil. In the mining realm, something similar has happened with the Spanish mines of the Rio Tinto region, the origin of the eponymous mining giant with modern-day bases in Australia and the United Kingdom. Six hundred years before Christ, when the Tartessian civilization exploited the Tarsis mine of this region, they did it because it was so rich in copper that the river that flowed through it appeared as red as wine— hence its name. Even in 1930, the Tarsis mine located in the area was so rich that copper ingots with a concentration of 75% were readily extracted from it with ease, with high percentages of gold (5%) and silver (20%) mixed in. Today the copper concentration is so low in the region that it is no longer profitable to extract this element; its wealth has also been overexploited.

Now, the oceanic mantles possess metallic resources in a virgin state, with the highest purity, and therefore require less energy to extract and process. Obviously, extraction at a depth of 960 meters, as in Tropic Mountain, is an altogether different game than at 3000 meters. But as Javier tells me, "A sign of the potential of these metallic nodules, and other underwater riches such as manganese crusts or rare earth-rich muds, are the recent disputes that are taking place over them." As in past colonization throughout history, we are already witnessing the first confrontations between states. Spain and Morocco have already brought their territorial claims to Mount Tropic to the UN. Both are requesting recognition by extending their exclusive economic zone waters from 200 nautical miles to 350, thus reaching the new oceanic booty.

They are not the only countries with this type of conflict. China and Japan, for example, are close behind. In this case it is a matter of sludge containing a plethora of rare earths instead of merely manganese, but the expectations for exploitation are just as high. The territorial dispute between Tokyo and Beijing over the Senkaku Islands is also a struggle to gain access to all the ocean resources associated with its waters, including the rich seabed. That is why Japan, seeking to secure its future supply of rare earths, is targeting other islands. This time it is the ocean floor of its conflict-free Ogasawara islands, where it intends to start prospecting before 2028. The state-owned exploration company will deploy an already proven technology on board its deepwater drillship Chikyu, capable of pumping and sifting some 70 tons of mud per day. The challenge here is the 6000-meter depth, but the advantage is that these muds, in addition to their richness in rare earths, have minimal amounts of radioactive elements like thorium and uranium. Japan wants private companies to enter the market starting from fiscal year 2028, but announced intentions to exploit its sludge, rich in rare earths, as early as 2024. According to official statements, there would be enough rare earths in these sludges to meet Japan's demand for rare earths for several decades.

As the concentration of minerals in land-based mines decreases, the seabed will become more attractive. The more the price of these metals increases, the more imperative the need for their supply becomes. In parallel, the more subsea mining techniques scale up and improve, the more relevant and desirable these ocean deposits will become. Reserves such as the Clarion-Clipperton fracture zone in the Pacific Ocean, so named because of its proximity to Clarion Island, located between Mexico and Hawaii, could represent an oxygen balloon for the world's supply of some rare metals older than 200 years, including rare earths. In particular, its cobalt and nickel reserves are thought to be greater than all current terrestrial reserves.

Times have changed since the Spanish landed in America more than 500 years ago, but the repetition of some patterns is very significant. Javier tells me about his voyages on the Spanish navy's flagship for scientific research, the *Hespérides*. I cannot help but recall how this alliance between Spanish state mining and Spain's navy was already foundational to the colonization of the new world. Spanish shipyards will also build, like those of the Japanese or the Dutch, the ships necessary for the new conquest, but this time the impediments will not be scurvy, lack of supplies, or the Doldrums. This time the main obstacle will be environmental groups—as well as inter-state rivalries.

Although the degree of contamination does not seem high compared to land-based mining, the truth is that, as Javier points out, "The impact is not yet sufficiently studied. The repercussions on the water column or on benthic communities, the populations of organisms on the bottom surface or the effects of strong noise pollution are not yet well known." What is known is that pressure from these environmental groups against underwater mining is just as forceful as that directed towards land mining, even though here you cannot be mining in anyone's backyard. According to him, "This could be due to the financing of some of these groups by companies with hidden interests. Fishing companies that do not want to see their fishing area become a mining reserve or even large land-based mining companies that are wary of a marine mining competition in which they have not invested."

The problem in this fight is that the referee is absent, and there are no clear rules. Although the UN has been obliged on demand to develop regulations governing the exploitation of the oceans, a request from the European Commission for a moratorium in order to study the environmental impact in depth has slowed its development. In other words, Javier clarified, "Each nation can declare mining reserves in its own waters or grant permits to exploit the seabed, but only permits for scientific research and exploration are granted in international waters."

Some countries are launching themselves head-first into seabed exploitation. Norway is one such pioneer in this new exploration. Norway knows well what it is like to go from living in poverty to being one of the countries with the highest per capita income in the world, thanks to its domestic exploitation of natural gas and oil resources. Now that these fossil materials are both depleting and losing their international glamour, Norway seems determined to be among the first to launch itself into the exploitation of seabed metals.

Another example is the Cook Islands, whose government is advised by fellow scientist and friend of Javier's, James Hein of the U.S. Geological Survey. Both have collaborated closely in past projects. Primarily a tourist paradise by nature, these islands have had to evaluate, lacking UN underwater mining regulation, the pros and cons of exploiting their seabed. Their exploitation shows a positive verdict of compatibility of both industries through proper management. The Canadian company Canadian Metals, formerly known as Deep Green, has already started this work. According to Javier, "One of the advantages of these polymetallic minerals is that they are almost fully exploited. It is as if you found a mine on land from which you could extract the metals usually contained in three or four mines."

The race to establish new settlements has begun. New sonars, with reduced noise pollution and triangulation methods similar to GPS, could revolutionize the exploitation and use of the seabed, enhancing geolocation. Naturally, these sonars owe their properties to rare earth elements. Let us hope that the International Seabed Authority (ISA) is invested with authority and that its laws have sufficient clarity and legal backing so that we avoid becoming spectators of new territorial wars.

## NEW LAWS

Given finite mineral resources and their intensive exploitation in new territories like the ocean floor, the arctic or the moon, the currently held reserves of the most critical and strategic of these resources, rare earths, could well lead to a redistribution of geopolitical power. Australia, Brazil, Canada, China, USA, India, Russia and South Africa have a sufficient level of governance to take advantage of their large domestic rare earth reserves. In other countries such as Angola, Congo, Zambia, Burundi, Madagascar, Tanzania, Malawi, Myanmar and Vietnam, these resource reserves could be more curse than blessing. The difference in the successful exploitation of these will lie in the development of an appropriate national strategy, supported by integrated institutions at the inter-ministerial level, which will enable them to channel help from allied countries or actors, or stop interference from unwanted external agents with harmful interests.

Some of these countries are beginning to react. Canada is a good example. Ottawa is finalizing the details of its new "Strategy for Critical Minerals" and is abandoning its traditional "laissez-faire" free market stance. On the one hand, it is introducing new protectionist measures, new laws, to defend itself against Asian mining companies. On the other hand, it embraces a new alliance to secure the rare earths needed for the energy transition. Thanks to its new regulations, Chinese companies instigated by Beijing will no longer be able to acquire ownership of mines or projects producing metals such as rare earths, lithium, or cobalt in Canada. Such purchases are now considered a threat to national security. Did recent acquisitions by Chinese state-owned companies of projects such as the Tanco Lithium or Neo Lithium mines set off alarm bells, or perhaps served as scapegoats?

It is questionable to what extent these measures are part of a political whitewash or are really intended to address the problem by nipping it in the bud. Three of Canada's largest mining companies, Teck Resources, Ivanhoe Mines Limited and First Quantum Minerals Limited, count Chinese state-owned enterprises as their biggest single shareholder despite producing critical metals such as beryllium, tin, germanium, indium, lithium, palladium, platinum ... and rare earths. The Canadian government has not yet forced the Chinese government to divest its shares in these companies.[351] According to the consulting

351 Divya Rajagopal, "Exclusive-Canada will not force Chinese state investors to divest stakes in Teck, First Quantum," *Yahoo! Finance,* March 8, 2023. https://uk.finance.yahoo.com/news/exclusive-canada-not-retrospectively-target-141833968.html

firm Refinitiv, the sovereign wealth fund China Investment Corp owns a 10.3% stake in Teck, China's state-owned CITIC Metal Group owns 26% in Ivanhoe Mines, while China's largest copper producer, Jiangxi Copper Corp Ltd, owns 18.3% in First Quantum Minerals. These giants are no exception, as according to Bloomberg data, Chinese companies have been involved in 89 announced acquisitions and investments in Canadian metals and mining companies over the past decade. The value of these transactions amounts to $14 billion. Many of the deals involve companies related to the thirty-one critical minerals identified by the Canadian government.[352]

On the other hand, Canada's new Western alliance includes not only the U.S. but also Australia, France, Finland, Sweden, Germany, Japan, United Kingdom, South Korea and the European Commission. The U.S. Under Secretary of State for Economic Growth, José W. Fernández, announced in June 2022 that "The U.S. has just created a new partnership specifically dedicated to securing the rare earth supply chains needed for the energy transition. This alliance seeks to channel public and private investments and share information on existing rare earth deposits[353]"

But as positive as these alliances are, they will be of little use if states, especially Canada, do not take strong protectionist measures. There are now mining companies, veritable giants in the sector, which have the solution in their hands. These companies not only have the capital available to make the requisite investments, but also the technical know-how and the production, storage, and distribution networks. The large international companies BHP Group Ltd., Rio Tinto PLC, Glencore PLC, Vale, Anglo American, Alber Male, among others, have turnover figures greater than the Gross Domestic Product of some countries. But they are very cautious when it comes to making new investments. These mining giants tend to prioritize the use of their profits to pay dividends and buy back their own shares. The aim is to benefit shareholders in the short term, instead of investing in new

---

352 Bloomberg News, "China has links to dozens of Canadian miners tied to critical minerals," *Mining.com,* November 11, 2022, https://www.mining.com/web/china-has-links-to-dozens-of-canadian-miners-tied-to-critical-minerals/

353 Reuters, "U.S. and partners enter pact to secure critical minerals like lithium," June 14, 2022. https://www.reuters.com/markets/commodities/us-partners-enter-pact-secure-critical-minerals-lithium-2022-06-14/

projects that would drive the energy transition and would be profitable in the medium and long term. The investment of the 10 largest mining companies in the Western world in 2022 and 2023 is only 40 billion dollars, compared to the 80 billion dollars invested in 2012, according to the Bank of America Corporation.

But this lack of investment is also due to increased regulation, pressure from environmental protection groups, and the obligation to meet ESG criteria under increasingly stringent social scrutiny. Consequently, mining companies are unsurprisingly focused on short-term shareholder satisfaction while avoiding risk. Western governments lack industrial strategies that sufficiently take safety into account and neglect to both help and "guide" them. New laws such as the EU Commodities Act or the American Inflation Reduction Act could be a good start that other Western countries should emulate and expand upon, in order to prevent the products of their large mining companies from escaping to China, or lying fallow in their mining remnants, as is currently happening. Rio Tinto, using Anglo-Saxon capital, sells the monazite extracted from Madagascar to China, when instead the American company Energy Fuels could process it to obtain uranium and thorium for nuclear fuel, as well as rare earth concentrates. The Brazilian mining giant CBMM, with a world monopoly on niobium, neither exploits nor bargains nor sells its tailings, within which rare earths remain abundant.

Unfortunately, none of the mining titans are so far replicating the pattern of exploiting rare earths as a by-product of mineral exploitation, as China does in its Bayan Obo iron ore mines. The reason is simple: for the time being the strategic importance and criticality of these metals have not been reflected in their costs. If they had been, the rare earths market (taking into account the value of all its already-separated oxides) would not have its current value of 7.29 billion U.S. dollars a year, but rather a value orders of magnitude greater. Still, the market value is growing progressively; five years prior, its value was less than half of what it is today. Without laws forcing the big Western mining companies to exploit these by-products and supply our own industries as a priority, they may face nationalization by states in order to get the job done or the competition of new state-owned enterprises. States should bear in mind that legally binding these corporations should never mean a new limitation, a new tax, an added expense, or burden for them. They are a part of the recipe for success in what is intended to be the fastest energy transition in history.

But there are laws that bind them both inside and outside our borders. Citizens of liberal democracies boast that our Western laws help prevent certain minerals from becoming a source of conflict or being used to finance conflict in developing countries. Moreover, Western laws also favor the development and control of fair trade and respect for human rights in mining areas in compliance with ESG criteria. We pride ourselves on our civility, even though these laws slow down and tie our companies' hands in the international competition for critical minerals. China has its human rights laws, too, reflected its 2021 "Human Rights Action Plan of China (2021–2025),"[354] which may restrain China from continuing to copy what has heretofore been the Western practice of outsourcing pollution. While Chinese workers adapt to the terrain and move with agility in environments filled with corruption and lack of respect for human rights, European companies are constrained by the moral scrutiny of shareholders, the conscientious consumer and bureaucratic morass. All Western mining companies need legal experts who are familiar with the myriad of regulations associated with mining. These include the 2012 UN Guiding Principles for Business and Human Rights, and Section 1502 of the Dodd Frank Act, which requires publicly traded companies in the U.S. to conduct due diligence on mining companies from the Democratic Republic of Congo and neighboring countries, the recent EU Conflict Minerals Regulation, the U.K.'s Modern Slavery Act, the U.K. London Metal Exchange's Responsible Sourcing Policy and Evolution of the Supply Chain Due Diligence Landscape, the list goes on.

While it is true that, excepting the U.K.'s Modern Slavery Act, these acts are not clearly supported by the criminal code of any country, following these regulations is a matter of prestige and reputation, which are fundamental to the success of a company in the West. If these laws are infringed, at least they are on the books, affording environmental activism an avenue of legal reference in support of their claims. Other new regulatory initiatives such as the EU's Digital

---

354 "China: Human Rights Action Plan (2021–2025) mentions encouraging Chinese businesses to abide by UN Guiding Principles," Business & Human Rights Resource Center, September 9, 2021. https://www.business-humanrights.org/en/latest-news/human-rights-action-plan-of-china-2021-2025/

Product Passport (DPP), which will collect data on the value chain of products, leave the problem in the hands of companies and citizens, with little room for reaction since they do not entail any kind of penalty. Transparency will help to increase social awareness, but for the moment these regulatory steps will not be sufficient to regenerate mining in our own soils, nor will it be enough to magically generate rare earths outside China.

In our (so far) globalized world, every economic gap left by one country is filled by another. In the case of mining, the problem is that this gap is filled by aggressive Chinese government directives facilitated by its state-socialist system; if the West does not voluntarily vacate, the Asian giant pushes us out. Only with the commitment of all actors could the integrity of a conflict prevention system for mineral resources be guaranteed. Our companies should start selling their products in our markets, such as the London Metal Exchange, but should rescue it first from Chinese hands. It is imperative to include the sale of rare metals, which are so far omitted from any specific legislation, in this market. Today, China has such a strong position in the rare metals market that it may have no interest in adopting common legislation in this regard. But if China does not accept the binding of its companies to coercive international legislation, or should fail to adequately enforce its own legislation, this would give them a great competitive advantage by exempting them from responsibilities that their Western counterparts would have to fulfill in Africa, South America, and other developing countries.

The same is true of Chinese trading centers, where these critical minerals are bought and sold, constituting an opaque market that makes it easier for the West, wittingly or not, to buy end products produced from rare earths and other critical materials mined under conditions considered illegal in Western canons. A clear example of how the enormous differences in legal and moral responsibility between the two blocs ends up with Chinese monopolization of minerals, market appropriation, and supply chain control can be seen in Congolese cobalt. This element, so essential for our modern technology, is mined and bought by Chinese companies constituting a monopoly similar to that of rare earths. Aware that the Democratic Republic of Congo holds 70% of the world's cobalt reserves, China has been systematically buying up all the American and European mining companies with cobalt holdings in the region. It should come as no surprise that China is already leading the global race for car batteries and power grids. Not only does it have control over seven of the largest cobalt mines via its Molybdenum company, but China buys almost all the cobalt in the Congo. These acquisitions include both part of the cobalt from Swiss Glencore, the only Western company that has survived the Chinese state-run market economy, as well as from retail mining, which was and continues to often be illegal and involve minors. All Western companies fled, harassed by Western public opinion and legislation that forced them to operate by Western standards on African soil. Glencore is the exception, and despite having to pay multi-million-dollar fines and face a multitude of complaints, it continues to make its operations profitable.

As a result of this advantageous situation, China is consolidating its monopoly on green metals. Thanks to them, it is trapping the downstream supply chain and becoming the Silicon Valley of electric cars. The Asian giant not only possesses the rare earths that provide the best electric motors, but also produces 80% of the world's high-grade cobalt, which, together with lithium and graphite, ensures the best batteries.[355]

Negotiations at the international level with China are crucial to make its critical metals market transparent, giving it traceability and opening it up to Western markets and international verification agencies. Today China merely has "guidelines," which fall short of legal or regulatory status. Its CCCMC (China Chamber of Commerce of Metals, Minerals and Chemicals Importers and Exporters) recently published the China Due Diligence Guidelines for Responsible Minerals Supply Chains. However, these guidelines, based on those of the EU and similar in name as well as being voluntary in nature have not yet been implemented,[356] unlike the European ones. Only with the agreement of China and all actors involved in mining in developing countries, will it be possible to positively transform mining slavery

355 Felix Todd, "China, cobalt, and the Congo: Why Xi Jinping is winning the 'batteries arms race,'" *NS Energy*, August 13, 2019. https://www.nsenergybusiness.com/features/china-cobalt-congo-batteries/

356 OECD, "Public consultation on the draft Chinese Due Diligence Guidelines for Responsible Mineral Supply Chains." October 12, 2015. https://www.oecd.org/industry/publicationsdocuments/38/

into honest work and criminal activities into respectable business activities. These countries are often not even aware of Western laws concerning mining companies operating in their territories.

Given that China could find it in its best interest to avoid any such legal arrangements, the West will have little choice but to return to mining on its soil. But due to outsourcing mining activity and the rejection of mining in our backyards,[357] there's been no impetus to update mining laws. Many countries have stopped developing laws that addressed the specificities of mining many rare metals. In the last interview I had with Teresa, the rare earth expert of the Geological and Mining Institute of Spain, she stated that, "Many of the authorities in charge of making decisions on the granting of mining permits do not have an adequate regulatory basis, but rather an outdated mining legislation. As a consequence, in order to approve or grant the opening of a new rare earth mine,[358] they have to resort on many occasions to the opinions of expert councils or request reports from other ministries, such as the Ministry of Environmental Protection."

As you can imagine, the decentralization of this system—having to collect reports through various ministries, councils, boards, and advisory bodies, to evaluate whether to grant mining permits—paralyzes processing times and leaves mining companies financially unprotected. Companies have no guarantee that their applications will be approved, and these ad-hoc processes lack both consistency and transparency regarding what criteria determine the approval or rejection of a permit. They turn the granting of a permit into an enigma, which hampers a company's planning and discourages applications for new licenses.[359]

Another friction point is the definition of the authority that grants the final license for the opening of a site. The more political the position of the person in charge of making the decision, the more likely it is that the decision will be made on the basis of political election cycles instead of objective, scientific criteria. Political entities can be

---

357 Michael Malone, "The Collapse of Western Metal Mining: An Historical Epitaph," *Pacific Historical Review* 55, no. 3 (August 1986): 463. http://www.jstor.org/stable/3639707

358 Teresa Llorens González, Geologist in charge of Strategic Minerals Spain S.L., Interview conducted on November 22, 2021.

359 Enrique Burkhalter, Matamulas REE Project Manager at Quantum Mining. Personal interview conducted on November 23, 2021.

more easily influenced by lobbying groups or environmentalist movements[360] that do not conform to scientific criteria, which are much more constant and transparent. A more developed mining law is needed[361] to minimize the political weight of the decision, or even leave it fully in the hands of non-partisan technical governmental bodies. Thus, the decision would be much more transparent and predictable for companies, and processing times would be reduced. Meanwhile, as the head of Human Resources at Strategic Minerals Spain commented to me, "Other companies should follow our example of starting by remediating old mines and taking advantage of the bargains and by-products from their tailings ponds and dumps with local workers. It is the best way to earn 'social license.'"

For a technical standpoint, the main legal problem with opening a new rare earth mine is thorium.[362] Mining authorities often lack national legislation or guidance specifically in reference to thorium. At present, as thorium is usually found in ores in combination with uranium, it was legally given the same consideration. However, there are ores, such as monazite, rich in rare earths and thorium, which have an exceptionally low concentration of uranium. This means that, after extraction of monazite, the thorium could be separated and the remnants of the ore containing uranium in low concentrations could be safely returned to the mine, without presenting a radiological problem, for backfilling during closure.[363]

Until about two decades ago, there had understandably been no governmental interest in regulating specific and detailed licensing

---

360 Sonja Kivinen, Juha Kotilainen, and Timo Kumpula. "Mining conflicts in the European Union: environmental and political perspectives," *Fennia - International Journal of Geography* 198(1–2), August 2020. https://www.researchgate.net/publication/343818442_Mining_conflicts_in_the_European_Union_environmental_and_political_perspectives

361 Rubén Esteban Pére, "Future challenges in international cooperation for the exploration and exploitation of mineral resources with high added value in Europe" *European Geologist* no. 42 (December 2016). https://eurogeologists.eu/european-geologist-journal-42-future-challenges-in-international-cooperation-for-the-exploration-and-exploitation-of-mineral-resources-with-high-added-value-in-europe/

362 "The 800-pound gorilla in all rare earth companies is the radioactive thorium and/or uranium residue that will be generated in mining, separation and refining operations," according to rare earth expert Jack Lifton.

363 Andrei Litvinjuk, CEO, Neo Performance Materials. Interview conducted in Estonia, Sillamae, on October 21, 2021.

criteria for mining radioactive ores containing rare earths. Thorium, and to some extent rare earths, were of no commercial interest, let alone a security interest. Therefore, the specific radioactivity of their ores simply represented a problem without any advantageous trade-off. Governments had no interest in favoring their exploitation.[364]

However, good mining laws can make a difference. Let's see this by comparing two rare earth mines, using as a common basis for measurement standards contained in the EU's Basic Safety Standards, which integrate all the regulations of the European Atomic Energy Community (EURATOM). The Norra Kärr mine in Sweden is an example of a rare earth deposit with a radiological content that is exempt from any control or licensing, while the uranium content of the Kvanefjeld ore in Greenland is sufficient for it to be considered an additional product.[365] However, each country applies its own national regulations,[366] and in many there are fundamental legislative gaps. These include the definition of the levels of radon gas exposure that can occur during uranium and thorium mining.[367] In fact, in some countries this level of exposure is also not reflected in their environmental legislation. The implications of the lack of regulations are enormous. If the concentration of thorium is low enough, without radiological implications, it can be returned to the earth. If, however, the radiological implications are low or medium, the waste ore must be stored in national repositories created for that purpose.[368] But thorium is unfairly equated to uranium under current mining laws; the mining and extraction of thorium from monazite is relatively

---

364 Constantine E. Karayannopoulos, CEO, Neo Performance Materials. Interview conducted in Estonia, Sillamae on October 21, 2021.

365 European Rare Earth Union (EURare), "Regulation of environmental and health impacts on the rare earth elements industry" (accessed 2021). http://www.eurare.org/regulation.html

366 Miranda Keith-Roach, Bertil Grundfelt, Lars Olof Höglund and Anne Kousa, "Environmental, Legislation and Best Practices in the Emerging European Rare Earth Element Industry," in *Rare Earths Industry* (December 2016), 279–291. https://www.researchgate.net/publication/299390404_Environmental_Legislation_and_Best_Practice_in_the_Emerging_European_Rare_Earth_Element_Industry

367 Miguel Ángel Alba Hidalgo, "Control and recovery of orphan radioactive sources," Spanish Association of Industrial Hygiene, May 16, 2020. https://www.aehi.es/2020/05/16/control-recuperacion-fuentes-radiactivas-huerfanas/

368 Teresa Llorens González, Geologist in charge of Strategic Minerals Spain S.L., Interview conducted on November 22, 2021.

easy, and significantly different from that of uranium from its ores. Exposure during extraction is much lower than for uranium, and the total production of radioactive waste in the mining operation is about two orders of magnitude lower than for uranium. The so-called radon impact is also much less than for uranium, due to the short lifetime of thoron gas (radon 220) compared to that of radon 222. Downstream, although monazite processing is more sensitive, there are also well-known options that have long proven to be effective and safe.[369]

If countries developed specific laws to address these different options, the mining industry could benefit from the extraction of these elements in a safe way, without carrying all the consequences of being considered a miner of radioactive materials.[370] But these current out-dated regulations burden mining companies with unnecessary costs and paperwork, making them less competitive and complicating our access to rare earths and thorium.

---

369 "In India, until recently, monazite used to be leached with alkalis, rare earths were separated as a mixture, and thorium stored in the form of thorium hydroxide in concrete silos. The hydroxide cake contained about 35% ThO2, 7% rare earth oxide, 0.6% U3O8 and nearly 28% insolubility and moisture. Recently, a project entitled 'Thorium Recovery, Uranium Recovery and Thorium Oxalate Restoration' (THRUST) has been completed to process monazite such that all thorium present is separated in the form of pure thorium oxalate (99% purity) which is much easier to handle, store and recover to prepare mantle grade thorium nitrate or nuclear grade thorium oxide as and when required. In addition, the major uranium fraction present in monazite is also separated in the form of crude uranium concentrate." *Thorium fuel cycle – Potential benefits and challenges* (International Atomic Energy Association, May 2005). https://www-pub.iaea.org/mtcd/publications/pdf/te_1450_web.pdf

370 In base metal production it is common to use terms such as "co-product" and "by-product." These mines often produce several metals, such as gold, copper, silver, zinc, lead, mercury, antimony, etc. By-product is used for resources where the primary product also contains a secondary or even tertiary product. Often, the secondary product is not itself economic, but its extraction may be facilitated by the production process of the primary product. Co-production occurs when more than one metal is present in economic concentrations. This is common in base metal ores where, typically, copper and nickel or zinc, lead and silver are produced from a single ore source. Thorium production is mainly from REE, which is usually considered as a feedstock that could contribute more than 80% of revenues. Thorium, a feedstock of little economic value at present, would then be referred to as a by-product. If several feedstocks are recovered, such as pure fractions of individual REE, other base metals, etc., all feedstocks, including thorium, would be referred to as co-products. *Thorium Resources as Co- and By-products of Rare Earth Deposits,* IAEA-TECDOC 1892 (Vienna: International Atomic Energy Agency, 2019).

## THE NUCLEAR POWER OPTION

History seems to give us a wink of complicity; when the chemical element thorium was discovered in Sweden in 1828, it was named after Thor, the god of lightning and storm in Nordic and Germanic mythology. Curiously, Thor controlled the climate, which today, due to man's actions, has gone out of control. Now, thorium-based nuclear reactors will provide a novel and efficient means of meeting our electrical energy needs. As the risk of hyperbole, these reactors are one of humanity's great hopes for combating climate change and developing energy sources that leave the smallest environmental footprint. Therefore, in addition to the strategic and safety interest of rare earths, we should not rule out the relevant future nuclear use of this metal, often found alongside rare earths. This new use could attract the interest not only of private companies, but also of governments, to pursue the exploitation of minerals that combine rare earths and thorium, such as monazite.

Renewable energies can help to curb climate change but the rare earth resources to develop them are physically not available at the quantity required by the current political agendas. Energy transition faces metals shortage accordingly with the Energy Transitions Commission.[371] Since 1992, when the world first became officially concerned about climate change, $CO_2$ emissions have never decreased for any significant period of time. We are now at record highs, with total annual emissions of 36.84 gigatons of carbon dioxide. In 2022 we were adding annually 50% more $CO_2$ of emissions to the atmosphere than in 1990 at the beginning of the fight against climate change.[372] Nuclear energy can be part of the solution to the environmental and climate change problem in some countries,[373] taking on a larger portion of the national and global energy mix.

---

371 Roberto Bocca, "Energy transition faces metals shortage unless investment rises, plus other top energy stories this week," World Economic Forum, July 25, 2023. https://www.weforum.org/agenda/2023/07/energy-transition-in-jeopardy-without-metals-investment-plus-other-top-energy-stories-this-week/

372 International Energy Association, *$CO_2$ Emissions in 2022,* March 2023. https://www.iea.org/reports/co2-emissions-in-2022

373 UNECE, "Application of the United Nations Framework Classification for Resources and the United Nations Resource Management System: Use of Nuclear Fuel Resources for Sustainable Development – Entry Pathways," March 2021. https://unece.org/sustainable-energy/publications/nuclear-entry-pathways

According to the International Energy Agency itself, the world needs to double nuclear power capacity by 2050 from the current 400 GW to 800 GW. Electricity production needs for decarbonization are set to triple in that timeframe. These figures assume the existence of sufficient mining and metallurgical capacity so that by 2050, according to the International Energy Association, 70% of the world's energy produced will come from renewable energies. But shortages or failures in the supply chains of the materials needed to develop solar and wind renewable energies, or to electrify automobiles, mean we are addressing this state of affairs at a surreal, dreamlike pace. This also implies a world energy storage capacity in batteries of 3100 GW when in 2020 it was only 8.5 GW. Many mining companies, specialized mining agencies, global metallurgy consultancies and other bodies such as the European Commission itself predict that with such an increase in demand, the risks of not meeting these gates are very high. In the words of Matt Sloustcher, vice president of MP Materials, the only large-scale producer of rare earths in the U.S., "One-third of the demand for rare earths in 2035 is projected to be unmet based on the investments currently being made."[374]

Bill Gates, author of the book *How to Avoid the Disaster of Climate Change*, sees nuclear energy as a large part of the solution to successfully fight climate change. In partnership with his friend Warren Buffet, considered the best world investor of the last 60 years, Gates invested their capital to create the company TerraPower, focused on the design of small molten salt reactors like the Molten Chloride Fast Reactor or the Natrium, which will soon perform an operational demonstration in the facilities of an old coal plant in Wyoming. This project has already received an $80 million grant from the U.S. Department of Energy.

In fact, thorium, a faithful companion of rare earths, has always been present as a nuclear fuel since the dawn of nuclear energy development. The primary reason that it was discarded as a nuclear fuel was the more propitious use of uranium for military purposes. At that time, the development of military and civilian projects was being combined. Therefore, the reactor models chosen to produce electrical energy

---

374 Tristan Bove, "You may be stuck paying high gas prices for years as a global metals shortage sabotages the electric car revolution," *Fortune*, June 10, 2022. https://fortune.com/2022/06/10/metals-supply-shortage-demand-electric-cars-renewables/

were very similar to the reactors used to produce material for nuclear weapons. It was a conservative bet by the U.S. government that would vilify the world of nuclear energy to the present day.

Until recently, the U.S. with its 98 nuclear reactors, and France with its 58, have been the global spearhead of nuclear power. But in the last five years, 87% of new nuclear power projects (27 out of 31) belonged to China and Russia. The Western world has lost nuclear power leadership at a time when it needs it most. Economies of scale and component supply chains in the Western nuclear world have been shrinking. So much so that by early 2022, only half of the 58 aging French nuclear power plants in the hands of Électricité de France (EDF) were operational. The problem was so systemic that the French government decided to completely nationalize EDF.

As the energy transition to renewables inevitably fails, the West will be locked into gas-fired power (in an effort to avoid coal), competing with other countries to secure sufficient supplies for an exponentially growing hunger for energy. While thorium's promise of energy independence awaits, it's overshadowed by our growing natural gas consumption, driven by a collective race towards a fatuous renewable paradise, with neither time nor oxygen to think straight.

But some democracies have already chosen to plot a safer course. Countries such as South Korea and Japan are leading the way to change, choosing nuclear energy as their primary source of production and hydrogen, as discussed above, as a means of transporting it. According to the World Nuclear Association, Canada, China, Russia, the USA and the U.K are among the countries that are developing or planning projects that use electricity from nuclear power plants to produce hydrogen using electrolysers.[375] China is betting hard on nuclear, planning the construction of 150 new nuclear power plants. Some other countries building new nuclear reactors initially not necessarily related with hydrogen are Argentina, Bangladesh, Brazil, Egypt, India, Iran, France, Turkey, Poland, Ukraine, the United Arab Emirates, Russia, Romania and Slovakia.[376] Only a rapid escalation of nuclear

---

375 World Nuclear Association, "Hydrogen Production and Uses," November 2021. https://www.world-nuclear.org/information-library/energy-and-the-environment/hydrogen-production-and-uses.aspx

376 Statista, "Number of nuclear reactors under construction worldwide as of June 2023, by country." https://www.statista.com/statistics/513671/number-of-under-

projects worldwide will make it possible to reduce energy costs and $CO_2$ emissions in the medium and long term. Nuclear projects such as Bill Gates' are a feasible option and can be included in nearly any political narrative. Given the smaller size and rapid manufacturing of these reactors, if their manufacture is governmentally incentivized, they can begin operation within a typical 4-year election period—the critical time period for decision-making in democratic countries. These reactors can provide jobs, develop technological efficiencies, and lower costs via economies of scale. Politicians would have arguments, accompanied by results, to show their voters for the next election. In Japan and South Korea, construction times before the nuclear moratorium resulting from the Fukushima accident ranged between 3 and 5 years for larger and more conventional plants—longer than the smaller thorium-based reactors being proposed today. Obviously, other western countries will have to recover this technology and their associated supply chains if they wish to avoid the yoke of the Chinese monopoly.

Only one problem remains to be solved, the management of radioactivity both in the mining of the precious raw material to produce nuclear fuel and in its waste. It is therefore important to differentiate between uranium and thorium mining, as discussed previously. The management of uranium's natural radioactivity presents serious problems for the mining industry, which in many cases has been outsourced to developing countries. Its extraction in Europe has been reduced in recent years to just two countries, the Czech Republic and Bulgaria.[377] As a result, many of Europe's nuclear reactors continued to operate with uranium from abroad, sometimes from former European colonies in Africa. The best example is Niger, which produces around 5% of the world's uranium. Most of these uranium mines are owned and operated by the French company Orano,[378] but in post-coup Niger

---

construction-nuclear-reactors-worldwide/

377 *Uranium 2020: Resources, Production and Demand,* A Joint Report by the Nuclear Energy Agency and the International Atomic Energy Agency (Nuclear Energy Agency Organization for Economic Co-operation and Development, 2020). https://www.oecd-nea.org/upload/docs/application/pdf/2020-12/7555_uranium_-_resources_production_and_demand_2020__web.pdf

378 World Nuclear Association, "Uranium in Niger," April 2021 (updated August 2023). https://world-nuclear.org/information-library/country-profiles/countries-g-n/niger.aspx

continuing French ownership may be uncertain. At the same time, there are very few facilities in Europe with the capacity to process uranium into nuclear fuel for reactors.[379] There is a big niche in Europe—gap in the capacity to process uranium and thorium—with this responsibility falling mainly on the French state-owned companies Areva-Orano and Belgian Solvay-Rhodia.[380] Many European and world nuclear power plants rely on Russian-made nuclear fuel, which has never yet been threatened by sanctions.[381]

However, the problems associated with uranium could disappear if it were replaced by thorium. In 2005, a report by the International Atomic Energy Organization recommended the use of thorium fuel for nuclear reactors. Thorium resources as co-products and by-products of rare earths are very significant and given the renewed interest in the use of thorium as a possible nuclear fuel, these resources could become increasingly important in the future.[382] This will open up their potential for recovery from mining by-products. While it is true that nuclear energy is slowly experiencing a renaissance, uranium reserves used at the current rate would only last 70 years.[383] This time it is India that is showing us the way forward, as it is the only nuclear world power that has long used thorium as a nuclear fuel.[384] Current nuclear reactors in other countries would have to be modified to run on thorium. However, some companies such as Norway's Thor-Energy are working on thorium-uranium nuclear fuel rods as a direct replacement.

The benefits of switching to thorium would solve many environmental and safety problems associated with nuclear power. TMSR

---

379 Andrea Wallner and Philipp Stein, *Uranium Mining In and For Europe,* (Vienna: Österreichers Ökologie Institut, September 2012). https://wua-wien.at/images/stories/publikationen/uranium-mining.pdf

380 Solvay, "Solvay and AREVA join their expertise in the development of new applications for thorium," December 20, 2013. https://www.solvay.com/en/press-release/solvay-and-areva-join-their-expertise-development-new-applications-thorium

381 Ashutosh Pandey, Why EU sanctions don't include Russian nuclear industry, *DW,* July 19, 2023. https://www.dw.com/en/russia-nuclear-industry-eu/a-66275352

382 Kevin Clark, "Is Thorium the Fuel of the Future to Revitalize Nuclear?," *Power Engineering,* August 13, 2019. https://www.power-eng.com/nuclear/reactors/is-thorium-the-fuel-of-the-future-to-revitalize-nuclear/

383 Lisa Zyga, "Why nuclear power will never supply the world's energy needs," *Phys.org,* May 11, 2011. https://phys.org/news/2011-05-nuclear-power-world-energy.html

384 IAEA, *Thorium fuel cycle.*

reactors[385,386] based on thorium use a cheap and overly abundant raw material, while producing much less radioactive waste. Moreover, their radiation decays to humanly tolerable limits in 300 years instead of uranium's million years. Their waste management is much easier. The safety of these fourth-generation reactors is light years ahead of that of second-generation reactors such as the Russian Chernobyl RBMK model. TMSR nuclear reactors are safe from earthquakes and power outages, with no risk of meltdowns as the fuel is already melted, and no risk of explosions as they operate at atmospheric pressure. These reactors could scale up beautifully from small portable generators to full-size power plants. As there is no need for evacuation zones, they could be located close to urban areas, providing a flexible response in the coming years to increasing or decreasing energy demand in different regions.

The World Nuclear Association notes the use of thorium as fuel in six different nuclear reactor models.[387] China, which aims to achieve energy independence by 2035, also relies on thorium as a nuclear fuel. The Thorium Molten Salt Reactor (TMSR) reactor model is the backbone of its plan to become a clean and cheap energy powerhouse beyond renewables.[388] In essence, a molten salt reactor is a vessel containing hot liquid salt, in which a nuclear reaction takes place. The salt is made up of nuclear fuel (thorium, in this case) and other compounds that optimize the reaction, heat transfer and salt stability. This means that the salt mixture is both the fuel and the coolant. This allows for very high heat production.

The question is not whether China will succeed in building a nuclear mega-industry with its own export capacity, already capable of supplying and assisting developing countries with their own energy transitions. The question is whether Western countries will have the capacity and will to catch up—to offer an alternative to China's new nuclear energy for the world, or at minimum for domestic use.

---

385 World Nuclear Association, "Thorium," Nov. 2020, https://world-nuclear.org/information-library/current-and-future-generation/thorium.aspx

386 Thorium Energy World, "China, Thorium Molten salt Reactor (TMSR)" (accessed November 28, 2021). http://www.thoriumenergyworld.com/china.html

387 World Nuclear Association, "Thorium," updated November 2020. https://world-nuclear.org/information-library/current-and-future-generation/thorium.aspx

388 Smriti Mallapaty, " China prepares to test thorium-fueled nuclear reactor," September 9, 2021. https://www.nature.com/articles/d41586-021-02459-w

The demonstration of the first Chinese molten salt reactor, designed and operated by the Shanghai Institute of Applied Physics (SINAP), occurred at Wuwei, on the outskirts of the Gobi Desert. This reactor proves the ability to safely obtain nuclear energy without the use of water and gives an implicit nod to many of the African countries in arid and desert climates, who could benefit from such an energy source. The $3 billion initially invested by China in this technology in 2011 could well turn into a super-investment, once these reactors begin to be commercialized, China can begin large-scale production.

China not only holds the title of the world's largest factory, but in recent years it has earned a reputation for being able to carry out pharaonic infrastructure projects in a very short time frame, and within budget. This contrasts with many Western nuclear projects, which are subject to much longer lead times and fall prey to continuous delays and cost escalation as the work progresses. Accordingly, China presents itself to the world as the perfect partner to solve energy problems triggered by a lack of materials. If the West does not react quickly, after escaping from the Asian giant's monopoly on renewable energies and control of green metals, its monopoly on the latest generation of nuclear energy will instead be waiting to ensnare us.

A chemical engineer such as Chinese President Xi Jinping is well aware of the physical limitations that chemical elements impose on the development of both renewable energy and nuclear power, and technology in general. China is already developing the capacity to use the "forgotten fuel" thorium, with which it will usher in a new era of nuclear energy[389] in a sustainable way. The minerals extracted from the Bayan Obo mines[390] will be used not only for iron but also for the associated rare earths and their thorium-rich residues.

Today Russia, China, and India have robust thorium-based nuclear programs, and their mutual cooperation will assist with creating the requisite economy of scale to spur widespread adoption of these reactors. China is again showing the world how it can copy an

---

389 Cindy Hurst, *Fuel for Thought: The Importance of Thorium to China* (Institute for Analysis of Global Security, February 2015). http://iags.org/thoriumchina.pdf

390 Timothy Ault, Stephen Krahn, and Allen Croff, "Radiological Impacts and Regulation of Rare Earth Elements in Non-Nuclear Energy Production," *Energies* 8, no. 3 (2015): 2066–2081. https://doi.org/10.3390/en8032066

abandoned Western technology and make it profitable through mass production and economies of scale. Just as the USA and Germany were the innovative powers that revolutionized the world of solar energy with their patents, so too was the USA the first country to develop a thorium-based molten salt nuclear reactor. As early as 1954, the U.S. Air Force was experimenting with a small molten salt reactor using thorium as nuclear fuel. Because of their high level of safety, researchers intended to equip the Air Force's fleet of long-range bombers with these reactors, until the project was shelved by the arrivals of ballistic missiles.[391] In the 1960s, Oak Ridge National Laboratory designed a molten salt reactor using thorium as fuel, which was operated as a demonstration model from 1965 to 1969. Today there is renewed interest in developing reactors of this type not only in China, but also in Japan, Russia, France, England, and the U.S. But it is China that has moved beyond theoretical intention and has already announced the construction of 150 nuclear power plants by 2035. If realized, China will develop in 15 years more nuclear power plants than has the entire world in the last 30 years.

If the West opts to use thorium as a nuclear fuel, we would perhaps at last see the opening of a major rare earth mine in Europe, and an optimal use of the residues or by-products of other mined minerals. The world quantity of rare earths produced annually would increase appreciably, and the deep Western dependence on China and the possibility of conflicts over the procurement of rare earths would be reduced. Preemptively, Western states could take the step of developing thorium processing and storage plants. Following the example of France and Belgium would help us to have thorium reserves available for use as nuclear fuel, providing cleaner and carbon-free energy for the future.[392,393] Finally, the commitment to nuclear thorium has the double benefit of optimizing the extraction and processing of minerals and of carbon-free energy production, with a very small radioactive waste footprint.

---

391 Wolfgang Kaufmann, "The Perfect Technology," *Preußische Allgemeine Zeitung,* March 14, 2022; posted by *The Thorium Network on* May 3, 2022 (consulted July 2022). https://thethoriumnetwork.com/category/china/

392 IAEA, *Thorium Resources as Co- and By-products of Rare Earth Deposits.*

393 Michael Montgomery, "Thorium: Rare earth passive or active?," *Investing News Network,* March 14, 2011. https://investingnews.com/daily/resource-investing/critical-metals-investing/rare-earth-investing/thorium-rare-earth-liability-or-asset/

If the world does not soon choose the nuclear option and renewable energies fail (as Gates predicts in his book), the world will be left to gamble on the emergence of some technological miracle. Despite betting on nuclear energy, Bill Gates maintains a dubious backup plan: solar geoengineering. Although solar geoengineering consists of several different techniques, the most popular one is aimed at blocking part of the solar radiation that reaches the planet by spraying sulfur particles into the atmosphere, simulating the cloud of a volcano. Gates himself has funded a Harvard University experiment to study the effect of spraying particles into the stratosphere that would create a global cooling effect. It's an instance where science and science fiction intersect, but there's only one planet to conduct experiments with.[394] The consequences of failure, miscalculation, or unconsidered side effect are not yet foreseeable; the proposed remedy could be worse than the disease. One is reminded of Gates' insistence that what the world needed when faced by COVID was a vaccine, and the mixed results and growing public skepticism of the efficacy of that. But here the issue does not concern hacking genetics to produce a vaccine for millions of humans. This time it is about how "hacking" our single earth atmosphere in order to allow 10.000 million people to continue to live in a technological world resembling today's modernity by 2050.

A reminder: should this technology be used, at that sad and dangerous moment, we should realize that in the end, by using it, we would only be treating the symptoms of global climate change, and not the causes.

## BRINGING IT ALL BACK HOME ...

The report of the last world economic forum, the Davos Forum (which was not attended by Russia or China) warned of a multi-crisis scenario. We find ourselves in an extremely unique historical moment, in which different crises are overlapping each other. They all have something in common—the once vaunted globalized economy is not only jeopardizing our political, economic, and social systems, but we are seeing our supply chains unravel and catching glimpses of the

394 David Vetter, "Solar Geoengineering: Why Bill Gates Wants It, But These Experts Want To Stop It," *Forbes,* January 20, 2022. https://www.forbes.com/sites/davidrvetter/2022/01/20/solar-geoengineering-why-bill-gates-wants-it-but-these-experts-want-to-stop-it/?sh=299026471842

material finiteness of our resources. The rare earth supply chain is the tip of the iceberg of unsustainable globalization. It is no longer a question of whether supply chains can be damaged, but rather what will be the first crisis (or combination of crises) to completely and irrevocably break these supply chains.

Time is money, or rather time is rare earths and critical metals. Most of us enjoy at least some of the advantages of globalization but these are the risks we have assumed, often thoughtlessly: the risk of new pandemics; the Western monetary debt crisis and Western and Chinese debt traps for developing countries; the global warming, climate change and energy crisis; the risks of cyber-attacks targeting power grids; the failure of international economic institutions; the loss of habitat and loss of arable land, and so on.

A crisis in supply chains seems to be the natural consequence of any of these crises, which can lead to extreme protectionist measures, abrupt cuts in production, border closures, disruption of communication and transport routes, conflicts, etc. These situations could leave countries completely out of supplies, hit by shortages of different materials critical to production. Prudence suggests the West should shift towards reindustrialization and seek a certain degree of self-sufficiency and autarky at the national level.

In general, global supply chains are made of cardboard, they decorate our economies nicely, but when a bad rainy day comes along, they fall apart easily.

The backdrop to this "multi-crisis scenario" is not much more flattering. A Western middle class that has been losing purchasing power for many years to an increasingly smaller group of individuals, and which is becoming more and more politically polarized risks political chaos within states and the deterioration of effective governmental planning. And finally, we face the most significant and likely threats: a shortage of natural resources in various sectors, whether energy or otherwise, and a heightened struggle for hegemony between the U.S. and China, which at times reaches pre-war stages through the militarization of information and the economy and drags its allied nations along with it.

As we try to put out these fires, the clock is ticking, metals are becoming scarce, and the earth's temperature is rising. Reaction time is decreasing, and the price of inaction is increasing. A critical mass of society must collectively awaken and act to tip the balance, demanding decisive action to avoid catastrophic consequences. This change must not happen randomly, as an impotent reaction to catastrophes as they happen, but with foresight, in an organized and decisive manner. Let us hope that the kind of women and men who in the past have helped humanity navigate other storms have not disappeared behind their cell phones—*let them give thought to the access to the more than 40 elements of the periodic table that it takes to make them*—and become insouciant or fateful, enjoying the fragile sweetness of the fruits of a capitalist way of life while it lasts, or have allowed themselves to be intimidated by their dictators. Let us hope that a critical mass of not only scientists, journalists, writers, and statesmen, but also artists, bloggers and internet celebrities will wake up the Western world.

We must start by stopping this erratic crusade to obtain from foreign lands materials that we have on our own soil, now being plundered in developing countries at such a dizzying pace that it will soon make hydrocarbon exploitation and the resulting conflicts pale in comparison. Sublimating the problem by focusing on other issues would leave the West in the hands of an Asian giant, China, which may be tempted to consider the current situation as a just reversal of centuries of Western colonialism. We need to correct the course of the energy transition and draw in the minds of every citizen a clear dividing line between renewable energy production (solar and wind) and the desired decarbonization—they are not synonymous. By themselves, renewable energies are a dead end in the fight against climate change, due to the scarcity of materials, the immense pollution associated with their production and the fossil fuel-based framework necessary for their production.

In the coming years, the balance will be tipped either towards the democratization of critical elements or towards competition and the resource curse. We can no longer ignore the implications of this new pollution paradigm and the fact that the quantity and rate of production of green metals are not sufficient to ensure a global energy transition designed to save ourselves from global warming. But in their chosen blindness, most of the world's nations remain committed to an energy transition based primarily on renewables. Thus, countries operating rare earth mines could be targeted by the economic interests of big business or by struggling Western governments trying to deal with the security challenges arising from their scarcity. We have seen similar patterns in the past with gold, diamonds and most notably cobalt and tantalum from the mineral[395] coltan. But these historical precedents in the world of mineral competition may be just a mere rehearsal compared to the intensity of future mineral resource wars.

So far, regulations and laws regulating rare metals markets[396] aimed at increasing traceability and protecting human rights[397] have had very limited success. Without universal, enforceable laws, the sharing of critical materials on a global scale is a chimera. If some regulate and others do not, if some prosecute the crimes associated with unethical mining and others look the other way, the pressure for access to scarce resources will seek an outlet and deepen its negative impact on developing countries. Therefore, there will continue to be manipulated or obscured markets for critical materials, unprotected countries with great mining potential but low levels of governance, and unscrupulous companies and countries willing to take advantage of the situation. Armed groups, governmental or otherwise, will be able to continue to use poorly regulated minerals as a means of financing[398] and competition between nations will intensify leading to violent conflicts over resources. To avoid this situation, we need to

---

395 OECD, *OECD Due Diligence Guidance for Responsible Supply Chains of Minerals from Conflict-Affected and High-Risk Areas: Third Edition* (Paris: OECD Publishing, 2016). http://dx.doi.org/10.1787/9789264252479-en

396 The main ones are:

- *Protocol of Accession to the World Trade Organization* (WTO), *General Agreement on Tariffs and Trade* (GATT), specifically Article XX of GATT paragraph G;
- China's export control law of December 1, 2020, the *Dodd-Frank Consumer Protection Act* (Section 1502 addresses international trade and the use of conflict minerals);
- the OECD *Due Diligence Guidance for Responsible Supply Chains of Minerals from Conflict-Affected and High-Risk Areas* (OECD Guidance) applied by the London Metal Exchange organization;
- the EU Conflict Minerals Regulation, which came into force throughout Europe on January 1, 2021;
- the regional certification of the International Conference on the Great Lakes Region (ICGLR).

397 London Metal Exchange, "LME responsible sourcing," HKEX, October 2019.

398 Global Witness, "Definition of Conflict Resources," Global Policy Forum, August 2007. https://archive.globalpolicy.org/component/content/article/198-natural-resources/40124-definition-of-conflict-resources.html

restart the struggle for rare earths—this time, with a new roadmap that puts science and security at the forefront.

## A NEW ROADMAP FOR RARE EARTHS SECURITY

Faced with the catastrophe posed by the shortage of rare earths and its consequences for the safety of citizens, well combined political-industrial decisions and legal measures represent a powerful fire extinguisher to put out emergencies, as we have seen with the coronavirus health crisis. But we do not need to wait for a fire to break out before we act. We need a strategy to build an industrial base that takes into account not only national security, but citizen safety, by ensuring a minimum of autonomy in vital supply chains. We can legislate early to curtail the problems, else we may find ourselves legislating late and poorly with national emergency laws, when a rare earth supply disruption finally emerges. We can legislate even 25 years from now as the climate deteriorates by enacting climate emergency laws.

The creation of national strategies[399] to orchestrate measures to avoid a rare earth supply disruption should have a preventive character. Inter-ministerial commissions focused on critical materials could assess risks, supply options, mitigation measures and medium-term solutions. Coordination at the international level is also of paramount importance. Proof of this is the now almost forgotten problem of the ozone layer. Thanks to the international coordination embodied in the Montreal Protocol, which banned the use of a total of 96 substances 35 years ago, the ozone layer is expected to be partially restored by 2040 and fully restored by 2060.

In our roadmap, the first step should be to obtain a minimum degree of self-sufficiency to avoid any kind of collapse. Beyond a first minimum supply of "war reserves"[400] and encouraging recycling and substitution, there are our own mines. Many Western countries have open mines in whose by-products there are sufficient concentrations of rare earths. These are tin or coal mines, for example. This reuse of minerals would not only reduce waste but would set an example of

399 U.S. Department of Commerce, *A Federal Strategy to Ensure Secure and Reliable Supplies of Critical Minerals,* June 4, 2019. https://www.commerce.gov/sites/default/files/2020-01/Critical_Minerals_Strategy_Final.pdf

400 The White House, "Fact Sheet: Biden-Harris Administration Announces Supply Chain Disruptions Task Force."

mining frugality worldwide. Large Western mining companies should be encouraged by governments by whatever means to take the lead in this with respect for the environment. Government intervention is urgent, as evidenced by the creation of thorium refineries and storage centers.

However, given the limited resources, a second step would be to obtain clean, emission-free, and cheap energy, beyond that coming from renewable energies (solar and wind) that should be qualified more with the color "black" for the coal that makes them possible than with green. The latest generation of nuclear energy, which uses thorium as fuel, a residue from the mining of rare earths, continues the process of using the by-products of the mines. Although scaling up this energy and transporting it through "pink hydrogen" would slow global warming, other technologies would continue to demand scarce critical metals. However, with sufficiently cheap energy, metals could be extracted without the need for ores with high concentrations of these elements. In other words, many common rocks outside of today's mines would become mineable.

Finally, if we want the energy transition to be completed in due time and in a fair and democratic way at the global level, we need to establish an accounting of the planet's resources and match the rate of extraction and recycling based on national and global needs, possibly leading to an international treaty specifically addressing mining and/or rare earths, addressing not just states but states' governance of non-state entities. If the states were to accede to such a treaty, which might include an adherence supervisory role to the UN, the extraction of metals could be done in an organized and equitable way to save the world from global warming, limiting pollution while avoiding countries falling into resource wars. The UN could not only draw up the roadmap for the treaty, but also oversee states' exploitation and distribution of resources and ensure compliance. On the other hand, the good news for humans (and the bad news for the planet) is that new territories affording the exploitation of resources are opening up. The discovery of a new underwater world exploration portends mineral wealth that must be exploited responsibly and that will give humanity more time to reach definitive solutions to climate change and resource scarcity.

In the absence of a ceding of authority via an international treaty or a similar mechanism created for this purpose, each country will be tempted to resort to subsidies, tariffs, and tax incentives that will further undermine the foundations of the World Trade Organization. Strategic alliances will provide only a partial solution to the supply problem and will aggravate tensions between blocs. It is necessary to review the network of institutions created after the Second World War, which are no longer effective today in guaranteeing our international security. These include the World Trade Organization and the World Bank. Global problems need global decisions, over and above the interests of individual states or their regional organizations. Humanity must survive climate change without leaving nature exhausted and without falling into a global crisis of scarcity that would lead to a multitude of conflicts and security problems.

On a more immediate horizon, enabling humankind to ramp up its support for the struggle, we will have to ask ourselves why we are living such a pernicious way of life on earth. What is driving us to the unrestrained predation of other species, both animal and mineral? The hope of massive and efficient recycling, the promise of unlimited energy from fusion or a great increase in the efficiency of solar energy may postpone the search for much-needed answers. But I do not believe that technology is the answer at the end of the road.

Perhaps it is a matter of controlling certain of our passions at the individual and global level. Frugality has to become our new ideal, paradoxically further enabling mass consumption, including information, ultra-communication and technification. This would entail a proportionate decrease in energy consumption, a reduction in food wastage and better food distribution, a reduction in the amount of material use, etc. It would imply that we would voluntarily limit our freedom in favor of Gaia, our beloved planet Earth. It cannot be all about maximizing benefits and profits. Just as citizens cede part of their freedoms to a State and the State protects them, this time citizens would have to cede part of their freedoms to the planet Earth, which in return would not extinguish them. Given the difficulty of establishing this pact with the planet, the best intermediary would be a world intergovernmental organization better structured to ensuring human security and the sustainability of life on the planet—a revamped UN unlike the UN of today, which has discredited itself by its many biases and by structurally entrenching the positions of the most powerful, while attaching subsidiary bodies enabling the rest of the world to, as Stephen Wertheim puts it, simply blow off steam.[401] Indeed, the most powerful and wealthy are the ones who have the most to lose, the most freedoms to give up, and the ones who must accept that their freedoms are limited by the finite resources of nature and the freedoms of beings far from their countries, as in Burundi, Congo, or Myanmar. We need an accounting of the resources consumed and a rationalization of their use according to their importance.

Maybe, in a few decades, as we assess our efforts in this struggle to secure access to rare earths, to stop climate change and to maintain and advance our technological way of life, we will realize that this present approach does not make sense either. In time we may realize that our "crusade" must become more about "stopping doing" than "doing," that frugality is better than voracity, that sustainable development is better than infinite growth and that the greatest pleasures are not given to us by technology but by nature.

---

401 See Stephen Wertheim, *Tomorrow, the World: The Birth of U.S. Global Supremacy* (Harvard University/Belknap Press, 2022).

# Index